OECD ECONOMIC SURVEYS

2002-2003

United States

OECD

ORGANISATION FOR ECONOMIC CO-OPERATION AND DEVELOPMENT

ORGANISATION FOR ECONOMIC CO-OPERATION AND DEVELOPMENT

Pursuant to Article 1 of the Convention signed in Paris on 14th December 1960, and which came into force on 30th September 1961, the Organisation for Economic Co-operation and Development (OECD) shall promote policies designed:

- to achieve the highest sustainable economic growth and employment and a rising standard of living in member countries, while maintaining financial stability, and thus to contribute to the development of the world economy;
- to contribute to sound economic expansion in member as well as non-member countries in the process of economic development; and
- to contribute to the expansion of world trade on a multilateral, non-discriminatory basis in accordance with international obligations.

The original member countries of the OECD are Austria, Belgium, Canada, Denmark, France, Germany, Greece, Iceland, Ireland, Italy, Luxembourg, the Netherlands, Norway, Portugal, Spain, Sweden, Switzerland, Turkey, the United Kingdom and the United States. The following countries became members subsequently through accession at the dates indicated hereafter: Japan (28th April 1964), Finland (28th January 1969), Australia (7th June 1971), New Zealand (29th May 1973), Mexico (18th May 1994), the Czech Republic (21st December 1995), Hungary (7th May 1996), Poland (22nd November 1996), Korea (12th December 1996) and the Slovak Republic (14th December 2000). The Commission of the European Communities takes part in the work of the OECD (Article 13 of the OECD Convention).

Publié également en français.

Table of contents

Boxes

Tables

Figures

BASIC STATISTICS OF THE UNITED STATES

THE LAND

Area (1000 sq. km)	9 629	Population of major cities, including their metropolitan areas, April 2000 (thousands):	
		New York	21 200
		Los Angeles-Anaheim-Riverside	16 374
		Chicago-Gary-Kenosha	9 158

THE PEOPLE

Resident population, July 1st 2002	288 369 000	Civilian labour force, 2003	146 515 667
Number of inhabitants per sq km	29.9	of which :	
Annual net natural increase (average 1998-2002)	1 592 400	Health services	11 812 800
		Unemployed	8 776 583
Natural increase rate per 1 000 inhabitants (average 1998-2002)	5.7	Net immigration (annual average 1998-2002)	1 116 000

PRODUCTION

Gross domestic product in 2003 (billions of US $)	10 988	Origin of national income in 2002 (per cent of national income[1]):	
GDP per head in 2003	38 073	Manufacturing	13.7
Gross fixed capital formation		Finance, Insurance and real estate	20.0
Per cent of GDP in 2003	18.4	Services	24.7
Per head in 2003 (US$)	6 997	Government and government enterprises	13.7
		Other	27.9

THE GOVERNMENT

Government consumption 2003 (per cent of GDP)	15.5	Composition of the 108th Congress as of November 5th 2002:		
Government current receipts, 2003 (per cent of GDP)	30.7		House of Representatives	Senate
Federal government debt held by the public (per cent of GDP), FY 2003	36.1	Republicans	228	51
		Democrats	205	48
		Independents	1	1
		Vacancies	1	–
		Total	435	100

FOREIGN TRADE

Exports:		Imports:	
Exports of goods and services as per cent of GDP in 2003	9.5	Imports of goods and services as per cent of GDP in 2003	14.1
Main exports, 2003 (per cent of merchandise exports):		Main imports, 2003 (per cent of merchandise imports):	
Foods, feeds, beverages	7.5	Foods, feeds, beverages	4.8
Industrial supplies	23.2	Industrial supplies	15.2
Capital goods	40.5	Capital goods	25.3
Automotive vehicles, parts	11.0	Automotive vehicles, parts	18.0
Consumer goods	12.4	Consumer goods	28.5

1. Without capital consumption adjustment.

Note: An international comparison of certain basic statistics is given in an annex table.

This Survey is published on the responsibility of the Economic and Development Review Committee of the OECD, which is charged with the examination of the economic situation of member countries.

•

The economic situation and policies of the United States were reviewed by the Committee on 10 March 2004. The draft report was then revised in the light of the discussions and given final approval as the agreed report of the whole Committee on 30 March 2004.

•

The Secretariat's draft report was prepared for the Committee by Hannes Suppanz, Thomas Laubach, Michael Kiley and Michael Wise under the supervision of Peter Jarrett.

•

The previous Survey of the United States was issued in November 2002.

Assessment and recommendations

Helped by supportive demand management, economic activity has accelerated

The US economy has performed very well since the early 1980s. Since then, real GDP growth has been the highest among G7 countries and well above the OECD average. In per capita terms real incomes remain much higher than in nearly all Member countries. Productivity gains picked up markedly in the second half of the 1990s, and there has been a further acceleration of late. Following a period of sluggish growth and massive policy stimulus, the economy has now enjoyed nearly a year of strong expansion, growing by about 5 per cent (annualised) over the past three quarters. Since mid-2003, the recovery has broadened – spreading from spending by households and government to business capital formation – and has gained considerable cyclical momentum. This should ensure continued growth at above-potential rates in the near term – even though macroeconomic policies are likely to become less stimulatory – so that the output gap that opened in 2001 may close around the middle of next year. To be sure, significant downside risks to this positive outlook remain. While the current account balance is not a policy target, the persistence of a large external deficit could put upward pressure on long-term interest rates. And the unusually slow improvement in the labour market might crimp confidence and spending. On the other hand, the further pick-up in productivity and hence potential output in recent years and the high level of profitability bode well for a continued robust economic expansion, increasingly led by business investment.

But sustaining good economic performance poses a number of policy challenges

The US Administration has emphasised strong economic growth as a top priority; assuring such an outcome will be a challenging task. Indeed, although the economy has been quite resilient, manifesting a solid capability to adjust to adverse shocks, policymakers face a number of hurdles, which need to be cleared in order to ensure a sustained recovery and continued strong growth over the medium and long run. Major policy challenges in this regard are to:

- Reduce public dissaving by strengthening budgetary discipline and placing the public retirement and health-insurance systems on sound financial footings.
- Ensure policy settings are consistent with an orderly unwinding of the external deficit, based on a strengthening of national saving and exports, rather than weaker investment and growth.
- Lock in price stability and adapt the central bank's communications policy to the new low-inflation environment.
- Continue to re-build financial-market confidence by vigorously implementing and enforcing corporate governance and accounting reforms.
- Further enhance product-market competition to maintain higher productivity growth.
- Avoid protectionism and continue to build support for free trade.

This does not mean that there are not other areas that need attention and where reform efforts or policy changes should be considered, especially to address environmental problems and tackle a broad range of social issues. These social and environmental challenges, in particular, were extensively covered in the last *Survey* and are hence not revisited in depth.

Budgetary discipline must be restored

The federal budget has moved from a surplus of nearly 1½ per cent of GDP in fiscal year 2001 to a deficit of 3½ per cent in 2003 and a projected 4¼ to 4½ per cent this year. This rapid deterioration is attributable to sharply reduced tax receipts following the recession and the demise of the stock-market bubble combined with tax cuts and the rapid expansion of defence, "homeland security" and other discretionary outlays. While the cyclical drag on public finances should fade soon, recent policy changes on both the revenue and outlay sides imply that, under realistic assumptions and absent corrective action, the deficit will remain substantial over the next ten years by both US historical and international standards. At that time, the retirement of the baby boom generation will be in full swing, putting enormous pressure on entitlement programmes. Now that the recovery has taken hold, measures to reduce the deficit are urgently needed if the beneficial effects on long-run national income from recent marginal tax-rate cuts are not to be outweighed by the adverse consequences of the fall in public and national saving. These measures should aim both at curbing outlays and, to the extent revenues have to be raised, broadening the tax base. In its 2005 Budget the Administration proposes to halve the deficit by 2009 through unprecedented restraint on non-security expenditure. However, even if that objective were achieved, it might nonetheless not be ambitious enough in view of the Administration's intention to make the recent tax cuts permanent, its defence aspirations, the need to deal with the surging numbers of taxpayers who will be subject to the Alternative Minimum Tax and the serious demographic effects on entitlement spending that would then be just around the corner.

This requires a renewed commitment to budget-control mechanisms...

Bipartisan agreement on the need for sustained deficit reduction was a critical factor behind the improvement in public finances in the 1990s. This agreement produced and sustained the 1990 Budget Enforcement Act (BEA). But its main provisions – statutory caps on discretionary spending and the pay-as-you-go requirements for mandatory spending and revenue measures – expired at the end of fiscal year 2002. Although fiscal discipline began to erode when surpluses emerged in the late 1990s, until then the BEA seemed to provide an effective restraint on both spending and revenue measures. The international evidence suggests that fiscal rules are unlikely to be effective in the absence of a strong underlying dedication to fiscal prudence. Should there be a new bipartisan commitment to deficit reduction, reinstatement of all of the BEA's main provisions would probably facilitate the return to budget balance. In this context, it would be useful to improve the transparency of the budget outlook by accounting more clearly for the rapid accumulation of liabilities under entitlement programmes and thereby focusing stronger attention on the key choices that will have to be made to put government finances on a sustainable path. Recent Congressional and Administration proposals, if implemented, would go a long way to address these issues.

... while long-term fiscal pressures need to be tackled as soon as possible

While the retirement of the baby-boom generation has drawn nearer and life expectancy has continued to increase, no progress has been made in recent years to put entitlement programmes on a sturdier financial footing. Under baseline assumptions, spending on Social Security, Medicare and Medicaid is projected to rise from just over 8 per cent of GDP currently to nearly 18 per cent by 2050. As time progresses, the cost of restoring the programmes to actuarial balance will rise rapidly. The Social Security programme should be safeguarded through a combination of revenue increases and benefit reductions, such as reducing replacement rates for high income earners and indexing the full-benefits age to life expectancy. The financial position of Medicare and Medicaid is considerably worse, given the rapid growth of health-care costs, and has deteriorated further as a result of the recent addition of a prescription drug benefit to Medicare. To keep its cost increases in check, it will be necessary to restrain the growth of costs per enrolee, particularly under the new prescription drug benefit. Controlling costs is an equally demanding and important challenge for Medicaid, where long-term care expenses are projected to rise rapidly as the eligible elderly population continues to grow. Allowing greater scope for the authorities to negotiate with producers the prices paid for drugs provided under the new prescription drug benefit might lessen the impact of projected increases in drug expenditures on the financial condition of both Medicare and Medicaid. Policymakers must recognise the unpalatable arithmetic of the current entitlement programmes and take early action to rein in the inexorable rise in their costs.

... as well as a broadening of revenue sources

Restraining both discretionary and mandatory spending, while necessary, is unlikely to be sufficient to restore the budget to balance over the longer term. To the extent that revenues have to be raised, this should be done primarily by broadening the tax base rather than by reversing recent reductions in marginal tax rates. Considering the low aggregate tax burden compared to other member countries, statutory and marginal effective tax rates remain rather high, reflecting the heavy reliance on income taxes, in particular at the federal level. To broaden the tax base of the personal income tax, the deductibility of mortgage interest (regardless of the use of the loan) and of charitable donations should be phased out, as should the unlimited exclusion of employer health insurance plan premia. As to the corporate income tax, base-broadening efforts should focus on exemptions that reduce revenues and create inefficiencies, such as sectoral tax shelters. In any case, there is significant scope to improve revenue yield by better enforcement. If the yield from broadening existing income tax bases is ultimately insufficient, a further move to a consumption-based tax system through the introduction of a nation-wide value added tax (VAT) should be considered. While introducing a VAT would be complicated in the US context, in which most states rely heavily on sales taxes for their revenues, such a step would be an efficient approach to raising revenues and might also help to boost household and national saving.

Such moves would contribute to a smooth unwinding of the potentially destabilising external deficit,...

The current account has been in almost uninterrupted deficit since the early 1980s. With the usual cyclical improvement hardly visible during the recent recession, it has reached record levels and is currently running at around 5 per cent of GDP. As a result, net external claims on US residents have grown to some 25 per cent of GDP, still less than the net liabilities of many other countries but rising of late by an average of several percentage points of GDP per year. An adjustment in the current account balance could involve a number of domestic and foreign factors that affect the global demand for dollar assets. At some stage, those assets may come to occupy too large a share of foreign portfolios, even though their relative returns remain favourable. The flow of private capital into the United States has slowed somewhat in the last two years. Although governments – especially in Asia – have stepped up their purchases of US assets, this slowdown may have contributed to the decline in the dollar on foreign exchange markets since early 2002. This should help arrest the rise in the external deficit but, in the interest of global growth prospects, stabilisation of the foreign debt ratio cannot rely exclusively on dollar depreciation. Faster domestic demand growth abroad will be required, as will an increase in US national savings and some long-lasting competitiveness gains independent of exchange-rate changes.

... which is attributable to a lack of domestic saving

Underlying the current account deficit is a rising gap between domestic saving and investment, which is covered by foreign saving. If that deficit is to be reduced in relation to GDP, either domestic saving will have to increase or investment to fall, again relative to GDP. Increasing saving can be achieved by raising net exports relative to domestic demand, decreasing consumption relative to income or reducing public spending relative to taxation. The fiscal stimulus of the past few years has been helpful in promoting recovery; but if current prospects of future budget deficits are realised, interest rates will be higher, barring a considerable rise in private savings. This would imply slower growth in the capital stock, productivity and economic potential. There are a number of factors that would allow the current account adjustment to occur gradually, including the dollar's role as a reserve currency and the scarcity of equally attractive investment alternatives, owing to the favourable features of the US economy (deep capital markets, a flexible labour market, a healthy investment climate and robust productivity trends). Nonetheless, ensuring a smooth adjustment process that avoids endangering both domestic and international growth prospects will require policies that bolster investor confidence by strengthening corporate governance and curbing emerging protectionism and, more fundamentally, effective measures to shrink the budget deficit over time.

In the current low-inflation environment, clear communication by the monetary authorities is particularly important,...

By keeping the federal funds rate exceptionally low, the authorities have successfully geared monetary policy to engineering the pick-up in activity. However, the unusual situation of having core inflation at a rate that is slightly *below* the perceived official comfort zone increases the need for clear communication between the monetary authorities and the public, for two reasons. *First*, if core inflation continues to slow, the Federal Reserve will have to prevent inflation expectations from falling, since that would raise real interest rates, braking the expansion unnecessarily. *Second*, in the more likely event that the recovery progresses sufficiently strongly to gradually eliminate spare capacity, the authorities will need to make it clear to investors that some increase in inflation from current levels is acceptable and should not be mistaken for a weakening of their commitment to price stability. In either case, the Federal Reserve should provide clear guidance to markets regarding its own assessment of the economic outlook and policy response conditional on prospective developments.

... while adjustments to the policy framework may enhance the effectiveness of managing expectations

Responding to this need for effective communication, the Federal Open Market Committee (FOMC) has recently made several changes to the contents of the statements released following its meetings. It has separated the balance of risks assessment for inflation from that for output growth. Moreover, it has added a more forward-looking element by its recent indications that monetary policy can remain accommodative for a "considerable period" or be "patient". While these changes have provided valuable information, further steps toward greater clarity could help to inform markets about the FOMC's assessment of future economic developments and policy responses. In particular:

- The FOMC may also want to release its own projections more frequently and for a broader range of variables and a longer horizon than currently.
- An earlier release of the FOMC meeting minutes – now published only after the following meeting – should be considered.

The Federal Reserve recently set up a group to study some of these questions. More fundamentally, with the explicit approval of the relevant Congressional committees, the FOMC should consider quantifying its working definition of the price-stability objective mandated by law, specifying a suitable price measure and a desired long-run average value or range.

Restoring financial-market confidence would be assisted by progress in corporate governance reform,...

Besides the bursting of the stock-market bubble and geopolitical uncertainties, corporate governance and accounting scandals have played an important role in denting investor confidence in the last few years. While the stock market has regained substantial ground, underlying concerns about governance and accounting remain latent, and a renewal of such shocks would be seriously detrimental. Further reforms in this area would be conducive to strengthening the foundations for sustained growth and underpinning the integrity of financial markets. In response to widespread corporate malfeasance, the 2002 Sarbanes-Oxley Act stiffened penalties for fraud, enhanced both auditor independence and regulation of the accounting profession and increased both disclosure requirements for public companies and the responsibility of their executives for financial reporting. Considerable progress has been made in implementing the legislation, and early assessments of the reform's impact are largely positive, though concerns have been voiced that some provisions of the Act – such as the requirement for chief executives to certify financial statements – would adversely affect business behaviour. In addition, the listing requirements of the major stock exchanges have been strengthened with respect to corporate governance provisions. However, renewed scandals in recent months (involving the New York Stock Exchange and the mutual funds industry) have demonstrated that there is still unfinished business in the area of corporate governance reform:

- Guaranteeing the independence and strengthening the oversight of corporate boards. The still complaisant attitude of compensation committees is an indication that more needs to be done by investors, the exchanges and the authorities.

- Enhancing shareholder rights by providing access to the director nomination process, as proposed by the Securities and Exchange Commission, which should allow investors to vote for and remove individual directors.

- Pressing ahead with governance reforms in the mutual funds industry given its major role in the US economy.

- Ensuring that regulatory agencies are provided with sufficient resources to complete the reform agenda and to upgrade enforcement, while encouraging them to become more pro-active in their operations.

- Reforming incentive-based executive compensation to further enhance managerial performance. Requiring the expensing of stock options would make compensation more transparent and avoid inappropriate incentives facing managers, such as boosting earnings in the short term at the expense of long-term outcomes.
- Achieving greater harmony between US and international accounting standards and resolving questions about auditor oversight, thereby reducing pressures for the extraterritorial application of US regulatory oversight in this area.

... eliminating the special status of government-sponsored housing finance companies...

Two of the leading government-sponsored enterprises (GSEs), Freddie Mac and Fannie Mae, which have become major players in financial markets, have also been investigated for accounting irregularities. In view of their rapid growth and systemic importance, their regulation and supervision needs to be tightened, and the Administration has made proposals to this end, including relocating the regulatory authority to the Treasury Department. But reforms should go beyond that by eliminating their special status. This status has led to the market perception of an implicit government guarantee and hence slightly lower borrowing costs, allowing them to expand strongly and move into activities beyond their original mandate of supporting the secondary market for residential mortgages. In any case, the marginal funding advantage is an inefficient way of promoting homeownership – most of the benefits go to the shareholders of the two GSEs – and such promotion is separately undertaken by multiple tax preferences granted to owner-occupied housing. Altering the GSEs' status, however, may not be sufficient to eliminate their implicit government guarantee. Without reducing the size of the GSEs' portfolios, investors may still perceive them as "too big to fail". Limits could be placed on the growth of their mortgage-related asset portfolios, so that mortgage-backed securities traded in public markets, and not GSE debt, become the dominant source of secondary-market funding for mortgages.

… and improved regulation of corporate pension plans to avoid under-funding

Given their adverse impact on corporate finance and potential risks to plan participants and the Pension Benefit Guaranty Corporation (PBGC), weaknesses in the regulatory framework applicable to defined-benefit corporate pension plans need to be addressed. They have allowed substantial under-funding and have led to a huge financial deficit of the PBGC. The Administration has made proposals to improve liability measurement, disclosure and safeguards against under-funding by financially troubled companies. A more comprehensive reform of the system will be necessary though, because its problems are partly structural, reflecting its poor incentive characteristics. In doing so:

- It would be ill-advised to provide funding relief, as is being discussed in Congress, with no simultaneous offsetting action to address systemic under-funding associated with lax funding rules.
- It would be prudent to use a conservatively low discount rate to calculate pension obligations, while aiming at greater accuracy and transparency.
- The government pension insurance agency should be given greater flexibility so as to charge higher premiums to firms generating more risk to the system.

Regulatory reform has enhanced competition in many sectors and boosted aggregate economic performance

The economy's good performance for more than a decade can in part be traced to regulatory reform efforts in a broad range of industries, aimed at enhancing competitive forces as a means to improving efficiency, thereby stretching production possibilities. These efforts began in the 1970s and accelerated in the 1980s and have meant that competitive forces have now been stronger in the United States than in most other OECD countries for some considerable time. Robust product-market competition has probably increased pressures for flexible adaptation in labour markets. This, in turn, has favoured the quick adoption of productivity-enhancing technologies and the re-employment of workers displaced both by such innovations and by trade liberalisation. Nonetheless, despite favourable productivity trends and the generally pro-competitive thrust of policies, improvements remain possible in various areas.

But there is room to improve the competition policy framework,...

Since basic competition law has not changed for decades, antitrust policy has evolved through court decisions. By international comparison, penalties and enforcement are severe, and private litigation is unusually important. The high risks of sanctions and treble damages for violations have encouraged efforts to undo or weaken enforcement actions and often entailed exemptions, special treatment or anti-competitive state regulation. Several changes seem appropriate:

- Anomalous exemptions from law or jurisdiction should be eliminated to improve coherence and promote competition.
- The antitrust immunity of government enterprises should be terminated; it has no logical basis, and, indeed, no other OECD country exempts government-related firms from competition enforcement.
- State constraints on competition should be vigorously challenged under the Interstate Commerce clause, as they undermine the national commitment to rely on competitive forces.

... and challenges remain regarding intellectual property rights,...

The strengthening of intellectual property rights (IPRs) since the early 1980s has been accompanied by an expansion in R&D and a surge in patents. Some problems have followed the shift to stronger IPRs, notably the increase in patent litigation. The United States has greater patent protection than most of its trading partners. The significant protection afforded to IPRs is one factor contributing to the much higher level of branded drug prices and hence of health spending than in other countries. In assessing whether the strength of patent rights in the United States has moved beyond the optimal level, the question is whether too much current income and output is sacrificed for the additional innovation generated. While a comprehensive assessment of the costs and benefits of IPR policies is still lacking, some measures may be advantageous, including:

- Considering the adoption of an opposition system for patents similar to that in the European Union (giving broader rights for grants to be challenged), with a view to limiting litigation costs and improving the quality of the patent review process.

- Making agreements that stop entry by generic drug firms through payments from branded drug firms illegal, while maintaining the possibility of patent dispute settlements without payments.

... telecommunications regulation...

The telecommunications industry has changed significantly over the last 20 years in response to both rapid technological progress and regulatory reform. Competition for long-distance service entered a new phase in the mid-1980s when AT&T was broken up, and the 1996 Telecommunications Act then began the national effort to spur local service competition. Over this period, alternative infrastructure competition and cable broadband competition have also emerged. While local service competition has recently taken root, policy changes may still be needed to ensure that entry in local voice services and broadband are not thwarted by dominant carriers. These changes should also be compatible with the need to increase overall investment by all carriers in advanced network facilities that provide broadband access to all areas. In this respect, an early resolution of outstanding policy issues would be desirable, in particular:

- Given its positive effects on competition in local voice services and on investment in new services, unbundling of certain network elements should be continued for the foreseeable future where competitors' ability to enter is impaired.
- With a view to aiding broadband deployment, unbundling requirements for incumbent telephone carriers should be maintained, and cable firms should be required to open their lines using older technology to independent internet service providers.
- Reviewing the inter-carrier compensation regime, including reduction of current access charges, should be high on the policy agenda.

... and, likewise, electricity regulation

Regulatory reform in the electricity sector was driven by many of the same factors that had influenced efforts in telecommunications: successful liberalisation in other industries, technological progress and dissatisfaction with induced distortions to prices across states and different customers. Unlike in other areas where the United States has often been a leader in reform, US experiments followed those in a number of other OECD countries. Despite the opportunity to learn from such experience, their success has been decidedly mixed. Although the California meltdown in 2000-01 reflected flaws in the regulatory framework rather than the impact of competition, it has chilled enthusiasm for reform throughout the country. Nonetheless, the August 2003 blackout in the northeast has highlighted the urgency of policy measures to increase regional transmission integration and encourage investment in generation and transmission in order to both improve security and efficiency. A number of initiatives could improve efficiency through increased competition, including:

- Encouraging the integration of electricity markets, which have developed on a state-by-state or small region basis, by implementing a proposed standard market design.
- Commencing reforms to the transmission system, which is currently characterised by balkanised asset ownership, in order to ensure efficient investment in capacity.
- Removing distortions to competition that are implemented through tax and subsidy systems (such as differential tax treatment of public utilities) or that arise from public ownership of some electricity generators.

Energy and environmental policies seem unlikely to achieve even timid objectives efficiently

While some progress has been made in the environmental field, there remain several areas of concern, including ozone protection, air pollution reduction and mercury targets. In its Clear Skies initiative, the Administration set a new target for reducing major pollutants through cap-and-trade policies, but it opposes targets for greenhouse gas (GHG) emissions. A credible alternative to the Kyoto protocol commitments on global warming is still lacking, although GHG emissions are heavy and hence in need of market-based restraint. Proposed energy legislation focuses almost entirely on supply increases through costly hand-outs to producing sectors, while measures to restrain demand by price or other means are notably absent. One result of this reticence is that the fuel efficiency of the automotive fleet has being stagnant over the past decade at some 6 per cent below earlier peak levels as the fleet has grown heavier and its typical engine more powerful. The government persists in setting separate ("CAFE") standards for cars and light trucks – although it has announced tighter standards for the latter for the coming three model years, narrowing the gap somewhat – tyhereby accommodating the increase in the light-truck share of new vehicle sales from one-tenth when the programme began in 1979 to around one-half most recently.

Agricultural and some trade policies need to change course

The United States is committed to further trade liberalisation in global, regional and bilateral contexts. However, its repeated resort to import-restricting measures – even though often consistent with WTO rules – has somewhat eroded its leadership role in the world trade arena. Anti-dumping and countervailing duty sanctions against Canadian softwood lumber and safeguard actions regarding steel and Chinese textiles are the most prominent examples. The United States has yet to implement certain rulings issued by the WTO's Dispute Settlement Body, notably those concerning the so-called Foreign Sales Corporation provisions in the US tax code. The recent discontinuation of the steel tariffs and a provisional agreement in the long-standing dispute on softwood lumber are welcome steps, although the former has been accompanied by the imposition of a licensing and monitoring programme and the latter would still severely limit market access by a quota system, adding permanently to the cost of homebuilding. Hence:

- Actions to restrict access to domestic markets or to impede firms' and governments' ability to source globally should be avoided, both because they imply higher prices and lower real incomes for consumers and tend to impede structural adjustment and flexibility and because they encourage protectionist tendencies worldwide.

- US leadership to successfully conclude the Doha round is essential. In this context, the authorities might need to consider how bilateral and regional trade agreements can best support and complement progress in multilateral trade liberalisation. The limited coverage of key protected sectors such as agriculture in bilateral agreements underlines the need to press for comprehensive trade liberalisation multilaterally.

Agriculture is both the source of many trade disputes as well as a sticking point in the present global trade negotiations. While agricultural support relative to farm revenues is below that in some other OECD regions, it is likely to increase as a result of recent policy changes. The gains from these support measures go overwhelmingly to large-scale farmers and entail losses to consumers, taxpayers and foreign producers, especially those in developing countries. Recent policy changes risk accentuating both production distortions and trade tensions and are not in line with the long-term OECD policy reform objectives. It would be desirable to roll back the extra support given to farmers in the past few years and reverse the move away from market-based outcomes implied by recent legislation. This would strengthen the United States' leadership role in the world-trade arena where it has tabled ambitious proposals for agricultural liberalisation in the context of the Doha Round.

Some social policies also need attention

There are also ongoing challenges on the social policy front. Health insurance coverage has begun falling again, following a temporary improvement in the late 1990s. This represents a significant economic cost to the extent that a lack of insurance leads to poorer health outcomes and earlier death. In contrast to health coverage, fears that the cyclical downturn would reverse the sharp drop in welfare caseloads following the reforms in the mid-1990s have proved unfounded. On the other hand, poverty rates have edged up again, and, although they are still below their previous peak in the 1990s, they are very high for some population groups. Continued efforts are necessary to ensure that improvements in social conditions in the 1990s, highlighted in the 2002 *Survey*, are not reversed.

Summary

Economic performance over the past two decades has been impressive. Underpinned by an increased reliance on competitive forces, which have been stronger than in most other Member countries for some time, productivity and output have accelerated significantly. In recent years, helped by timely macroeconomic policy responses, the economy has demonstrated its capacity to adjust to adverse shocks, so that the per capita growth gap against other countries has widened further. The outlook is for this to continue in the next few years, with real GDP expanding by around 4 per cent per annum. Nonetheless, there are a number of challenges that need to be addressed to sustain these laudable economic outcomes. By far the top priority is to confront the current and projected federal budget deficits. The fiscal stimulus of the past few years has been helpful in supporting the recovery, but if public dissaving is not reduced, interest rates may be higher, ultimately implying slower growth in economic potential. Increased budget discipline, and indeed significant reform on both the spending and revenue sides of the budget, will be necessary because of the impending demographic pressures on government finances. Corrective fiscal measures will also assist the unwinding of the current account deficit, which is unusually large for this stage of the cycle. As the Federal Reserve begins to move the federal funds rate back to a more neutral level, it will need to be especially attentive to the clarity of its communications with the markets. Further corporate-governance and accounting reforms would help to underpin confidence of domestic and foreign investors, thereby facilitating orderly current-account adjustment. Less reliance on import restrictions and maintaining a leadership role in trade liberalisation would favour structural adjustment at home. Furthermore, despite the generally pro-competitive thrust of antitrust and other regulatory policies, a number of areas deserve attention, notably intellectual property rights, telecommunications and electricity, where further reforms would be welfare enhancing.

I. Sustaining strong growth and social cohesion: key challenges

The economic situation

After a very weak start, the recovery from the 2001 recession finally gained momentum in the spring of 2003. Until then, the recovery had proceeded very unevenly, with GDP increasing by only 2.1 per cent over the four quarters to the first quarter of 2003, despite enormous amounts of monetary and fiscal stimulus. Growth during this period remained entirely driven by household and government spending (Table 1.1). Real business fixed investment contracted in each quarter between the first quarter of 2001 and the first quarter of 2003, despite very low interest rates

Table 1.1. **Contributions to GDP growth**
Percentage points, volume terms, chain 2000 prices

	1999	2000	2001	2002	2003
Private consumption	3.4	3.2	1.7	2.4	2.2
Private residential investment	0.3	0.0	0.0	0.2	0.4
Private non-residential investment	1.1	1.1	–0.6	–0.8	0.3
Government consumption and investment	0.7	0.4	0.5	0.7	0.6
Final domestic demand	**5.5**	**4.6**	**1.6**	**2.5**	**3.5**
Stockbuilding	0.0	–0.1	–0.9	0.4	0.0
Total domestic demand	**5.4**	**4.5**	**0.7**	**2.9**	**3.4**
Net exports	–1.0	–0.9	–0.2	–0.7	–0.4
GDP	**4.5**	**3.7**	**0.5**	**2.2**	**3.1**
Memorandum items:					
Growth rate of:					
Private consumption	5.1	4.7	2.5	3.4	3.1
Private non-residential investment	9.2	8.7	–4.5	–7.2	3.0
Core PCE inflation	1.5	1.7	1.9	1.7	1.2
Output gap	2.5	2.2	–1.1	–1.8	–2.0

Source: Bureau of Economic Analysis.

and the special depreciation allowances legislated in March 2002. The weakness in capital spending owed to the remaining capital overhang following the investment boom of the late 1990s and a pervasive sense of uncertainty ahead of the conflict in Iraq, as well as renewed efforts at cost cutting and balance sheet improvements in the wake of corporate governance scandals (further discussed in Chapter IV).

During the final three quarters of 2003, however, GDP grew at an annual rate of around 5 per cent, and business fixed investment has finally joined the expansion (Figure 1.1). The combination of the swift resolution to the conflict in Iraq, a strong rebound in corporate profits driven by a substantial decline in unit labour costs since the beginning of 2002, and further easing of financial conditions (see below) has led to a clear improvement in the fundamentals for corporate capital formation. Household consumption, which had been well maintained throughout 2002 and early 2003, surged in the third quarter, as disposable income was lifted by the 2003 income tax reductions, and household net wealth was boosted by a continued strong housing market and a rebounding stock market (Table 1.2). Mortgage refinancing activity has picked up again recently, and equity extraction from residential real estate through turnover or home equity loans has remained strong. Moreover, residential investment has been boosted by some of the most favourable financing conditions since the early 1960s. In several respects, this recovery resembles the previous one, notably in the delay with which GDP and employment picked up and with the persistent disinflation. There are, of course, also differences, such as the larger and more protracted decline in business fixed investment following the investment boom of the late 1990s, and the greater contribution to growth from government purchases, reflecting the enormous expansion of federal discretionary spending after the terrorist attacks of September 2001 and military operations in Afghanistan and Iraq. Furthermore, the contribution from net exports during the current expansion has been smaller, as the current business cycle has been more synchronised across the major regions than was the case in the early 1990s.

In terms of productivity gains, however, this recovery differs sharply from its predecessor. In the late 1990s labour productivity, as measured by output per hour in the non-farm business sector, began to accelerate compared to the previous 20 years, from an annual growth rate of 1.5 per cent during 1975-95 to a rate of 2.5 per cent during 1996-2000. Since the beginning of 2002, however, productivity has increased at an annual rate of 4.8 per cent (Figure 1.2), compared to a rate of 2.6 per cent over the first two years of the previous recovery. Although productivity tends to grow rapidly during the early stages of recovery, this typically follows a period of weak productivity growth or even declines, neither of which happened before or during the 2001 recession. Since investment was particularly weak for much of this period, the recent acceleration has not been driven by capital deepening. Instead, the gains may reflect firms' efforts to better utilise the capacity put

Figure 1.1. **Aggregate economic indicators**
Per cent

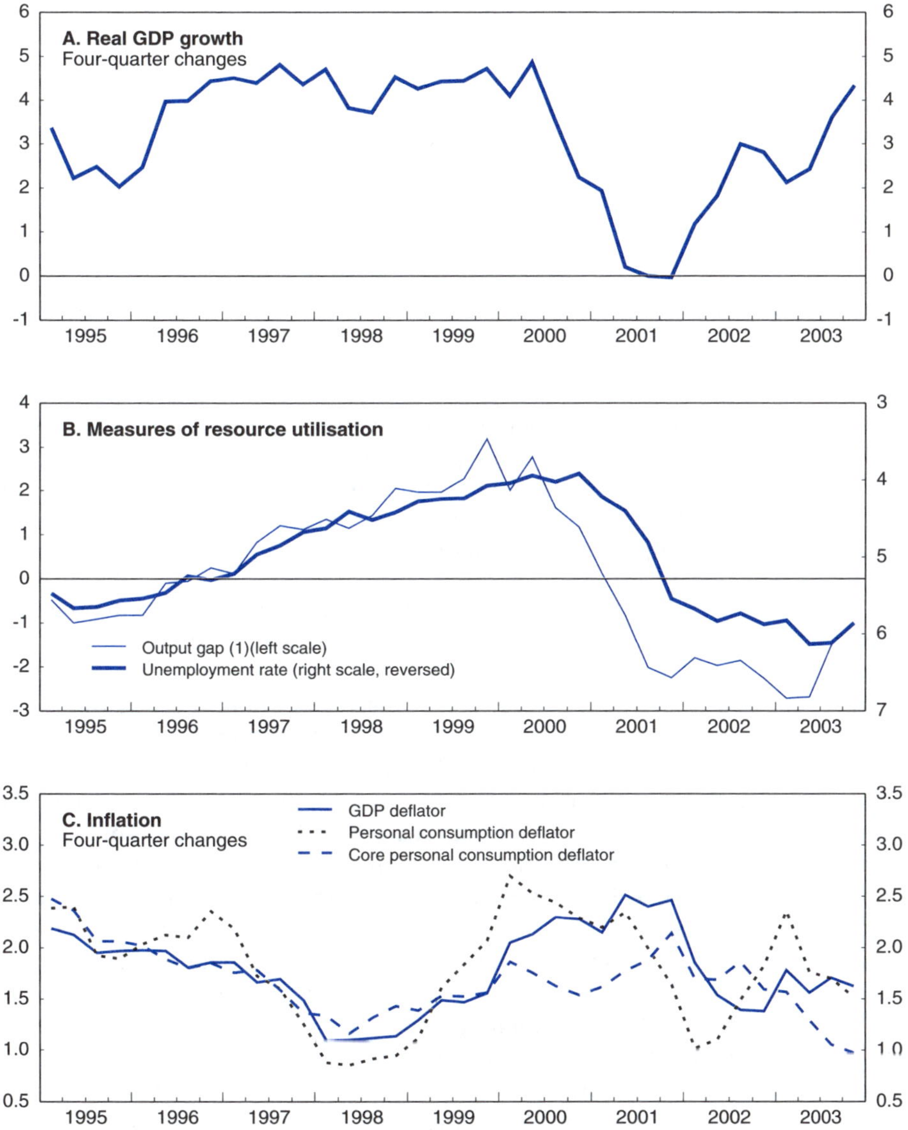

1. Per cent difference between actual and estimated potential output.
Source: OECD.

Table 1.2. **Labour market and household indicators**
Per cent

	1999	2000	2001	2002	2003
Unemployment rate (level)	4.2	4.0	4.7	5.8	6.0
Labour force participation rate (level)	67.1	67.1	66.8	66.6	66.2
Private non-farm employment growth[1]	2.5	2.1	–0.3	–1.7	–0.4
Personal income	5.1	8.0	3.4	2.3	3.1
Disposable personal income	4.7	7.5	3.8	5.2	4.4
Personal saving rate (per cent of disposable personal income)	2.4	2.3	1.7	2.3	2.0
Household net worth	13.3	–0.8	–1.6	–3.7	11.7

1. Establishment survey.
Source: Bureau of Labor Statistics; Bureau of Economic Analysis; and Board of Governors of the Federal Reserve System.

in place during the investment boom of the late 1990s (Kohn, 2003), thereby raising multifactor productivity. Most likely productivity will decelerate as the expansion matures. Much uncertainty therefore attaches to current estimates of its trend growth rate, but for now nothing suggests that the increase in the growth rate seen during the late 1990s will be fully reversed.

The enormous productivity gains combined with modest average GDP growth during the recovery has meant that economic slack did not bottom out at the end of the recession but continued to expand until the beginning of 2003, with the output gap reaching about 2½ per cent. This view of only recently diminishing excess capacity in the product market is consistent with the fact that industrial capacity utilisation continued to decline through June, and that the labour market has only recently shown signs of improving, even if only modestly. Although there has been some debate recently about the accuracy of different labour-market statistics (see Box 1.1), according to the most widely used measure total non-farm employment has declined by 323 000 between the end of the recession in November 2001 and March 2004. This impression of labour market weakness is confirmed by the fact that the unemployment rate peaked in June 2003, 18 months after the business cycle trough, at 6.3 per cent, and its decline since then reflects not only moderate employment gains (according to the household survey), but also a decline in the labour force participation rate, particularly pronounced among those aged 16 to 19. The various measures of compensation show either little acceleration or deceleration. With spare capacity at firms only gradually dissipating, and absent labour cost pressures, core inflation measures have declined considerably over the past two years, but have stabilised more recently, so that the risk of outright deflation in the near future seems now small (see Chapter III).

Figure 1.2. **Labour costs, productivity and profits**
Per cent

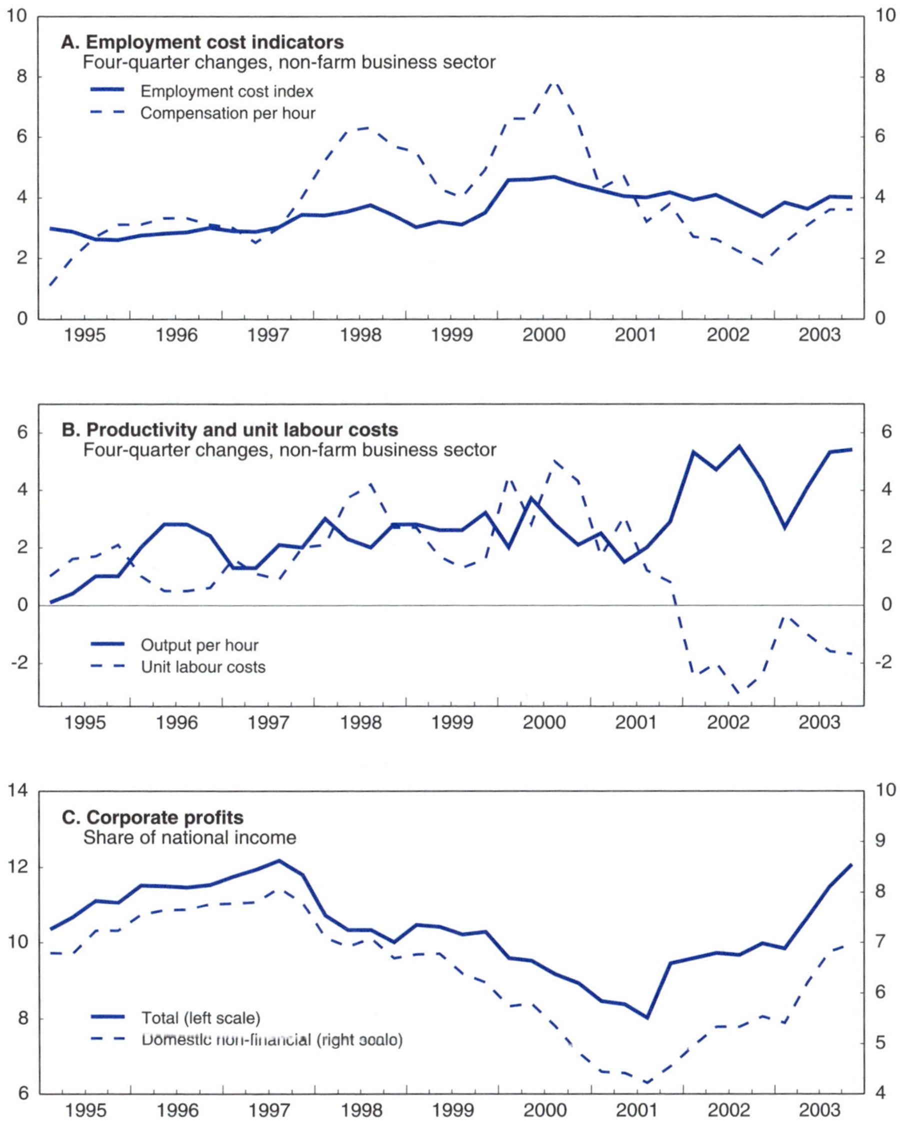

Source: Bureau of Economic Analysis and Bureau of Labor Statistics.

Box 1.1. Jobless recoveries

The two most important sources on aggregate US employment data are the Current Population Survey (informally known as household survey) and the Current Employment Statistics Survey (commonly referred to as the establishment survey). The household survey, which is conducted monthly by the Bureau of Labor Statistics (BLS) and the Bureau of the Census, is based on a random sample of about 60 000 households. Each household contacted is asked for the employment status of each person aged 16 or older, *i.e.* how many persons are currently employed, are searching for but unable to find employment, or are neither working nor looking for work. Although the household survey provides information on the level and change of employment, the most widely known statistic based on this survey is the unemployment rate. The establishment survey conducted monthly by the BLS, by contrast, is based on payroll records of about 400 000 business establishments, covering about one-third of total non-farm payroll employment. Moreover, with a lag of about one year the employment estimates from the establishment survey are benchmarked to an almost complete count of payroll employment based on state unemployment insurance tax records. The statistic of the establishment survey that receives the most attention is the monthly change in non-farm payroll employment.

The discrepancies between the changes in aggregate employment reported by the two surveys have received considerable attention of late because they have provided somewhat different views on the extent to which the current recovery is "jobless". While according to the household survey employment rose by more than 1.5 million over the two years following the business cycle trough in November 2001, according to the establishment survey it fell by 844 000.[1] In part these differences are explained by differences in coverage between the two surveys. Employment in the household survey includes unincorporated self-employed workers, unpaid family workers, private household workers and farm workers, none of which is included in payroll employment in the establishment survey. On the other hand, the household

Table 1.3. **Reconciliation of household and payroll employment**

Seasonally adjusted, in thousands

	November 2001	November 2003	Change
Household employment[1]	136 602	138 158	1 556
Less:			
Agriculture[1]	2 234	2 411	177
Self-employed[1]	8 878	9 515	637
Unpaid family and private household[1]	901	855	–46
Multiple job holders[1]	7 171	7 282	111
Adjusted household employment	131 760	132 659	899
Non-farm payroll employment (establishment survey)	130 871	130 027	–844

1. Adjusted for updates to population estimates.

Source: Bureau of Labor Statistics; OECD calculations.

Box 1.1. **Jobless recoveries** (*cont.*)

survey counts the number of employed persons whereas the establishment survey counts the number of jobs, so that a person holding two jobs counts once in the household survey, but twice in the establishment survey. Table 1.3 provides a rough estimate of the effects of these differences in coverage.[2] The gap between the two surveys' changes narrows somewhat, in part because growth in agricultural employment and the number of self-employed has been unusually strong during the current recovery. Even after accounting for these differences, however, employment in the household survey rose by about 900 000 over the two years since the recession ended.

The question therefore arises to which survey one should pay more attention. Some have argued that the establishment survey initially underreports employment in the early part of expansions because much employment is created by newly formed businesses that are systematically underrepresented in the establishment survey.[3] However, the BLS has expended much effort on improving the adjustments made to the raw data to account for births and deaths of establishments. Moreover, the benchmark revisions to the level of employment as of March 2002 and March 2003 have both been negative. As mentioned above, after the benchmark the establishment survey's employment data are based on an almost complete count of payroll employment. By contrast, the household survey employment estimates are obtained by scaling the responses of the 60 000 households to the overall population size. They are therefore sensitive to population estimates, and there is

Table 1.4. **Labour market indicators during and after recessions**

	Recession		
	1957-82 average	1991	2001
Decline in employment from its peak to its trough, per cent			
Household survey	1.8	1.5	1.5
Establishment survey	2.5	1.5	2.0
Rise in unemployment rate from its trough to its peak, percentage points	3.2	2.8	2.4
Change over first 24 months of expansion[2]			
Employment (per cent)			
Household survey[1]	5.2	1.6	1.1
Establishment survey	6.6	1.3	–0.6
Unemployment rate (percentage points)	1.7	0.2	0.3
Change over first 8 quarters of expansion[2]			
Productivity (per cent, annual rate)	3.8	3.0	4.7

1. Adjusted for updates to population estimates.
2. 1980 recession omitted from 1957-82 averages.
Source: US Bureau of Labor Statistics; OECD calculations.

Box 1.1. **Jobless recoveries** (*cont.*)

some evidence suggesting that in recent years population may have grown more slowly than assumed by the population estimates used in the household survey (Juhn and Potter, 1999; Nardone *et al.*, 2003). If so, the household employment estimates would be biased upward. In summary, while neither survey provides a completely accurate picture of employment, the bleaker picture presented by the establishment survey cannot be discounted.

Table 1.4 provides some historical perspective on the jobless nature of the current recovery. The first three rows give some impression of the severity of the last two recessions in terms of the labour market indicators discussed above and compare them to the average of the previous six recessions, using the recession dates of the National Bureau of Economic Research (NBER). Specifically, the percentage decline in employment from its peak, typically right before the onset of the recession, to its trough, usually shortly after the end of the recession, are reported, as well as the increase in the unemployment rate from its trough to its peak. By all three measures, the past two recessions were slightly milder than the average of the previous six, but not by much. Thus, the sluggish recoveries of the labour market after the past two recessions are not simply a reflection of small job losses during those recessions. The next three rows report the percentage changes in employment and the change in the unemployment rate over the 24 months following the end of the recession. By these measures, the past two recessions are indeed strikingly different from the previous five (the recession of 1980 is omitted because the 24-month horizon extends into the following recession). This impression is confirmed by the timing of the peak in the unemployment rate: 15 months after the end of the 1991 recession, and 19 months after the end of the 2001 recession compared to an average of 5 months following the previous six recessions.

The reasons for the different labour market experiences during the past two recoveries compared to earlier norms are not yet well understood. One recent study (Groshen and Potter, 2003) has focused on structural change, as measured by the trend rise or decline of employment in different industries, as a potential source for the protracted labour market weakness. These authors noted that, contrary to earlier recessions, during the past two recessions those industries in which employment fell during the recession continued to contract afterwards, whereas many of those industries that had been gaining employment during the recession continued doing so afterwards. This decline in the cyclicality of employment within industries is consistent with the fact that the great majority of layoffs during recent recessions have been permanent, not temporary. Besides structural change, another contributing factor in the most recent recovery has undoubtedly been the high rate of productivity growth. As shown in the last line of Table 1.4, output per hour in the non-farm business sector rose much faster during the first eight quarters of the current recovery than during the comparable previous periods, in fact faster than during the two years following any of the previous seven recessions. Without a proportional pickup in demand, businesses were able to expand output sufficiently without expanding employment. Finally, the deterioration in the US trade balance over the past decade has probably

Box 1.1. Jobless recoveries (*cont.*)

gone hand in hand with the acceleration in the long-run trend decline in manufacturing employment, in particular since a large part of the change in trade expand output sufficiently without expanding employment. Finally, the deterioration in the US trade balance over the past decade has probably gone hand in hand with the acceleration in the long-run trend decline in manufacturing employment, in particular since a large part of the change in trade flows has taken place in manufactured goods (Bernanke, 2003). In fact, manufacturing employment declined by almost 1.5 million over the 24 months following the end of the recession, far above the decline in overall payroll employment during that period.

1. The household employment numbers have been adjusted for updates to population that the BLS does not carry backward.
2. The reconciliation is only approximate because the figure for multiple job holders includes for example self-employed and farm workers, but at the same time simply adding this number does not correct for persons holding more than two jobs. Moreover, no correction is made for unpaid absences, which count as employment in the household but not the establishment survey. For a more detailed reconciliation of the 1994 and 2000 employment estimates involving data not regularly published by the BLS see Nardone *et al.* (2003).
3. Kitchen (2003) presents some evidence that in the past the establishment survey initially underestimated employment growth early in expansions. However, it is unclear to what extent these results still apply given the methodological changes that the BLS has introduced over recent years.

Financial conditions have eased since the beginning of 2003. While long-term Treasury yields and mortgage rates currently stand at roughly the same level as then, spreads of corporate yields over Treasuries have decreased compared to their previously elevated levels (Figure 1.3). Moreover, the stock market has rebounded, and broad market indices have reversed roughly half of the losses between its peak in 2000 and the trough in late 2002. The rise in the stock market and the continued strong housing market have pushed household net worth in the fourth quarter of 2003 above its previous record level in early 2000. Despite rapid growth in home mortgage debt, homeowners' debt burden, as measured by the ratio of financial obligations to disposable income, has fallen slightly since the end of 2002 as they have locked in low mortgage rates. The financial obligations ratio for other households has also declined over the same period. The fact that households' net acquisitions of financial assets rose rapidly over the past two years suggests that the proceeds from home-equity withdrawal have largely been used for balance-sheet improvements. The aggregate balance-sheet of the non-financial corporate sector too has improved since the recession, as profits have rebounded sharply while capital spending has picked up only recently. Corporations have also sought to take advantage of the low interest rates by

Figure 1.3. **Financial indicators and current account**

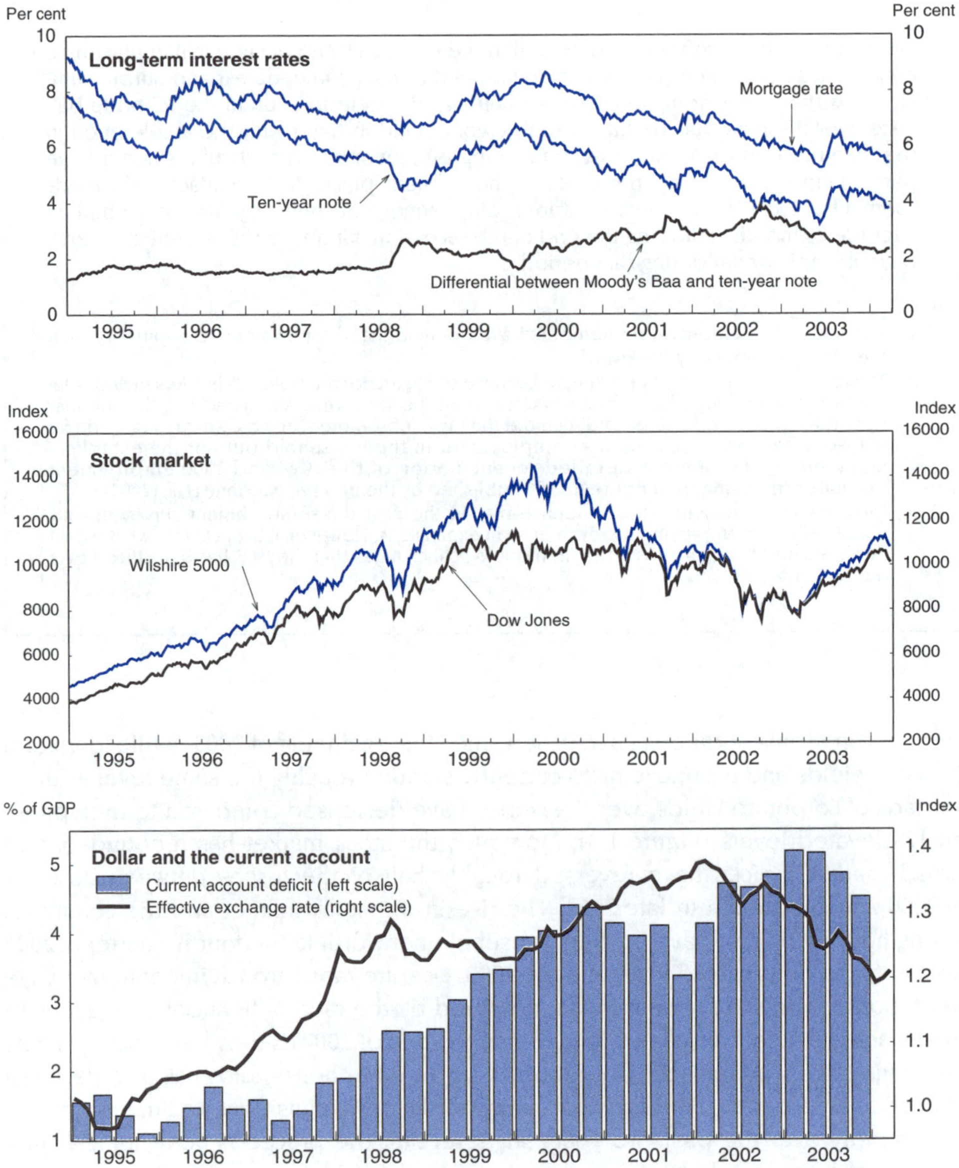

Source: Board of Governors of the Federal Reserve System, Bureau of Economic Analysis, Thomson Financial.

Table 1.5. **Balance of payments**
$ billion, seasonally adjusted, annual rate

	2001	2002	2003	2002	2003			
				Q4	Q1	Q2	Q3	Q4
Current account balance	–394	–481	–542	–514	–557	–559	–541	–510
of which:								
Exports of goods, services and income	1 285	1 230	1 294	1 244	1 239	1 246	1 294	1 398
Imports of goods, services and income	1 632	1 652	1 768	1 697	1 727	1 737	1 768	1 839
Net unilateral transfers abroad	–47	–59	–68	–62	–70	–68	–67	–69
Balances:								
Goods	–427	–483	–549	–529	–544	–552	–545	–557
Non-factor services	69	65	59	65	58	56	58	65
Investment income	11	–4	17	12	–1	5	12	50
Private transfers	–29	–37	–41	–39	–41	–40	–39	–44
Official transfers	–17	–22	–27	–23	–29	–28	–28	–25
Memorandum:								
As per cent of GDP								
Current account	–3.9	–4.6	–4.9	–4.8	–5.2	–5.2	–4.9	–4.5
Foreign assets in the United States (flows)	7.6	6.7	7.8	7.4	9.0	9.7	4.3	8.2
US assets abroad (flows)	–3.5	–1.7	–2.5	–1.7	–3.8	–4.1	–0.5	–1.8
Net position	4.1	5.0	5.2	5.7	5.3	5.5	3.8	6.4
Statistical discrepancy	–0.2	–0.4	–0.3	–0.9	–0.1	–0.3	1.1	–1.9

Source: Bureau of Economic Analysis.

restructuring their debt, and net interest payments as a share of this sector's GDP have continued to decline. The dollar continued its fall that started in early 2002, having depreciated by about 12 per cent in trade-weighted terms as of March 2004 and reversing about half of the rise from the beginning of 1997. With the substantial depreciation over the past two years, the balance on goods and services may have stopped its rapid decline from a deficit of about 1 per cent of GDP in early 1997 to 4.6 per cent of GDP in the second quarter of 2003, narrowing slightly in the second half of the year (Table 1.5). Exports have been slow to pick up, as export market growth has remained subdued, while imports have been growing apace following a brief pause during the recession. As will be discussed further below, at this stage the United States is not yet experiencing any difficulties in financing its current account deficit, partly because the favourable outlook compared to other major economic regions means that it remains an attractive destination for foreign investment. Moreover, it seems unlikely that the depreciation of the dollar alone will substantially reverse the trend in the foreign trade position.

The policy stance

Monetary policy has remained highly accommodative since the end of the recession in late 2001. By most measures, the real federal funds rate has fluctuated around zero or has been negative for the past two years. This stimulus has been transmitted to the economy through very low yields on long-term private and government securities, resulting in exceptionally low mortgage rates and, especially since the stock-market trough in late 2002, in a low cost of capital for businesses. After the aggressive easing of 2001, the Federal Reserve kept its federal funds target at 1.75 per cent for most of 2002. At its November 2002 meeting the Federal Open Market Committee (FOMC) reduced the funds rate target by another 50 basis points in response to signs of renewed output deceleration and ongoing labour market weakness. It attributed the weakness in both product and labour markets to greater uncertainty, in part due to heightened geopolitical risks. As productivity growth remained robust, the weak GDP growth in late 2002 and early 2003 implied a substantial further widening of the output gap and hence intensified disinflationary pressure. In the statement following its May 2003 meeting was understood by markets as signalling that it was concerned about the risk of substantial further disinflation, and declines in various measures of inflation expectations during the spring of 2003 suggested that this concern was shared by the private sector. At its June 2003 meeting the FOMC reduced its funds rate target by another 25 basis points to 1 per cent. Around that time, the first signs emerged that the recovery was finally gaining momentum, and over the next few weeks long-term interest rates reversed earlier declines. Since then, the risk that the recovery could stall again has faded, and monetary policy turned towards fostering the recovery by indicating that, in the presence of extremely low inflation, an accommodative stance could be maintained for "a considerable period", and that the FOMC can be "patient in removing its policy accommodation".

Fiscal policy has also continued to support aggregate demand through strong growth in government purchases of goods and services as well as further reductions in personal and corporate taxes. Real purchases of goods and services at the federal, state and local levels combined have expanded at an annual rate of 3½ per cent since the beginning of 2001, about three times as fast as during the previous decade. Spending on defence and homeland security has of course grown vigorously since September 2001, but discretionary spending outside of these areas has also expanded rapidly. Following the two major rounds of tax cuts and investment incentives of June 2001 and March 2002, the revenue legislation passed in May 2003 brought forward many of the personal income tax reductions originally legislated in 2001, expanded the previously implemented investment incentives and reduced the taxation of corporate dividends and longer-term capital gains. The reductions in marginal tax rates on personal income in particular not only provided timely support for household incomes but should also have beneficial effects on labour supply in the long run. However, the combination of sharp increases in government spending, income tax cuts and plunging tax revenues due to sharply reduced capital gains realisations have led to ballooning deficits at the federal level as well as to severe budget shortfalls at the state level. The deficit in the unified budget of the federal government rose from 1.5 per cent of GDP in fiscal year (FY) 2002 to 3.5 per cent in FY 2003.

Near-term prospects and risks

The near-term outlook for the US economy is favourable (Table 1.6). The recent rapid pace of the expansion is expected to moderate over the coming quarters, but GDP growth should exceed its potential rate of about 3¼ per cent for the foreseeable future.[1] The sizeable depreciation of the dollar – about 12 per cent in trade-weighted terms from its peak in early 2002 – and a gradual acceleration in worldwide demand are expected to reduce the drag from net exports on growth. The improvement in foreign trade, however, may not be strong enough to reduce the current account deficit much below 5 per cent of GDP. Consumption expenditures will receive another boost in early 2004 from large income tax refunds reflecting tax cuts retroactive to the beginning of 2003, and are expected to remain well maintained thereafter as employment gains begin to support household incomes. Business fixed investment is expected to advance rapidly, although the expiration of the partial expensing provisions at the end of 2004 is likely to reduce the growth of spending on equipment in early 2005. Residential investment, on the other hand, will tend to weaken after its recent torrid expansion, especially as monetary policy is assumed to tighten beginning in mid-2004 and long-term interest rates could well rise substantially when this occurs. Nonetheless, the momentum from consumption and investment should keep real GDP expanding at a rate of 3¾ per cent even as federal spending decelerates in 2005 after the current round of spending increases has run its course. The result is that the output gap is expected to close in the middle of 2005. With spare capacity only gradually diminishing, core inflation is likely to remain near its current low level for the next two years.

There are substantial risks to this outlook, but they appear more evenly balanced now than during the earlier stages of the recovery. On the upside, the recent strong productivity performance may spark another cycle of optimism concerning business profits and household incomes and may fuel business investment and household spending. Continued strong productivity growth would also likely prevent inflation from rising anytime soon and allow monetary policy to remain on hold for longer than projected. On the downside, it is unclear how fast the factors that have held back hiring by companies are subsiding. If firms continue to exercise great caution in hiring, consumption may decelerate more than currently projected once the stimulus from tax cuts has faded. Moreover, given the enormous run-up in residential construction, housing investment may contract sharply once long-term interest rates begin to rise. The high federal budget and current-account deficits increase the risk of disorderly exchange-rate movements and a larger rise in long-term interest rates than projected, which might stifle the recovery in business investment. Finally, if productivity were to decelerate more sharply than anticipated and the decline in the labour force participation rate turned out to be more lasting, excess capacity would be reduced more rapidly and inflation expectations might rise, calling for an earlier tightening of monetary policy.

Table 1.6. **Near-term outlook**[1]

Percentage change over previous period, volume terms (chain 2000 dollars, s.a.a.r.)

	2003	2004		2003	2004	2005
	Q4	Q1	Q2			
Private consumption	3.2	3.4	3.3	3.1	3.7	3.1
Government consumption	0.7	3.3	3.4	3.9	2.5	1.9
Gross fixed investment						
Private residential	7.9	3.0	3.0	7.5	6.1	1.9
Private non-residential	10.9	5.8	8.9	3.0	9.1	8.9
Government	–3.6	4.2	4.2	1.5	3.7	3.5
Final domestic demand	**3.6**	**3.6**	**3.8**	**3.4**	**4.1**	**3.5**
Stockbuilding[2]	0.7	0.3	0.2	–0.1	0.3	0.2
Total domestic demand	**4.3**	**4.0**	**4.1**	**3.3**	**4.4**	**3.7**
Exports of goods and services	20.5	2.0	12.0	2.0	9.7	10.6
Imports of goods and services	16.4	1.5	9.0	4.0	7.3	8.1
Foreign balance[2]	**–0.4**	**0.0**	**–0.1**	**–0.4**	**–0.1**	**–0.1**
GDP at market prices	**4.1**	**4.1**	**4.1**	**3.1**	**4.5**	**3.7**
GDP price deflator	1.5	1.6	1.0	1.7	1.3	1.3
Private consumption deflator	1.0	2.2	0.9	1.8	1.3	1.1
Output gap	–1.3	–0.8	–0.5	–2.0	–0.5	0.0
Potential output	3.2	2.3[3]	3.3	3.2	2.9[3]	3.2
Unemployment rate	5.9	5.6	5.6	6.0	5.5	5.2
Federal funds rate	1.0	1.0	1.0	1.1	1.2	2.8
Ten-year Treasury note rate	4.3	4.0	4.2	4.0	4.4	5.3
Net lending of general government						
$ billion	–485.3	–573.7	–578.2	–522.4	–574.7	–495.4
Per cent of GDP	–4.3	–5.0	–5.0	–4.8	–4.9	–4.1
Current account balance						
$ billion	–510.5	–540.7	–554.0	–541.9	–561.6	–604.2
Per cent of GDP	–4.5	–4.7	–4.8	–4.9	–4.8	–4.9
Household saving rate[4]	1.7	2.1	2.3	2.1	2.5	2.8

1. Preliminary projections prepared for *Economic Outlook* 75.
2. Contribution to GDP volume growth.
3. Values for 2004 Q1 and 2004 are below trend growth rank of 3.2 per cent due to BLS population controls.
4. OECD definition.
Source: OECD.

Key challenges

Although the US economy has proved remarkably resilient in the face of serious adverse shocks and the near-term outlook is for continued robust growth, a number of challenges remain that will need to be addressed in order to sustain robust expansion over the medium and longer term. It is important that the external deficit, which is unusually large for this stage of the cycle and would seem to be difficult to sustain at current and projected levels, unwind in an orderly fashion. This will require, above all, that the unusually large budget deficit be corrected and put on a sustainable footing, the issue addressed in the next chapter. The following chapters pick up three further challenges: the maintenance of price stability both through appropriate monetary management and adjustments to the current framework; the restoration of financial-market confidence that has been tainted with corporate scandals; and the further strengthening of product-market competition with a view to sustaining higher productivity growth. Assuring robust expansion is the objective focused on in this *Survey*. But there are other important challenges, such as those in the human capital development, environment and social areas, which are briefly addressed at the end of this chapter, having been covered extensively in previous *Surveys*. A comprehensive overview of progress in structural reform can be found in Annex 1.1.

Coping with the external deficit

The current external account, which had basically been in a slight surplus position since the late nineteenth century, has displayed substantial deficits over most of the past 20 years. At around 5 per cent of GDP in 2003, the current account deficit reached the highest level ever recorded, although it declined somewhat over the course of the year. As a result, the US net international investment position, which was still in broad balance in the late 1980s, has moved to a net negative position equivalent to around 25 per cent of GDP of late (Figure 1.4). To some extent, the rising external deficit reflects a higher import propensity and a stronger economic expansion than abroad, with the growth gap widening since the mid-1990s (reaching more than ½ and nearly 1 percentage point per annum against the OECD and European Union, respectively). It could be argued that the deterioration in the current account should not be of great concern to the extent that it was related to the favourable productivity shock, which not only attracted foreign capital but also prompted lower saving as households discounted the steeper future path of real income increases ("consumption smoothing"). Moreover, special factors have played a role: while the rise in the dollar contributed, part of the lack of the usual cyclical improvement during the recent recession can be related to the downturn in international demand for ICT goods, which hit US exporters particularly hard. More fundamentally, however, the external imbalance reflects a rising gap between domestic investment and saving (Figure 1.5, Panel A). During the second half of the 1990s, this gap was partly held in check by higher government saving, but that effect

Figure 1.4. **Net international investment position of the United States**

Year end, percentage of GDP

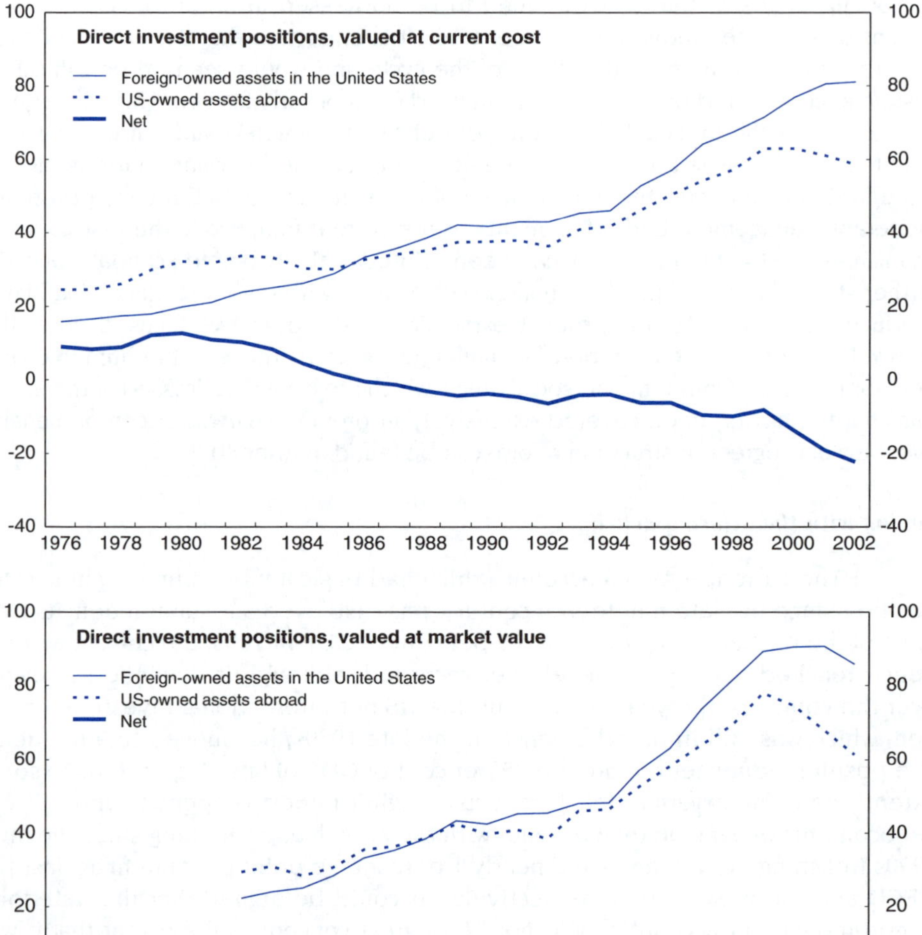

Source: Bureau of Economic Analysis.

Figure 1.5. **Gross saving and investment**

Per cent of GDP

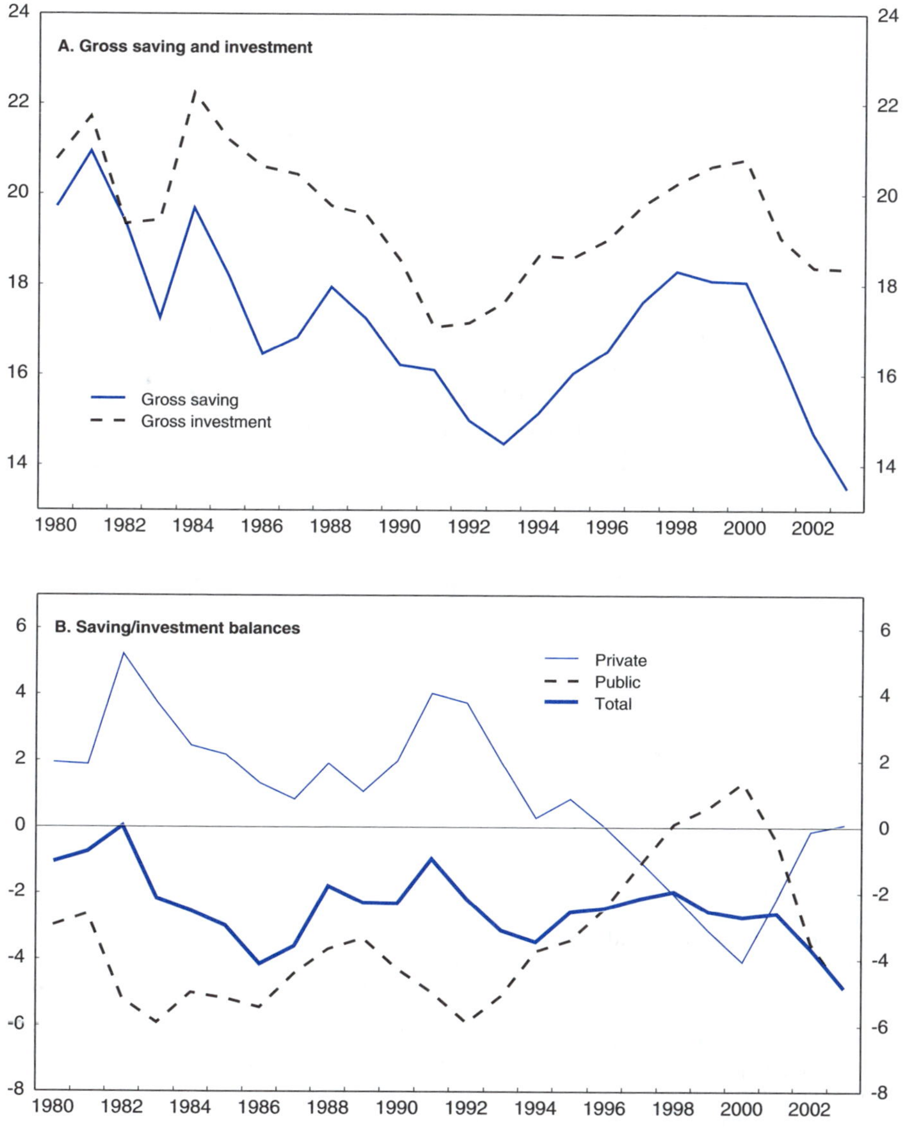

Source: Bureau of Economic Analysis.

reversed subsequently as the budget slipped back into deficit (Panel B). At the same time, although the private sector eliminated its financial deficit as firms reduced investment outlays, its saving/investment balance has remained lower than at this stage of most previous recoveries, given the persistently low household saving rate.

A large and persistent current account deficit portends rising financial payments arising from the increasingly negative international investment position, which could become more and more difficult to finance. However, the build-up in net external claims on US residents is relatively recent, and hence the net servicing cost of the debt still very small. And to the extent that foreign capital inflows have helped quicken productivity gains, the resulting increase in GDP growth enhances the country's capacity to service the debt. Yet, even though the US economic expansion is again more vigorous than most others', foreign investors may in the future become less willing to finance the gap between US spending and output. Indeed, while remaining high, the flow of private capital into the United States has slowed somewhat in the last two years. Although governments – especially those of Japan and China – have stepped up their purchases of US assets (Table 1.7), this slowdown may have contributed to the fall of the dollar on foreign-exchange markets since early 2002 (see Chapter IV). Still, the capability of the United States to incur foreign debt has been

Table 1.7. **Capital flows into the United States**

$ billion

	1999	2000	2001	2002	2003
Foreign official purchases of US Treasury securities	12.2	–10.2	10.7	43.1	128.5
Foreign official purchases of other government securities	20.4	40.9	20.9	30.4	24.8
Other foreign official purchases of US assets	11.0	7.0	–26.6	21.3	54.4
Foreign direct investment	289.4	321.3	151.6	39.6	82.0
Other foreign purchases of US Treasury securities	–44.5	–76.9	–7.4	96.2	139.9
Other foreign purchases of other US securities	298.8	455.3	406.6	291.5	238.7
Other foreign purchases not included elsewhere	152.9	288.8	209.7	184.8	188.5
Total inflows	740.2	1 026.1	765.5	707.0	856.7
Memorandum items:					
US purchases of financial assets abroad	–503.6	–569.8	–349.9	–179.0	–277.7
Current account deficit	290.8	411.5	393.7	480.7	541.8
Stock of foreign official assets in the United States	–	–	–	–	1 343.1
Held as Treasury securities	–	–	–	–	827.3
Held in Asia	–	–	–	–	928.1

Source: Bureau of Economic Analysis.

greater than in other deficit countries, given its ability to finance its external deficit in a reserve currency (Greenspan, 2003). Indeed, less than 10 per cent of aggregate US foreign liabilities are currently denominated in non-dollar currencies.

Looking forward, the weight of US investments in global portfolios will impose an increasing restraint on current account deficits. The marginal allocation of US assets in the global portfolio has risen sharply over the 1990s, absorbing most of the increase in net financial wealth earlier in this decade outside the United States. The foreign accumulation of US assets is likely to slow if they come to occupy too large a share of the world's portfolio. What constitutes "too large" will depend on confidence in the ability of the borrower to meet its obligations and on relative expected rates of return, although governments have other motivations than the private sector. After rising to over two-thirds during the course of the 1990s, the US dollar share of global central bank foreign exchange reserves has declined somewhat while the euro's share is approaching one-fifth. But strong central bank purchases of dollar assets over the past year – aimed at limiting exchange-rate movements – may have reversed or halted this trend (abstracting from exchange-rate effects). Approximately half of private cross-border holdings are denominated in dollars, with one-third in euros. If global investors seek greater diversification in non-dollar assets, then US spending will need to match production more closely, and more production will need to be exported abroad (Kohn, 2004). In this regard, the declining exchange value of the dollar will be helpful, despite repercussion effects on foreign growth and hence US exports. A crucial issue is what kind of domestic spending will bear the brunt of restraint. With a reduced availability of foreign saving, domestic saving will need to increase or investment – which is not especially high in cross-country comparison, albeit apparently highly efficient – has to be cut back. Increased saving can be achieved by decreasing household consumption relative to income or by decreasing public spending relative to taxes. If the fiscal outlook does not change, then unless there is a considerable rise in private saving, it is investment that could be expected to adjust. The mechanism would be higher real interest rates than otherwise, ultimately implying slower growth in the capital stock, productivity and economic potential, which would itself reduce the relative interest in US assets. Hence, in one way or another, the situation of a high current account deficit and strong capital inflows will need to unwind, with the timing and nature of the adjustment remaining uncertain.

Ensuring fiscal sustainability and budgetary discipline

Reining in the fiscal deficit will be essential in order to avoid passing a heavy burden onto future generations, and will also facilitate the necessary external adjustment. The federal budget has moved from a surplus of nearly 1½ per cent of GDP in fiscal year 2001 to a deficit of 3½ per cent in 2003 and a projected 4¼ to 4½ per cent this year. The income tax cuts of 2001 and 2003 and the investment incentives of 2002

Figure 1.6. **Baseline and adjusted federal budget surplus**
Fiscal years, per cent of GDP

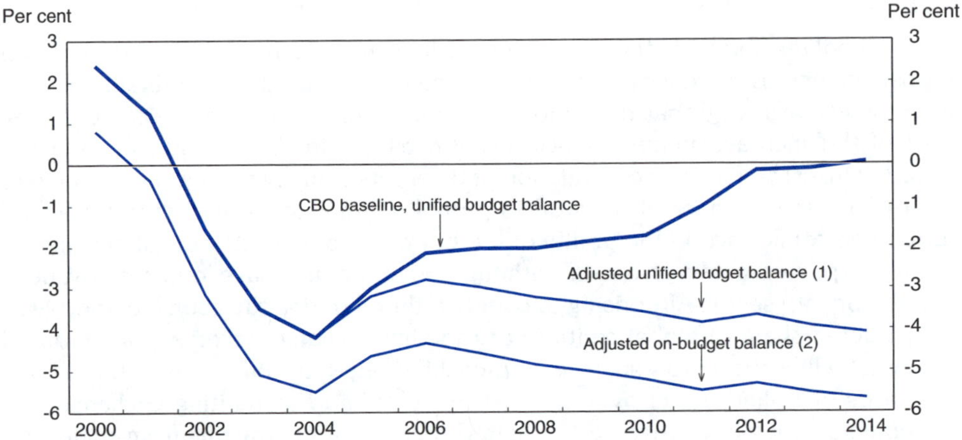

1. Adjusted for alternative policies; see Chapter II.
2. Adjusted surplus excluding Social Security trust fund surplus.
Source: Congressional Budget Office.

helped keep the recent recession short and shallow. They also provided timely support to the economy during the subsequent period when the recovery was held back by the effects of stock-market declines and corporate scandals and by a pervasive sense of caution toward hiring and capital spending. In principle, the reductions in marginal income-tax rates should also have beneficial supply-side effects over the medium term. However, while a return to budget deficits in the wake of the recession was appropriate, the revenue measures combined with the recent strong expansion in outlays mean that, without corrective action, large budget deficits will persist. Indeed, Secretariat calculations suggest that, if some plausible adjustments are made to the official baseline projections, the federal unified budget deficit including the surpluses accruing to the Social Security trust funds is unlikely to fall much below 4 per cent of GDP over the next ten years (see Figure 1.6 and Chapter II). By reducing national saving and therefore the domestically owned capital stock, deficits of this magnitude threaten to more than offset the beneficial effect on national income from the marginal tax rate reductions. The reduction in national saving could also be expected to put upward pressure on interest rates.

The projected large budget deficits are especially problematic because of the impending demographic stresses on public finances associated with the retirement of the baby boom generation beginning towards the end of the decade. Not much has been done in recent years to put Social Security on a sounder financial footing. Without any changes to current payroll taxes and sched-

Figure 1.7. **Long-term projected entitlement spending**
Per cent of GDP[1]

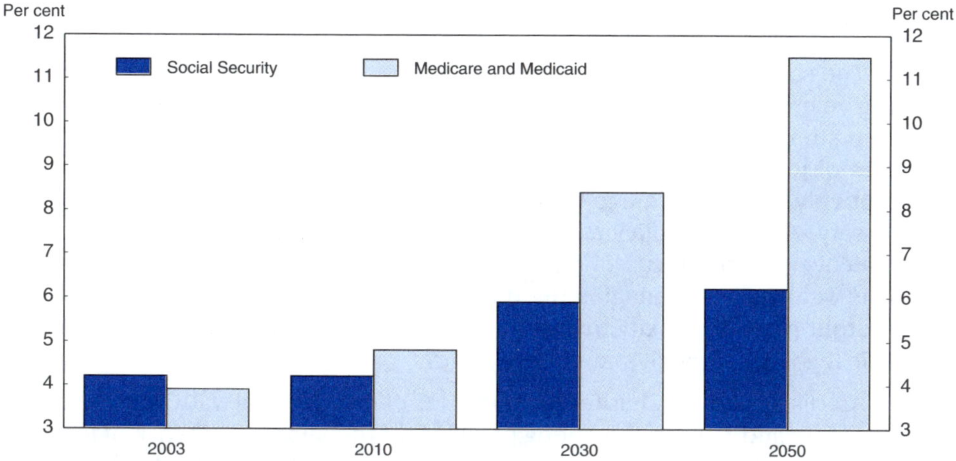

1. Intermediate spending path.
Source: Congressional Budget Office, *The Long-Term Budget Outlook.*

uled benefits, the trust funds will begin running deficits in 2018 and be exhausted by 2042. The financial outlook of the Medicare programme is much more uncertain because of the unknown growth of future medical costs, but in all likelihood this programme is in substantially poorer condition. On the one hand, the effects of demographic changes on public health spending are particularly sensitive to the rise in the retired population since it is at this point that the primary burden shifts from private to public insurance; on the other hand, it would seem politically difficult to pass rapid increases in medical costs largely driven by technological advance on to Medicare enrolees through premium or other cost-sharing increases. The recent addition of a prescription drug benefit to the programme has made matters considerably more difficult from this point of view, despite the use of deductibles and co-payments. Prescription drug expenses among the elderly are highly concentrated, and the structure of the co-payments makes it likely that the benefit will be disproportionately used by those with extremely high expenses. The Medicaid programme too is facing sustained projected cost increases, resulting from prescription drug expenses as well as growth in demand for long-term care. Based on conservative assumptions regarding cost increases per enrolee, spending on Medicare and Medicaid together is projected to increase from the current 4 per cent of GDP to 8½ per cent in 2030 and to 11½ per cent in 2050 (Figure 1.7). As time progresses, the cost of restoring the entitlement programmes to financial balance will rise rapidly. Hence, reform of all of them must remain a policy priority.

Maintaining price stability

The recent acceleration in demand makes it increasingly likely that within the next year the Federal Reserve will have to begin withdrawing some of the monetary stimulus that is currently being imparted to the economy. With core measures of inflation near the lower end of their desirable ranges, tightening as pre-emptively as a decade ago to head off incipient inflationary pressures seems unnecessary. Although policymakers can probably be more patient now than in earlier recoveries, the focus of policy has to be shifted from forestalling further economic weakness to managing the risks associated with the prospective closing of the output gap – the "exit strategy" from the recent overriding goal of achieving economic recovery through stimulatory policy.

As discussed in Chapter III, both the efforts to deal with the increasing deflation fears and risks in the spring of 2003 and the subsequent task of fostering the upswing by keeping real long-term interest rates low in the face of strong growth have highlighted the value of clear communication between the central bank and the private sector. Because the transmission of monetary policy through long-term interest rates relies importantly on private-sector expectations of future short-term interest rates, the Federal Open Market Committee's own view of the likely future course of the economy and its policy responses would be a useful element of its discourse with the public. Communicating this information effectively and in a manner that clarifies the contingent nature of their commitments regarding future interest rates is a major challenge for monetary policymakers. Moreover, in an environment of effective price stability, firmly anchored long-term inflation expectations are especially important, not only to maintain public confidence in the durability of low inflation achieved over the past two decades, but also to limit the risk of a potentially self-reinforcing deflationary spiral in the face of a hypothetical negative shock. Improvements to the monetary framework that anchor long-term inflation expectations without limiting the ability of policymakers to respond flexibly to shocks would probably be valuable.

Improving confidence and reducing distortions in financial markets

Corporate governance and accounting scandals undermined investor confidence and exacerbated the stock-market decline in the early part of the decade (Chapter IV). In this way they contributed to the uneven pace of the recovery from the 2001 recession and continue to pose a latent threat to financial stability in the sense that further scandals could easily re-ignite negative market behaviour. Underlying the corporate scandals have been weak governance structures, compounded by questionable accounting practices and executive compensation schemes that provided undue incentives to boost short-term share prices, even at the expense of longer-term value. The 2002 Sarbanes-Oxley Act responded to these and other concerns by calling for measures, among other things, to increase penalties for fraud, to enhance both auditor independence and regulation of the accounting profession, and to increase both disclosure requirements for public companies and the responsibility of their executives for financial reporting. Considerable progress has been made in implementing this agenda, but challenges remain, such as pressing ahead with improvements in the accounting for stock options, ensuring the independence of corporate boards, enhancing shareholder rights and achieving greater harmony between US and other international accounting standards. Moreover, renewed scandals in recent months, involving the New York Stock Exchange and the mutual funds industry, have demonstrated that there is still unfinished business in the area of corporate reform.

The substantial under-funding of defined-benefit corporate pension plans also poses significant financial, regulatory and accounting issues. Although they have become less widespread, such plans remain an important source of retirement security for 44 million American workers. Under-funded pension obligations have acted as a drag on corporate profits and credit ratings for a number of major US corporations. The failure of several large companies with significantly under-funded plans has also weakened the finances of the agency that insures such private pensions. Given the adverse impact on corporate finance and potential risks to financial-market stability, weaknesses in the regulatory framework and accounting practices that have allowed these problems to arise need to be addressed. In view of the rapid growth and systemic importance of some government-sponsored enterprises, their regulation and supervision will have to be tightened, too. Indeed, the two leading housing-finance enterprises, Fannie Mae and Freddie Mac, which have become major players in financial markets, have both admitted substantial accounting irregularities. An ongoing issue is these enterprises' special status, which has led to the market perception of a government guaranty, significant rents to their shareholders and a marginally lower cost of funds to home purchasers, a distortion that is incremental to the tax preferences already provided.

Enhancing competition to sustain higher productivity growth

Regulatory reform efforts in a broad range of industries, which began in the 1970s and accelerated in the 1980s, have resulted in increased importance of competitive forces as a means to allocate resources and improve economic efficiency. A number of indicators suggest that such forces have been stronger in the United States than in most other Member countries for some time. This has contributed to sizeable productivity gains and good economic performance by international comparison over the past decade or so. Nonetheless, despite the generally pro-competitive thrust of policies, a number of challenges remain (see Chapter V).

Although there are few sectors of the economy from which competition policy and law are completely excluded, given the high risks of sanctions and damages for violation, many anomalous exemptions and special regimes have found their way into US legislation. Contrary to other Member countries, government-related firms are exempted from competition enforcement. Intellectual property rights (IPRs) create special challenges for competition policy, as their purpose is to limit competition temporarily to capture the long-run benefits of innovation. The strengthening of IPRs over the past 20 years has been accompanied by a surge in patents. But the evidence linking this to increased innovation is slight, and some problems have followed the shift to stronger IPRs, such as the soaring cost of patent litigation.

The generally favourable experience with deregulation created pressure for liberalisation in network industries, where the United States has rather been a laggard, at least in the electricity sector. Reforms in the 1990s have entailed some positive results but also some setbacks, reflecting both the difficulties in ensuring competition in such industries and policy mistakes. As to telecommunications, the advent of competition for voice services in local markets following the reforms in the mid-1990s has started to bear fruit, but policies are still needed that make sure that entry in local voice services and broadband are not thwarted by dominant carriers. Introducing competition in the electricity market has proved particularly difficult, and restructuring has stalled in the wake of the California meltdown in 2000-01, which reflected flaws in the regulatory framework rather than the impact of competition. The urgency of further regulatory reform was highlighted by the August 2003 blackout, which has been traced in part to weaknesses in supervision and co-ordination.

The trade policy challenge

The United States continues to place great importance on free trade and competition in its commercial relations with the rest of the world. Controversially, it believes that it is appropriate to advance on all fronts – "competitive liberalisation" *via*"complementary courses" – despite the implications for the most-favoured nation (MFN) principle and the inability to deal properly with agricultural subsidies. It is therefore busily negotiating bilaterally and regionally, in addition to assuming its key role in the Doha Round. In 2003, new free trade agreements were concluded with Chile and Singapore, both including commitments to dispute settlement and compensation mechanisms in case capital controls were ever implemented. More recently, agreements, still to be approved by Congress, have been reached with five Central American nations and with Australia. They both avoid full liberalisation in sugar and the former in clothing as well. Negotiations are still underway with Morocco, Panama and the Dominican Republic, and are imminent with the Southern African Customs Union and four Andean nations. Despite these bilateral developments, US officials have not given up their hopes to have a Free Trade Area of the Americas (involving 34 countries) in place before mid-2005 when fast-track authority expires, arguing that narrower agreements will buttress and not undermine such plans.

On the multilateral front, negotiations in the Doha Round stalled with the Cancun ministerial meeting in September 2003. The United States had proposed to abolish tariffs on all manufactures by 2015 and have faster elimination for some other products. However, unlike the EU, it did not wish to include the so-called Singapore issues (customs procedures, transparency in government tendering, competition rules and investment). Efforts are now underway to restart the talks in order to have some chance of reaching the 2005 deadline. If that is not met, the risk is that the pace of protectionist tendencies will increase further, as seems to be happening in the matter of foreign outsourcing ("offshoring").

Foreign outsourcing has become controversial

While comprehensive data are not available, it appears that there has been an increase in outsourcing, at least in the services sector. It can tentatively be asserted that while globalisation in the manufacturing sector has been a feature throughout the half-century following World War II, this trend seems to have accelerated in recent years as an international value chain has been formed in many industries. In the IT-hardware sector alone this may have boosted real GDP growth by 0.3 percentage points per annum since 1995 (Mann, 2003b). Moreover, with the continued digitisation of economic activity and the ability to transmit increasingly large amounts of information at ever lower cost, it has become possible and profitable to shift the production of a rising number of services abroad,[2] just as earlier occurred with manufactures, even though such job transfers are unlikely to be responsible for the meagre overall job gains during this expansion. In any case, in accordance with comparative advantage, the life cycle of these goods and services often calls for their production to move to low-wage environments, once they have been standardised to some extent,[3] especially if the destination country has an abundance of skilled labour. Both source and host countries gain real income from the resulting specialisation. A recent study suggests that offshore outsourcing generates an average of about $1.46 of value to the world for each dollar of activity shifted offshore from the United States to India, of which 78 per cent (about $1.13 – that is, a net gain of 13 per cent) is retained in the US economy (McKinsey Global Institute, 2003).

For the United States the gains depend importantly on the degree to which workers whose positions are outsourced can find new employment. Concern over the lack of net job creation during the current recovery (see Box 1.1 above) has provided fuel for those opposed to employers' ability to outsource abroad, although job creation is projected to pick up from now on. The difficulty in finding employment for those whose positions have been eliminated is not a new phenomenon, even though in the 20 years to 1999 a clear majority of those displaced from their jobs in import-sensitive industries both in- and outside of manufacturing found new employment within a fairly short time at wage rates that were broadly equal to their previous levels (Kletzer, 2001). However, this still leaves a sizeable minority who lost out, especially concentrated among females and the low-skilled: indeed, about a quarter took longer than six months to find another job, and even among those successfully re-employed, more than a fifth had to take pay cuts of 30 per cent or more.[4]

The United States has long had legislation on its books that provides trade adjustment assistance to workers in manufacturing who are displaced by the side-effects of liberalisation. But that may be inadequate in the current context. As a result, Congress has a whole series of draft bills before it intended to deal, at least in part, with the problem. One would extend the existing training, health care and other benefits to displaced service-sector workers. Another would require firms to provide three months' advance notice of outsourcing moves. Other legislators have gone further in a restrictive direction by advocating that: the federal government should bar loans, grants and guarantees to any firm laying off more workers domestically than abroad; federal contracts should not be awarded to firms that intend to use offshore labour;[5] and tax deductions should be denied for corporate expenses to move workers abroad or hire foreign contractors. Earlier, some observers had proposed the implementation of a wage insurance scheme.[6] For its part, the Administration has recommended a system of "personal re-employment accounts", which would provide as much as $3 000 for displaced workers to spend on education, re-training or counselling at an estimated cost of $3.6 billion per year, but Congress has not yet voted on this proposal. As many as 30 states have recently been considering (and four have passed) legislation that would restrict international outsourcing by, for example, limiting the use of offshore contractors in state and local government procurement and requiring call centre employees to disclose their locations. The challenge for policy-makers will be to avoid protectionist responses to these developments, possibly by pre-empting such measures in the Doha Round (Mattoo and Wunsch, 2004) and focus instead on growth-promoting policies and improved adjustment assistance and social protection, so as to maintain the economy's ability to adjust flexibly to future developments.

Several important trade disputes

In that regard, there have been a rising number of commercial disputes, many of which have involved the WTO. Anti-dumping investigations still dominate, but safeguard cases are growing more strongly, both in number and importance. While the United States is a major user of these measures, it was supplanted by India as the heaviest anti-dumping user in 2002. Easily the most attention has been devoted to the safeguard tariffs of up to 30 per cent imposed by the United States on steel imports in March 2002 for three years (with subsequent exemptions for about one-third of total imports). In 2003, the WTO ruled that such duties were illegal, and the EU and Japan prepared to impose sanctions. A September 2003 study by the US International Trade Commission on the impact of the steel tariffs noted steep price increases and considerable associated earnings losses in steel-consuming industries, along with a modest ($42 million) fall in US welfare, despite estimated tariff revenue of $650 million.[7] With international steel prices firming, the dollar at a much lower level and progress in restructuring the steel industry, the United States agreed to eliminate the measures in December 2003. However, it simultaneously announced the continuation of the licensing and monitoring programme that had been in effect during the safeguard period and a possible change to the way anti-dumping duties are calculated, and pressures have surfaced to ban exports of scrap steel in view of prospective shortages. Still, the early elimination of the tariffs has given a lift to the prospects of reaching a steel-subsidies agreement at the OECD-led talks this year.

Another dispute, which may be near resolution, is that concerning Canadian softwood lumber. A provisional accord reached in December 2003 would give Canada duty-free access to 31.5 per cent of the US market, somewhat below its present market share and the pre-dispute quota level. Yet, complications have arisen with subsequent rulings by NAFTA and the WTO, the first of which objected to the countervailing part, while the second validated the anti-dumping part of the combined 27 per cent current duty on Canadian softwood lumber. In any case, import quotas are at best only a second-best solution, and it would be preferable to agree on the amount and eventual removal of alleged Canadian subsidies to the industry.

There are also several ongoing important disputes with the EU. One is over the so-called Foreign Sales Corporation (FSC) provisions in the US tax code, which the WTO ruled are not consistent with international agreements. In 2003, the WTO considered that US actions to abide with this ruling were not sufficient and entitled the EU to levy tariffs on US exports, which the EU started implementing in March. At the time of writing, there was no agreement in Congress on legislation addressing this issue, but proposals being considered would cut the corporate income tax rate for manufacturers progressively over the next five years by amounts in line with the foreign sales of the firm. Other disputes concern anti-dumping legislation. First, under the so-called Byrd amendment (the Continued Dumping and Subsidy Offset Act of 2000), the US authorities have been giving several hundred million dollars per year in revenues collected under anti-dumping and countervailing duties to the plaintiff companies, a procedure the WTO recently ruled to be in contravention with its rules. The WTO has also ruled that the Anti-Dumping Act of 1916 is not consistent with its rules and authorised the EU to suspend trade obligations on a corresponding amount of US exports. Judicial proceedings, especially in the latter case, have been especially burdensome for foreign exporting firms.

Finally, two sectors that have traditionally been subject to frequent disagreement continue to be sensitive. One is textiles and clothing, where the United States recently imposed safeguard quotas on certain imports from China (which has recently become a WTO Member), a move that has to be seen in the context of the impending expiration of the Multi-Fibre Agreement. The other is agriculture, where an explicit "peace clause" agreed at the foundation of the WTO has just expired. That clause prevented Member countries from resorting to its dispute settlement procedures with respect to farm subsidies, except if such subsidies rose beyond their 1992 levels. The current level of support relative to revenue in the US agricultural sector is relatively low by international comparison. In 2000-02, producer support estimates were 21 per cent in the United States, 35 per cent in the EU and 59 per cent in Japan. However, the 2002 farm bill demonstrates a marked shift away from the goal of greater market orientation embodied in the 1996 farm legislation. It increases and extends support, tightens the link between payments and production parameters and imposes higher costs not only on US taxpayers but also on other countries. It thus risks accentuating both production distortions and trade tensions, despite ambitious US proposals for agricultural liberalisation in the context of the Doha round, and is not at all in line with long-term OECD policy reform objectives.

The energy/environment challenge

With official estimates of dependence on foreign oil and natural gas being revised upwards and the reliability and cost of electricity supplies called into question by the August 2003 blackout and the California electricity crisis of 2000-01, the attention of the authorities has been focused for some time now on improving supply conditions in the industry and hence longer-term energy security. Legislation under consideration in Congress would provide tax incentives to most energy-producing sectors, including nuclear power and coal. It would encourage the production of ethanol to mix with gasoline, despite the fact that ethanol is widely considered to be far more expensive than other possible sources of transportation fuel (International Energy Agency, 2004), even when account is taken of its environmental advantages. But it would not tighten the "CAFE" standards on fuel efficiency by motor vehicles, even new vechicles' fuel efficiency has stagnated for the past decade at a level some 6 per cent below the 1987 peak level, as light truck sales have gone from one in ten to one in two and both weight and horsepower have continued to increase within each market segment. Criticisms levelled at the draft energy legislation include that it puts excessive emphasis on traditional petroleum over other kinds of energy and conservation, which means that greenhouse gas (GHG) emissions will rise inexorably. However, the Administration has separately succeeded in raising the "CAFE" standard for light trucks for the model years 2005 to 2007 by a cumulative 6 per cent. It would be useful to tighten up the definition of what constitutes a light truck so that the comparatively lax standards they face are not an artificial advantage in the market place.

The authorities continue to oppose efforts to reduce GHG emissions through the Kyoto protocol, claiming that existing technologies for their reduction would not be cost effective, harming economic growth excessively and allowing no role for new technology. They thus prefer to support climate science and related research focusing on "breakthrough technologies" such as carbon sequestration, hydrogen use, clean coal and nuclear fusion (specifically the ITER project). A July 2003 research plan calls for 21 separate reports on varying aspects of climate change to be produced over the next four years. US policies nevertheless aim at cutting the emissions intensity of output by 18 per cent relative to past trends by 2012, which would still allow a rise in actual emissions by 14 per cent relative to recent levels and 31 per cent over the 1990 (Kyoto baseline) outcome. In late 2003, the authorities announced that they intend to toughen the rules of the voluntary GHG registry, established in 1994 in order to make it more credible, and to launch a system of tradable credits. Firms exceeding a certain CO2 threshold would have to report emissions from all their plants and get credit only for the reductions achieved since 2002. The federal position is to some extent undercut by the states, with some of them having adopted policies to reduce or register GHG emissions, and others co-operating to decrease power plant emissions. Many private firms have announced their intention to cut emissions voluntarily, and a number of them have joined the city of Chicago to form the Chicago Climate Exchange to trade emission credits. In a related matter, the United States has asked for exemptions from the agreed January 2005 ban on methyl bromide (used in agriculture) in the context of the Montreal protocol on ozone protection.

In other energy policies with clear environmental impacts, in August 2003 the Administration weakened the New Source Review rules – requiring the installation of pollution-reducing technology when facilities are expanded or modernised – by allowing an escape clause if firms say that they are "upgrading" rather than modernising their plant and equipment. Neither will routine maintenance, repair and replacement bring about an enhanced pollution abatement requirement. In its view this requirement had been a barrier to carrying out such investments. A Congressionally mandated study had found that the existing system had failed to curb pollution by the nation's oldest plants and recommended that the latter should be given 10 years to clean up or shut down. In its Clear Skies initiative, the Administration set a target of reducing SO_2/NO_X/mercury pollution by 29 per cent by 2007 and 70 per cent by 2018, but it opposes recommendations to include GHG emission targets. In December 2003, it proposed to meet the mercury target by a cap-and-trade system rather than the previous administration's policy of requiring individual plants to respect specific mercury targets, which would have led to a reduction of at least 90 per cent by 2007. More recently, the Environmental Protection Agency has been studying the proposal rule to ensure that it would indeed achieve the target over the promised horizon and not as much as a decade later.

The social/equity challenge

Apart from the fiscal aspect mentioned above, the strong rise in health care costs also has a social dimension. Many Americans from all socio-economic groups lack health insurance, although it is among the poor, those with low educational attainment minorities and youth that the lack is most severe (Table 1.8). The overall proportion without health insurance picked up to over 15 per cent in 2002, after temporarily receding from its previous peak of over 16½ per cent in 1998. Public programmes, especially Medicaid, covered more people, but not enough to offset the decline in private coverage. The trend increase in the share of the uninsured is likely to continue as soaring costs discourage both employer-sponsored coverage and the purchase of individual insurance. This also has a significant economic impact. One study (Institute of Medicine of the National Academies, 2003) put the cost of poorer health outcomes and earlier death because of the lack of health insurance at 1¼ per cent of GDP. This is far greater than the estimated cost of providing the extra services that the uninsured would receive if they were covered, probably implying an efficiency loss of around ½ per cent of GDP. The public policy challenge of health care is the problem of maintaining some degree of equity in the face of technological change that persistently increases the cost of meeting that goal (Glied, 2003).

In contrast to health coverage, latest figures show that the fears that the cyclical downturn would reverse some, or all, of the sharp drop in welfare caseloads following the 1996 reforms have proved unfounded. While the downtrend has been slowing, it continued through mid-2003. The cumulative reduction in welfare caseloads since the 1993-94 peak is now some 60 per cent, and related to individuals (rather than families) it is now down to levels witnessed at the beginning of the 1960s. Probably half of the decline is attributable to a fall in *entry* to programmes, rather than beneficiaries being removed from the roles (Grogger, 2003). On the other hand, poverty rates have risen again. Although, at 12 per cent of the population, the overall poverty rate in 2002 was still 3 percentage points below the previous peak in 1993, poverty is likely to have kept growing in 2003. Moreover, it remains at around one-fifth for ethnic minorities and female householder families with no husband present. At the same time, there is notable hardship among the poor, with 40 per cent of poor single-parent working mothers' spending at least half of their income on childcare and a significant and rising proportion of poor households paying more than half of their income for housing.

Table 1.8. **The non-elderly without health insurance**

1998

	Current Population Survey	Per cent	Survey of Income and Program Participation	Per cent	Medical Expenditure Panel Survey	Per cent	National Health Interview Survey	Per cent
A. Absolute numbers (in millions)								
Uninsured for the entire year	–	–	21.1	9.1	31.1	13.3	n.a.	–
Uninsured at a specific point in time	–	–	40.5	16.6	42.6	18.3	39.0	16.5
Uninsured at any time during the year	–	–	56.8	24.8	59.0	25.3	n.a.	
Other[1]	43.9	18.4	–	–	–	–	–	–
	Spells beginning from July 1996-June 1977					Spells in progress in March 1998		
B. Duration of uninsured spells (%)								
Four months or less		44.5					87.9	
Five to 12 months		26.2					14.4	
13 to 24 months		13.4			}		77.8	
More than 24 months		15.9						
	Uninsured at any time during the year				Uninsured for the entire year		Distribution of the population uninsured for the entire year	
C. Selected characteristics (%)								
i) Race/ethnicity:								
White, non-Hispanic		18.4			6.3		48.4	
Black, non-Hispanic		33.4			10.7		15.3	
Hispanic		47.4			22.5		30.8	
Other		31.1			10.9		5.5	
ii) Family income (% of poverty level)								
Less than 200		47.9			19.5		74.9	
200 to 399		17.4			5.3		19.8	
400 or more		6.0			1.6		5.3	

Table 1.8. **The non-elderly without health insurance** (*cont.*)

1998

	Uninsured at any time during the year	Uninsured for the entire year	Distribution of the population uninsured for the entire year
C. Selected characteristics (%)			
iii) Highest education level among adults			
No high school diploma	50.4	24.6	28.4
High school graduate	33.1	12.7	36.4
Some college	22.1	7.3	26.6
Bachelor's degree or higher	9.9	2.6	8.7
iv) Family employment status			
At least one full-time worker all year	15.0	5.9	42.9
Part-time or part-year work only	46.1	16.1	46.6
No work	32.8	13.1	10.6
v) Age			
Less than 19	26.8	7.3	24.9
19 to 24	41.9	14.4	13.7
25 to 34	31.1	12.3	21.9
35 to 44	20.2	9.3	19.7
45 to 54	15.1	7.6	12.6
55 to 64	14.0	6.7	7.2
vi) Health status			
Excellent	23.7	8.9	28.8
Very good	25.1	9.3	32.8
Good	24.6	9.1	24.5
Fair	25.1	8.7	8.9
Poor	25.3	10.3	5.1

1. The CPS figure is intended to measure the number uninsured for the entire year but is believed to be up-biased and closer to a measure of those uninsured at a specific point in time.

Source: CBO (2003).

Finally, overall income inequality has stopped rising after its continuous run-up since 1979.

The education challenge

The current Administration has made reform of the compulsory education system one of its priorities. Already a decade ago the Committee termed its effectiveness "mediocre at best", pointing to low scores on international tests and high minority dropout rates as evidence and a lack of standards and incentives as culprits (OECD, 1994, p. 136). The costs of poor-quality compulsory schooling are multiple:

- greater numbers of dropouts;
- more remedial courses required among college students;
- more training needed by employers;
- an inability to handle new, productivity-enhancing technologies; and
- a reduced capacity to adjust to both temporary and permanent shocks, especially those related to "offshoring", that is shifting business functions to low-cost, foreign sites.

The Administration of the time tried a strategy of voluntary national standards for the public school system and for vocational studies, with little tangible success. Test scores later in the 1990s continued for the most part to show modest results in view of the comparatively high spending levels in the United States.[8] According to the most recent figures (1998), spending remains well above other countries' outlays, suggesting that value for money is still lacking. And upper secondary graduation rates are still on the low side by OECD standards.

A new and more ambitious approach is embodied in the 2002 No Child Left Behind (NCLB) Act, whose goal is not only to boost academic achievement overall but to bring all students up to a challenging standard labelled "proficiency". While the controversial idea of vouchers was dropped during Congressional debate, the legislation imposes mandatory standards – albeit ones that states are left to define completely for themselves[9] – and increased accountability on teachers, schools and administrators. Last year the states had to define a level of proficiency in reading and mathematics which they pledged to achieve for all pupils by 2013-14. In order to monitor progress annual tests for all those between 8 and 14 have to be set by 2005. Other deadlines include the fixing of standards in science and the guarantee that all teachers be "highly qualified" in their subject areas, each by 2005-06.

A key requirement in coming years will be for schools to achieve "adequate yearly progress" (AYP). AYP is being determined by test outcomes[10] and any school found wanting (either across the board or by race, income or disability group) will be sanctioned with increasing severity. In the first year the school is to receive "technical assistance". After two consecutive years students are supposed to be allowed to transfer. However, few have been able to do so thus far because of a lack of available space at better schools (though this is not supposed to be a legitimate excuse). Extra tutoring is called for under the law if a third straight year of underperformance is registered, but again the reality is that only a minority of those eligible so far have benefited from such help because of financial constraints.[11]

This may be symptomatic of a more general problem:[12] many state and local officials have claimed that the NCLB mandates have not been adequately funded by the federal government.[13] For example, it initially provided $360 million per year ($410 million is proposed in 2005) to pay for testing, but the National Association of State Boards of Education charged that it would cost many times more than that. Yet the federal government *has* been ramping up its aggregate discretionary education spending in recent years: since 2001 the average increase has been 8 to 9 per cent per year through to the Administration's proposed 2005 figures (depending on whether the calculation is made using outlays or budget authority), including double-digit average annual growth in funding the NCLB Act. But these are merely marginal increases in total government spending on schooling in kindergarten through twelfth grade, for which federal dollars are only about 7 per cent of the total. On the other hand, states have been in a severe although improving financial position, and education has been one area where dramatic cutbacks[14] have been made in some cases – even, ironically, in the very teacher training that is needed to achieve the NCLB Act objective of having only "highly qualified" teachers. It is clear that the situation will bear close monitoring in the coming years.

Notes

1. This growth rate of potential output is predicated on conservative assumptions for trend multifactor productivity growth (just below 2 per cent), growth of the capital stock (rising from 2 per cent in 2004 to 2½ per cent in 2005) and trend labour force growth (1¼ per cent). The implied growth rate of trend labour productivity in the business sector is about 2¼ per cent.
2. There are no official data on the magnitude of the phenomenon of outsourcing. One aggregate private-sector estimate, by the IT research firm Forrester, points to 400 000 US jobs that had been moved abroad cumulatively by July 2003, with a prediction of 3.3 million by 2015. These are of course small proportions of total job creation and destruction in the US economy, which average more than 30 million per year. Bardhan and Kroll (2003) judge that US employment in occupations at risk to outsourcing was around 14 million in 2001 (11 per cent of total employment), the majority of which were in office and administrative support categories with mean annual salaries some 25 per cent below average. However, about 5 million were comprised of business and financial support occupations and computer and mathematics professionals with salaries at least a third above average. The industries in which these occupations are prevalent all experienced worse employment outcomes in the nine quarters to the second quarter of 2003.
3. Furthermore, many jobs are simultaneously being "insourced", that is, being moved to the United States by foreign firms. Indeed, the United States habitually runs a surplus on its external trade in private services.
4. Those displaced from industries that were deemed relatively insensitive to import competition experienced similar re-employment and earnings change outcomes.
5. The Senate passed such legislation in March 2004. It would not apply to countries that have liberalised their public procurement rules.
6. Kletzer and Litan (2001) suggest that employers subscribe to such insurance with annual payments of up to $10 000 per worker for as long as two years at a yearly premium cost of some $5 billion. Agrawal and Farrell (2003) extend the idea and suggest that full-time workers could be covered for 70 per cent of all the wages lost until re-employment as well as healthcare subsidies for up to two years.
7. Similar negative assessments can also be found in a series of papers by Hufbauer and Goodrich (most recently, 2003).
8. Recent tests have included another eighth grade test in mathematics and science in 1999 (the so-called TIMSS-R), where US results were both quite low; and below-average outcomes in reading, mathematics and science literacy in the OECD's 2000 PISA programme for 15 year-olds. (The dispersion of reading outcomes was also especially marked.) However, in the 2001 PIRLS reading literacy test for fourth graders

US results were better than average, confirming that the real problem lies in later grades. Another piece of evidence suggesting sub-standard outcomes comes from the prevalence of incoming college students enrolling in remedial courses: according to the National Center for Educational Statistics, almost half of all freshmen at two-year colleges and nearly one in five at four-year schools enrolled in at least one remedial course in 2000 and they spent a longer time in remediation than in 1995 (OMB, 2004, p. 109). Eventually, 53 per cent of all college students take at least one remedial class in English or Mathematics (The American Diploma Project, 2004). Finally, by one count more than 60 per cent of employers rate high school graduates' basic language and mathematical skills as only "fair" or "poor" (The American Diploma Project, 2004).

9. Indeed, states also create their own tests and set their own thresholds for a student to be determined "proficient". Obviously, there is a risk of "dumbing down" both teaching and the tests so that the "standards" are met.

10. This is viewed as dangerous by teachers' unions, which fear the conflation of effects of teacher competency and school efficiency on the one hand and other exogenous factors such as innate ability, background and class size in the assessment of "proficiency". Critics have also charged that teaching will be increasingly tied to the tests. In any case many states have set their AYP targets such that the need for significant improvement is postponed until late in the 12-year adjustment period. Nonetheless, initial results and predictions are that a very high share of schools will fail to meet their targets right from the outset, even though some have even adjusted their scoring systems to downgrade what defines "proficiency" for the purposes of the NCLB Act. The American Diploma Project (2004) has established a set of English and Mathematics benchmark skills for college and workplace readiness. It urges all states to adopt them and the federal government to align its 12th grade testing on them and ensure that all students in the nation take that standardised test, as the NCLB Act requires at 4th and 8th grades.

11. After four years of failure to achieve AYP, schools must replace their staff, and after five the state must either run the school itself, transform it into a charter school or turn it over to a private manager.

12. More fundamental concerns that have been voiced (Ryan, 2003) are that NCLB creates perverse incentives:

- for states to lower academic standards, thereby creating a race to the bottom;
- for administrators to increase segregation by class and race and to push out low-performing pupils; and
- for the best teachers to avoid problem schools.

13. The Democrats contend that the FY 2004 appropriations bill passed in January underfunds the NCLB programme by around $ 7 billion or 13 per cent.

14. Compulsory education is not the only component to bear the brunt of state cutbacks: higher education has suffered trend declines since the late-1980s because of spending pressures emanating in part from Medicaid demands. This has led to upward pressure on tuition increases at public colleges and universities and a widening quality gap with their private counterparts (Kane and Orszag, 2003).

Bibliography

Agrawal, V. and D. Farrell (2003), "Who Wins in Offshoring", *The McKinsey Quarterly*, No. 4.

Bardhan, A.D. and C.A. Kroll (2003), "The New Wave of Outsourcing", Fisher Center for Real Estate and Urban Economics, University of California at Berkeley, Fall.

Bernanke, B.S. (2003), "The Jobless Recovery", Speech given at the Global Economic and Investment Outlook Conference, Carnegie Mellon University, Pittsburgh, 6 November.

Congressional Budget Office (2003), *How Many People Lack Health Insurance and For How Long?*, Washington, D.C., May.

Council of Economic Advisors (2004), *Annual Report*, Washington, D.C., February.

Glied, S. (2003), "Health Care Costs: On the Rise Again", *Journal of Economic Perspectives*, Vol. 17, No. 2, Spring.

Greenspan, A. (2003),"Remarks at the 21st Annual Monetary Conference", The Federal Reserve Board, Washington, D.C., 20 November.

Grogger, J., S.J. Haider and J. Klerman (2003), "Why Did the Welfare Rolls Fall During the 1990s? The Importance of Entry" , AEA *Papers and Proceedings*, Vol. 93, No. 2, May.

Groshen, E.L. and S. Potter (2003), "Has Structural Change Contributed to a Jobless Recovery?", Federal Reserve Bank of New York, *Current Issues in Economics and Finance*, Vol. 9, No. 8, August.

Hufbauer, G.C. and B. Goodrich (2003), "Next Move in Steel: Revocation or Retaliation?", Institute for International Economics, Policy Brief 03-10, Washington, October.

Institute of Medicine of the National Academies (2003), *Hidden Costs, Value Lost: Uninsurance in America*, Washington D.C.

International Energy Agency (2004), *Biofuels for Transport: An International Perspective*, Paris, April.

Juhn, C. and S. Potter (1999), "Explaining the Recent Divergence in Payroll and Household Employment Growth", Federal Reserve Bank of New York, *Current Issues in Economics and Finance*, Vol. 5, No. 16, December.

Kane, T. J and P. R. Orszag (2003), "Higher Education Spending: The Role of Medicaid and the Business Cycle", Policy Brief #124, Brookings Institution, Washington, D.C., September.

Kitchen, J. (2003), "A Note on the Observed Downward Bias in Real-Time Estimates of Payroll Jobs Growth in Early Expansions", unpublished manuscript, August.

Kletzer, L. (2001), *Job Loss from Imports: Measuring the Cost*, Institute for International Economics, Washington, D.C.

Kletzer, L. and R. Litan (2001), "A Prescription to Relieve Worker Anxiety", Policy Brief 01-2, Institute for International Economics, Washington, D.C., February.

Kohn, D.L. (2003), "Productivity and Monetary Policy", Speech given at the Federal Reserve Bank of Philadelphia Monetary Seminar, 24 September.

Kohn, D.L. (2004), "The United States in the World Economy", Remarks at the Federal Reserve Bank of Atlanta's Public Policy Dinner, 7 January.

Mann, C.L. (2003), "Globalization of IT Services and White-Collar Jobs: The Next Wave Productivity Growth", Institute for International Economies, Policy Brief 03-11, Washington, D.C., December.

Mattoo, A. and S. Wunsch (2004), "Pre-empting Protectionism in Services: The GATs and Outsourcing", Institute for International Economics, Washington, D.C., January.

McKinsey Global Institute (2003), "Offshoring: Is It a Win-Win Game?", San Francisco, August.

Nardone, T., M. Bowler, J. Kropf, K. Kirkland and S. Wetrogan (2003), "Examining the Discrepancy in Employment Growth between the CPS and the CES", paper presented to the Federal Economic Statistics Advisory Committee, US Bureau of Labor Statistics, 17 October.

OECD (1994), *Economic Surveys: United States*, Paris, November.

Office of Management and Budget (2004), *The Budget for Fiscal Year* 2005, US Government Printing Office, Washington, D.C.

Ryan, J. E. (2003), "The Perverse Incentives of the No Child Left Behind Act", University of Virginia School of Law, Public Law and Legal Theory Research Paper No. 03-17.

The American Diploma Project (2004), *Ready or Not: Creating a High School Diploma That Counts*, Achieve, Inc., The Education Trust and the Thomas B. Fordham Foundation, Washington, D.C., February.

Annex 1.1

Progress in structural reform

Labour markets

Previous recommendations

- Avoid increasing the federal minimum wage.
- Identify strategies to increase employment of the disabled.
- Tighten work requirement for welfare recipients.

Action taken

- A tightening of work requirements for welfare recipients, which currently have little bite, is under consideration in Congress.

Education

Previous recommendations

- Bring more schools up to the standards now in place.
- Expand competition in primary and secondary schooling.
- Reduce funding disparities across school districts and reconsider the design of state programmes.

Action taken

- The 2002 No Child Left Behind Act provides for testing, greater accountability, increased choice in public schooling and additional federal funding for schools in lower-income areas; it remains to be seen if the Act is sufficiently adapted or financed to achieve these objectives.

Product markets

Previous recommendations

- Improve competition in local telephone industry.
- Improve energy infrastructure, particular in electricity transmission and generation.
- Roll back the extra support given to farmers in recent years.

Action taken

- Unbundling of network elements has boosted competition for local voice services and provided incentives for investment and new services.
- The energy bill still considered in Congress focuses on increasing energy supply. Some of its provisions might help foster regional electricity transmission integration and related investment.
- The 2002 farm bill further increases support and distortions in the agricultural sector.

Financial markets

Previous recommendations

- Reassess bankruptcy and patent laws with aim of curbing abuses.
- Break links of government-sponsored enterprises with the federal government.
- Create independent regulatory board for, and limit consulting services by, auditors.
- Consider move toward principles-based accounting rules.
- Examine expensing of stock options.

Action taken

- Bankruptcy reform legislation has been stalled in Congress.
- The 2002 Sarbanes-Oxley Act created a regulatory board for auditors, the Public Company Accounting Oversight Board, and limited their non-auditing activities.
- As mandated by the Sarbanes-Oxley Act, the Securities and Exchange Commission carried out a study that recommended a prudent move toward principles-based accounting.
- The Financial Accounting Standards Board has recommended the mandatory expensing of stock options but there is still opposition in Congress.

Taxation

Previous recommendations

- Increase the limits for contributions to tax-free savings accounts.
- Eliminate deductions for mortgage interest and state and local income tax.
- Reform indirect taxation.
- Extend Earned Income Tax Credit.

Action taken

- Recent legislation has expanded tax-free Health Savings Accounts (HSAs) and the Administration has proposed the creation of tax-exempt Lifetime Savings Accounts (LSAs) and Retirement Savings Accounts (RSAs).

Environment

Previous recommendations

- Consider introducing a domestic cap-and-trade system for CO_2 emissions.
- Make evaluation of environmental costs and benefits of agriculture when providing support to this sector.
- Increase fuel taxes in lieu of tightening "CAFE" standards.
- Consider a carbon tax on all carbon-based energy products, including coal and natural gas.

Action taken

- While opposing efforts to reduce GHG emissions through the Kyoto protocol, the Administration has implemented a suite of policies to slow the growth of GHG emissions including aggressive technology investments in carbon sequestration, hydrogen, and fusion energy..
- The 2002 farm bill increases the size and scope of environmental programmes in this sector.
- The Administration has implemented a significant increase in fuel economy ("CAFE") standards for light trucks and SUVs over the coming three model years.
- The Administration has sent legislation to Congress and proposed regulations to cap emissions of SO_2, NO_x, and mercury from power plants by 70 per cent and has also proposed regulations to reduce emissions from diesel engines and diesel fuels. Taken together, these regulations are intended to satisfy the new National Ambient Air Quality Standards (NAAQS) for ozone and fine particulate matter by 2020.

II. Ensuring fiscal sustainability and budgetary discipline

Over the past three years, actual and projected federal budget balances have worsened more sharply than expected. Broadly, the deterioration to date of the federal budget reflects lower economic growth over most of the period, substantial personal income tax cuts and other revenue-reducing legislation, and a pronounced acceleration in outlays, notably on defence and homeland security. The current projections of large deficits in the unified budget persisting through the rest of the decade are especially problematic because towards the end of the decade the retirement of the baby-boom generation will begin, greatly increasing the stresses on public finances thereafter. At the state and local levels, where there are generally stringent requirements on balancing the budget year by year, significant cut-backs in current spending are beginning to alleviate fiscal strain following the collapse in revenues over recent years. This chapter focuses on the challenges posed by the deterioration in the fiscal outlook. It begins by analysing the recent changes to federal budget outcomes and projections for the next 10 years and their underlying causes, in particular the contributions from recent legislation. The chapter continues by reviewing recent developments in state and local finances and programmes shared between the federal and state levels. It then discusses projections of spending under entitlement programmes through 2050 and briefly reviews recent reform proposals for Social Security and Medicare. In view of the sharp rise in projected deficits, a return to budget discipline now that the recovery is gaining momentum is of utmost importance if recent tax reductions are to succeed in raising long-run income. To this end, the Chapter concludes by analysing recent developments in the presentation and transparency of the budget outlook and discussing options for reinstating the recently expired budget enforcement procedures.

The federal fiscal position and outlook

The deterioration of the 10-year budget projections

Figure 2.1 illustrates the successive downward revisions since January 2001 to the Congressional Budget Office's (CBO) baseline projections for the unified

Figure 2.1. **CBO's changing unified budget projections**

Surplus or deficit, fiscal years, $ billions

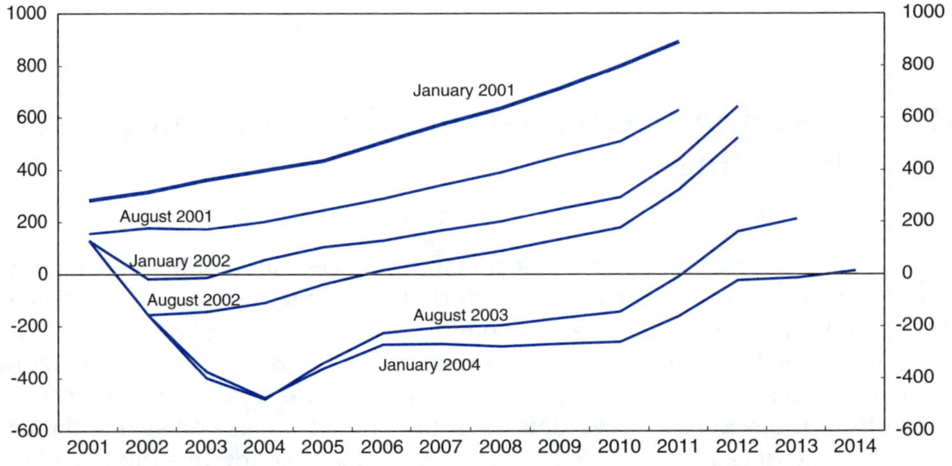

Source: Congressional Budget Office.

budget surplus for fiscal years (FY) 2001-11.[1] For several reasons the January 2001 projections are an appropriate starting point. Those projections were made immediately before the onset of the latest recession, and before the passage of several laws with major budget implications, among them the Economic Growth and Tax Relief Reconciliation Act of 2001 (EGTRRA), the Job Creation and Worker Assistance Act of 2002, and the Jobs and Growth Tax Relief Reconciliation Act of 2003.

The unified budget posted deficits in FY 2002 and 2003 of $158 billion and $375 billion, or 1.5 and 3.5 per cent of GDP, respectively. As recently as January 2003 the CBO projected a budget deficit for FY 2003 of only $199 billion, or 1.9 per cent of GDP. As discussed further below, the recent worsening of the fiscal balance was caused by further tax cuts, increases in discretionary spending and weaker-than-expected revenues from 2002 tax returns. Summing over the 11 fiscal years 2001-11, the projected and actual surpluses declined between January 2001 and January 2004 by $8.6 trillion, from a $5.6 trillion surplus to a $3 trillion deficit. Using the CBO's current projections for GDP, this decline amounts to an average of 6 percentage points of GDP. As mentioned, a large portion of the surplus reductions are caused by the much weaker economic conditions compared to what was anticipated as of January 2001. With the recovery taking hold, this source of drag on the federal budget will diminish, and accordingly the projected deficits tend to narrow in 2005 and 2006. However, downward revisions to the fiscal balance have not

Figure 2.2. **Sources of change in unified budget projections**
Surplus or deficit, fiscal years, $ billions

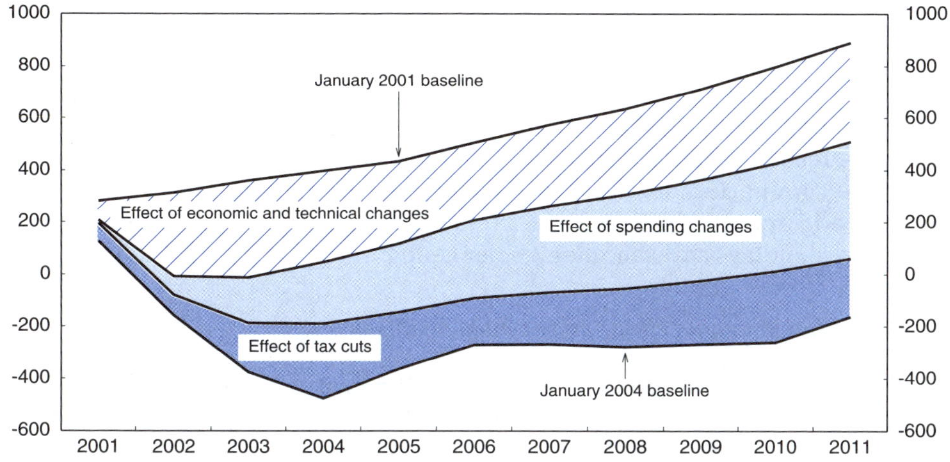

Source: Congressional Budget Office.

been confined to the recent past or near future but, under CBO's baseline assumptions, are upward of 6 percentage points of GDP in each year through 2011. This long-lasting deterioration in the budget outlook owes much to recent legislation and raises risks for sustainable economic growth as discussed further below.

When the CBO revises its projections, it classifies the changes to projected revenues and outlays into three categories: changes caused by recently enacted legislation, changes caused by adjustments to its economic projections and other, so-called technical factors that affect the budget.[2] Figure 2.2 presents a decomposition of the total revisions to the CBO's baseline between January 2001 and January 2004 into revenue changes due to legislation (labelled as "effect of tax cuts"), outlay changes caused by legislation ("effect of spending changes") and the effect of economic and technical revenue and outlay changes on the budget. To reflect the effects of tax cuts and outlay changes accurately, the increase in debt-service costs caused by revenue-reducing legislation such as an income tax reduction, which the CBO classifies as a legislative increase in outlays, has been subtracted from the CBO's projections of legislative outlay changes and added to its projections of legislative revenue changes.[3]

Slightly more than half of the downward revisions for FY 2002 and 2003 was caused by economic and technical factors, notably weakness in revenues. While some of this weakness is cyclical, based on its analysis of tax receipts from previous years the CBO concluded that a large part of this revenue weakness will be long-lasting.[4] Thus, technical factors are partly responsible for revenues as far into the future as 2011 being currently projected considerably lower than in January 2001. From 2004 on, however, about two-thirds of the downward revisions to surplus projections are due to legislative changes over the past three years. Moreover, even after assigning the debt-service cost associated with revenue-reducing legislation to the budgetary effect of the tax cuts, from FY 2005 forward more than half of the recent and projected legislative changes are driven by the enormous recent expansion in (mostly discretionary) spending. Over the second half of the current decade, the tax cuts enacted over the last three years are projected to add about 1.6 per cent of GDP to the federal deficit, while the projected expansion in outlays adds another 2.6 per cent.

Recent legislation and its effects on the budget outlook

Revisions to the budget outlook over the past year have been dominated by four legislative measures: the passage in May 2003 of the Jobs and Growth Tax Relief Reconciliation Act (JGTRRA), the supplemental appropriation acts of March 2003 and October 2003, and the Medicare Prescription Drug, Improvement, and Modernization Act signed into law in December 2003. JGTRRA brought forward some of the provisions of the 2001 tax legislation and reduced tax rates on certain capital gains and dividends (see Box 2.1). It reduces revenues in FY 2003-05 by a total of $265 billion, or on average about 0.9 per cent of GDP. Thereafter, its budgetary effects are small. The supplemental appropriations act passed in March 2003 provided budget authority of $79 billion for 2003, and the one passed in October 2003 provided budget authority for FY 2004 for another $87 billion. The bulk of this funding was provided for the war and subsequent occupation in Iraq and for ongoing military operations in Afghanistan. Because the CBO's baseline projections are required to assume that annual appropriations for discretionary programmes will continue at their current level with increases for projected inflation, the supplemental appropriations have boosted projected discretionary outlays for the period 2005-14 by a total of $880 billion, or on average about 0.6 per cent of GDP. While it is questionable whether the supplementary appropriations will be extended by the full amount as assumed in the CBO baseline, the current build-up in defence spending is likely to consume some of these funds for a sustained period. Discretionary spending outside of defence has also grown rapidly, on average by 9 per cent annually over 2001-03, and this higher level of non-defence outlays is also projected forward in the baseline, though its growth rate is expected to decline significantly.

The Medicare Prescription Drug Act presents the largest expansion of the Medicare programme since its creation in 1965 (see Box 2.2). The prescription drug benefit covers expenses for outpatient medication; after an initial deductible, 75 per cent of expenses are covered until a threshold of $2 250 of qualifying

Box 2.1. Provisions of the Jobs and Growth Tax Relief Reconciliation Act (JGTRRA)

Income tax provisions

JGTRRA brought forward the reductions in the regular income tax rates that had been scheduled under the Economic Growth and Tax Relief Reconciliation Act of 2001 (EGTRRA) for 2004 and 2006. Table 2.1 presents the reductions under previous and current law.

Table 2.1. **Marginal income tax rate provisions**

Calendar year	28 per cent rate reduced to:		31 per cent rate reduced to:		36 per cent rate reduced to:		39.6 per cent rate reduced to:	
	EGTRRA	JGTRRA	EGTRRA	JGTRRA	EGTRRA	JGTRRA	EGTRRA	JGTRRA
	Per cent							
2001	27.5	27.5	30.5	30.5	35.5	35.5	39.1	39.1
2002	27	27	30	30	35	35	38.6	38.6
2003	27	–	30	–	35	–	38.6	–
2004-05	26	–	29	–	34	–	37.6	–
2006-10	25	–	28	–	33	–	35	–
2003-10	–	25	–	28	–	33	–	35

Source: Congressional Budget Office (2003*c*); Joint Committee on Taxation (2003b).

The taxable income ceiling for the new 10 per cent tax bracket introduced by EGTRRA was initially $6 000 ($12 000 for married couples) through 2007, and $7 000 ($14 000 for married couples) from 2008 through 2010. JGTRRA raised the income level for 2003 04 to $7 000 ($14 000 for married couples).

JGTRRA also expanded the 15 per cent tax bracket and increased the standard deduction for married couples, so-called marriage penalty relief. Table 2.2 compares the provisions under previous and current law.

In 2001, EGTRRA committed to increasing the child tax credit from the previous $500 to $600 in 2001 04, $700 in 2005 08, $800 in 2009, and $1 000 in 2010. JGTRRA raised the child tax credit in 2003-04 from $600 to $1 000. After 2004 it returns to its level under EGTRRA.

JGTRRA also increases in 2003-04 the amount of individual income that is exempt from the alternative minimum tax, from $49 000 to $58 000 for married couples and surviving spouses, and from $35 750 to $40 250 for single taxpayers. After 2004, the exemption amounts return to pre-EGTRRA levels of $45 000 for married couples and $33 750 for singles.

Box 2.1. Provisions of the Jobs and Growth Tax Relief Reconciliation Act (JGTRRA) (*cont.*)

Table 2.2. Marriage penalty relief provisions

Calendar year	End point for 15 per cent rate for joint returns relative to single taxpayer end point		Standard deduction for joint returns relative to single taxpayer standard deduction	
	EGTRRA	JGTRRA	EGTRRA	JGTRRA
	Per cent			
2003	167	200	167	200
2004	167	200	167	200
2005	180	180	174	174
2006	187	187	184	184
2007	193	193	187	187
2008	200	200	190	190
2009-10	200	200	200	200

Source: Congressional Budget Office (2003*c*); Joint Committee on Taxation (2003b).

Provisions for capital gains and dividend taxation

JGTRRA reduced the tax rates for capital gains realised between 6 May 2003 and 31 December 2008, and for dividends received in 2003-08. Under previous law, individual income taxes applied to dividends as ordinary income tax rates. Individual income taxes on long-term capital gains were 20 per cent, with a lower rate of 10 per cent applying to taxpayers who are taxed at rates of 10 or 15 per cent on ordinary income. Under JGTRRA, the 10 and 20 per cent rates are reduced to 5 per cent (zero in 2008) and 15 per cent, respectively, and these rates are applied to dividends as well as long-term capital gains. These lower rates apply to the alternative minimum tax as well.

Expensing provisions

The Job Creation and Worker Assistance Act of 2002 introduced a special 30 per cent up-front depreciation deduction for qualifying equipment investment undertaken by businesses. Equipment has to be acquired between 11 September 2001 and 10 September 2004. JGTRRA raised this deduction to 50 per cent for investments undertaken after 5 May 2003 and extended the time period for acquisition until 31 December 2004. In addition, JGTRRA raised the amount of investment undertaken by small businesses that can be fully expensed through 2005.

Box 2.1. **Provisions of the Jobs and Growth Tax Relief Reconciliation Act (JGTRRA)** *(cont.)*

Budgetary effects

The budgetary effects of the law are summarised in Table 2.3.

Table 2.3. **Effects on budget deficit**[1]
$ billion

Calendar year	2003	2004	2005	2006-13	2003-13
Income tax provisions	31	88	46	6	171
Capital gains and dividend taxation	4	18	21	105	148
Expensing provisions	12	36	15	–53	10
Other	14	6	–	–	20
Net increase in budget deficit	**61**	**149**	**82**	**57**	**349**
As per cent of GDP	0.57	1.32	0.69	0.06	0.27

1. Total may not add up due to rounding.
Source: Congressional Budget Office (2003*c*); Joint Committee on Taxation (2003b).

expenses per year is reached. No coverage is provided for the next $3 600 of prescription drug expenses, after which catastrophic coverage sets in. The CBO estimates that for FY 2004-13 the prescription drug benefit will raise federal government non-interest outlays by $410 billion, with annual expenses reaching $73 billion (0.4 per cent of GDP) in 2013 (Congressional Budget Office, 2003*d*). While the negotiations in the Congress considered several proposals for a more comprehensive reform of the Medicare programme to address its prospective insolvency (see below), in the end the law achieves almost no cost reductions, so that its net effect is to add $394 billion to the cost of Medicare over the next 10 years.[5] The legislation concerning the prescription drug benefit itself contains a clause that "in order to promote competition", the Secretary of Health and Human Services "may not interfere with the negotiations between drug manufacturers and pharmacies and prescription drug plan sponsors" (Subpart 2 (i)). The inclusion of the clause reflects concern that the government might use its market power to achieve large savings on prescription drug prices, with negative effects on profitability and innovation in the pharmaceutical sector. The clause has been criticised on the grounds that prices (and thus programme outlays) would be higher without government intervention, assuming that prices that were administered by Medicare would be lower than those obtained by competing health plans. While there is considerable uncertainty about the potential for savings if this clause were modified, the CBO estimates that there is some potential if the

Secretary were to have the authority to negotiate prices of single-source drugs that do not face competition from therapeutic alternatives (Congressional Budget Office, 2004b); at the same time Medicare involvement need not stifle innovation, as Medicare has a history of accounting for public goods in designing payment formulas, for example the practice by which it reimburses expenses at teaching hospitals. Beyond the prescription drug benefit, the law contains provisions for greater competition among private insurance providers and fee-for-service (FFS) Medicare beginning in 2006, replacing the current Medicare+Choice programme (see Box 2.2). While proponents of these provisions argue that increasing competition would serve to contain FFS Medicare costs, there is concern that private insurers will design benefit packages so as to appeal to healthier groups, leaving FFS Medicare saddled with a riskier pool of beneficiaries (the so-called "adverse selection" problem). To minimise the potential for adverse selection, the Medicare programme is beginning to risk-adjust premium contributions to private plans, paying plans more for taking on greater risks, and paying plans less that attract lower predicted risks. By 2007, all of the government's contribution to private plans will be risk-adjusted. While risk adjustment systems remain imperfect predictors of future medical expenses, such adjustment of payments to private plans should mitigate these selection concerns.

The Medicare prescription drug legislation has also important implications for future expenditures under the Medicaid programme, and hence for state as well as federal finances. Under current programme rules, Medicaid covers prescription drug outlays for roughly 6 million "dual eligibles", persons who are fully eligible for both Medicare and Medicaid benefits. The prescription drug legislation makes these persons eligible for the new Medicare drug benefit as of 1 January 2006. States are required to finance most of the cost of providing the prescription drug benefit to dual eligibles through monthly payments to the federal government. These payments will be determined as a specific share of the amount a state would have spent on prescription drug coverage under Medicaid, depending on the state's per capita expenditures on Medicaid prescription drugs for dual eligibles in 2003, trended forward by per capita growth in prescription drug spending nationwide between 2003 and 2006, and the number of dual eligibles who are enrolled in the Medicare prescription drug benefit in the month in question. The share is initially set at 90 per cent, and is scheduled to decline to 75 per cent by 2015. Although this share is less than 100 per cent, it is unclear whether the prescription drug benefit will reduce or raise states' expenditures. In particular, because prescription drugs to dual eligibles will be provided under the Medicare benefit, states lose the ability to negotiate discounts for these drugs with producers. Prescription drug expenses of dual eligibles under Medicaid exceeded $13 billion in 2002 (Kaiser Commission, 2003), accounting for roughly half of prescription drug spending under Medicaid. The fact that these expenses will be covered under Medicare may therefore weaken the states' ability to secure discounts on their remaining prescription drug expenses.

Box 2.2. The Medicare Prescription Drug, Improvement, and Modernization Act of 2003

The Medicare Prescription Drug, Improvement, and Modernization Act (henceforth "the Act"), which the President signed into law on 8 December 2003, contains numerous provisions besides a prescription drug benefit for Medicare beneficiaries. This box summarises some of the act's most important elements.

The prescription drug benefit

In terms of its budgetary effects, by far the most important provision of the Act is the coverage of outpatient prescription drug expenses for Medicare recipients. Previously, with few exceptions, only drug expenses in hospitals were covered through Medicare. However, in 2000 (the latest year for which numbers are available) about 75 per cent of Medicare beneficiaries had some form of coverage of outpatient prescription drug expenses through employer-sponsored retiree benefits, Medicaid, individually purchased "medigap" policies, or through a Medicare+Choice plan (Holtz-Eakin, 2003a). The new benefit under Medicare will take effect at the beginning of 2006. Between June 2004 and December 2005, an interim programme will be in place in which Medicare beneficiaries can purchase Medicare-endorsed prescription drug discount cards offered by private companies for an annual fee of up to $30. Medicare estimates that discounts will be 10 25 per cent or more for many drugs. Moreover, beneficiaries with incomes below 135 per cent of the poverty line that are not eligible for prescription drug coverage through Medicaid are eligible for a $600 credit to use with the cards in 2004 and again in 2005.

Once the full programme takes effect in 2006, Medicare recipients can enrol in the voluntary plan, which could be offered by competing private companies that may charge different annual fees and reimburse drug companies by different amounts for the same package. Participants would pay an average monthly premium of $35. There is a $250 annual deductible, and 25 per cent co-payments for the next $2 000 in drugs, until the total cost reaches $2 250. Thus, a patient who purchases $2 250 of prescription drugs annually would pay for one third ($250 deductible and $500 in co-payments) and the government would pay for two thirds ($1 500) of the costs. Having paid $420 in premiums, the net financial benefit for the patient is $1 080. This estimate of the net benefit does not reflect the value of having insurance against catastrophic drug costs (see below). There is no additional benefit until a patient's annual prescription drug expenses reach $5 100, at which point out-of-pocket expenses excluding the insurance premium total $3 600. Finally, 95 per cent of prescription drug expenses beyond $5 100 per year are paid for under catastrophic coverage. The Act prohibits the sale of private insurance policies reducing out-of-pocket expenses for those enrolling in the Medicare prescription drug benefit. However, out-of-pocket expenses are reduced for beneficiaries with incomes below 150 per cent of the poverty line, with those below the poverty line who are fully eligible for Medicaid receiving full premium and deductible subsidy, and facing only minimal co-payments.

Box 2.2. **The Medicare Prescription Drug, Improvement, and Modernization Act of 2003** *(cont.)*

The Medicare Advantage programme

The Medicare Advantage programme builds upon and replaces the Medicare+ Choice programme created by the Balanced Budget Act of 1997 (BBA). Medicare+ Choice had expanded the opportunities for private health plans to participate in Medicare, and by 2001 about 14 per cent of Medicare beneficiaries were enrolled in a private plan, with the remaining 86 per cent being covered by Medicare's traditional fee-for-service (FFS) programme. Under Medicare+Choice, private health plans receive a monthly capitation payment for each enrolee that is based on the amount Medicare pays per beneficiary in the geographic area served by the plan. Prior to Medicare+Choice, only health maintenance organizations were allowed to participate in Medicare; under Medicare+Choice, preferred provider organizations and private fee for service plans in combination with tax-preferred medical savings accounts (MSAs) became eligible.

In part because of the payment rate changes to private plans implemented following the BBA, which uncoupled payment rate increases to private plans from cost increases in FFS Medicare, the number of participating plans fell sharply between 1998 and 2003. To encourage private plan participation, the 2003 Act stipulates that beginning in 2004 all plans will be paid at a rate at least as high as FFS Medicare, and that payments will grow at least at the same rate as FFS Medicare. A so-called "comparative cost adjustment" programme is scheduled to begin in 2010 on a six year trial basis in six metropolitan areas in which there are at least two private plans with at least 25 per cent market penetration among Medicare beneficiaries. Under this programme, plan bids from private plans and rates for FFS Medicare will be averaged to create a benchmark for competitive bidding. To address adverse selection problems, plans (including FFS Medicare) would be paid based on the demographic and health risks of enrolees. If the traditional Medicare plan would end up disproportionately enrolling poor risks, beneficiary premia would be adjusted accordingly. If a plan bids below the benchmark, 75 per cent of the savings accrue to the beneficiary and 25 per cent to the government (House Ways and Means Committee, 2003b).

Health Savings Accounts (HSAs)

The HSAs created by the Act are expanding and replacing the Archer Medical Savings Accounts (MSAs) originally created in 1996. Whereas MSAs were available only to the self-employed and employees of small businesses with qualified high deductible health plans, everyone below the age of 65 with a high deductible health plan (*i.e.* an annual deductible of at least $2 000 for a family plan or $1 000 for a single plan) can set up an HSA. Contributions to HSAs and earnings in the accounts are tax-free. Distributions for qualified medical expenses are also not taxed. Contributions can be made by individuals, their employers and family members. MSA contributions were limited to 75 per cent of the health plan deductible for joint tax filers (up to $3 788 in 2003) and 65 per cent of the deductible

Box 2.2. **The Medicare Prescription Drug, Improvement, and Modernization Act of 2003** *(cont.)*

health plan (*i.e.* an annual deductible of at least $2 000 for a family plan or $1 000 for a single plan) can set up an HSA. Contributions to HSAs and earnings in the accounts are tax free. Distributions for qualified medical expenses are also not taxed. Contributions can be made by individuals, their employers and family members. MSA contributions were limited to 75 per cent of the health plan deductible for joint tax filers (up to $3 788 in 2003) and 65 per cent of the deductible for single filers (up to $2 178). Contributions to HSAs are allowed up to 100 per cent of the health plan deductible, up to $5 150 for family policies and $2 600 for single policies. Distributions can be used among other purposes to pay for retiree health insurance, Medicare expenses and prescription drugs.

Discretionary spending in the near term is likely to continue rising at a brisk pace. Discretionary budget authority, which refers to the amount of spending authorised by appropriations bills for a given fiscal year, increased by slightly less than 3 per cent between FY 2003 and FY 2004. However, discretionary outlays, which provide a timelier picture of spending, are projected to rise by nearly 9 per cent, from $826 billion to $896 billion. In part this higher growth rate reflects funds authorised under the supplementary appropriations passed in March 2003 that are being spent only in FY 2004. In passing the appropriations bills, the Congress also assigned budget authority back to FY 2003, thus reducing the rate of increase in budget authority. Defence outlays, including spending out of supplementary appropriations, are projected to grow by more than 11 per cent in FY 2004, whereas growth of outlays outside of defence is projected at just under 6 per cent. Beyond the current fiscal year, the Administration's budget proposes to limit growth in discretionary spending in FY 2005 to 4 per cent, with budget authority for defence excluding the supplementary appropriations rising by 7 per cent, for homeland security by 10 per cent, and budget authority outside of defence and homeland security remaining essentially unchanged. The budget request does not include funding for operations in Afghanistan and Iraq; instead, the Administration intends to submit another supplementary appropriations request sometime in 2005 when spending requirements should be better understood.

Adjusting the baseline for alternative policies

The CBO's baseline projections discussed above are by law projections of federal spending and revenues under current policies. They are intended to be a

Figure 2.3. **Budget outcomes under alternative policies, 2004-2014**
Fiscal years, per cent of GDP

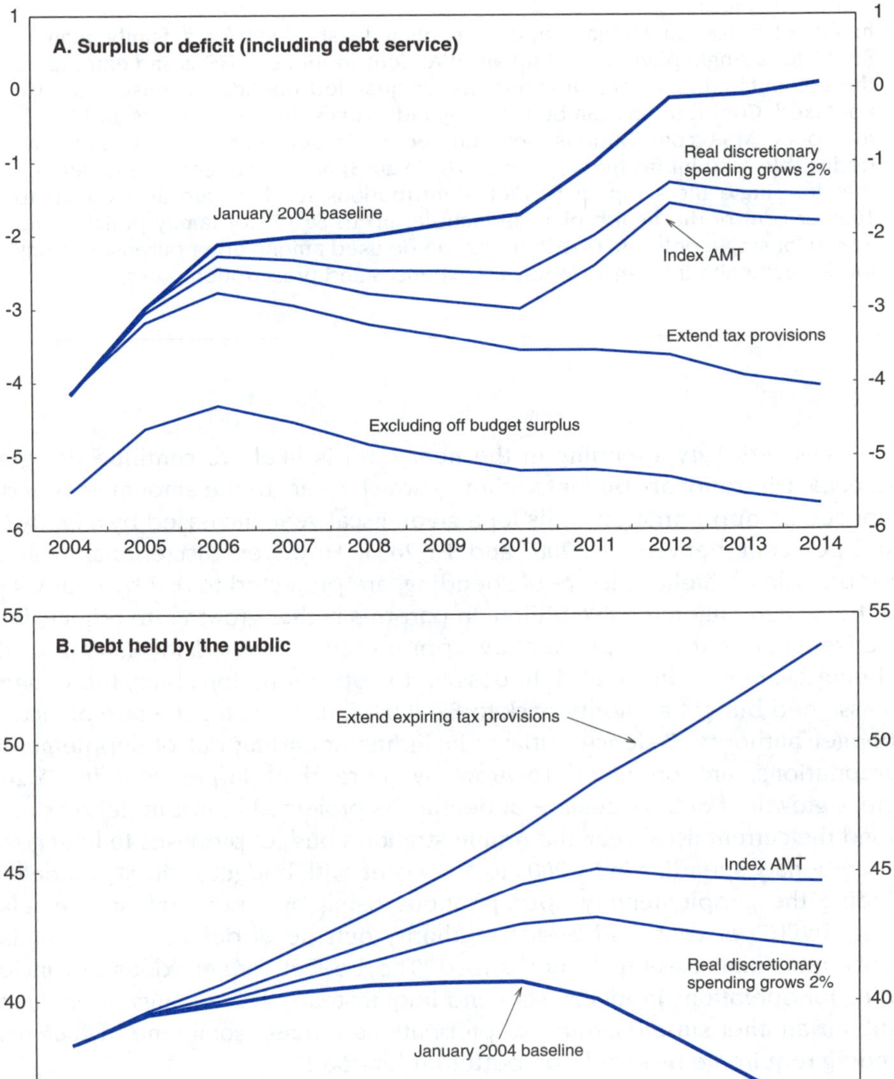

Source: Congressional Budget Office, OECD calculations.

benchmark against which to evaluate alternative policies, not a prediction about future budgetary outcomes. Figure 2.3 presents several adjustments to the latest baseline projection, focussing on scenarios that address several policy issues. One such scenario is that discretionary spending is unlikely to remain constant in real terms at its FY 2004 level, as assumed in the CBO's baseline. This assumption implies that discretionary spending would decline from 7.8 per cent of GDP in 2004 to 6.4 per cent in 2014. A similar decline occurred between 1993 and 2000; however, this was largely achieved through nominal declines in defence spending, a scenario whose probability seems remote under foreseeable circumstances.[6] The line labelled "Real discretionary spending grows 2%" shows the revision to the baseline projection if real discretionary spending were to rise at its post-1975 average pace, a rate far below the nearly 7 per cent real growth in discretionary outlays over the past three fiscal years.

A second adjustment concerns the steadily expanding coverage of households by the individual alternative minimum tax (AMT). As discussed in Box 2.3, the share of tax filers subject to the AMT is projected to increase from the current 1.8 per cent to 22.4 per cent by 2010. This is a concern in part because the AMT effectively eliminates eligibility for many exemptions and credits that are a feature of the regular income tax code. The increasing reach of the AMT is a long-standing problem that has, however, become much more acute with the enactment of EGTRRA. The revenue effects of different AMT reform proposals are very uncertain. As a point of reference, the scenario labelled "Index AMT" in Figure 2.3 would index both the AMT tax brackets and the exemption at its current (JGTRRA) level to inflation.[7] The effects of this, as well as alternative AMT reform proposals are discussed in Box 2.3. Another issue concerning taxation, which will be discussed further below, is the widespread use of sunsets in both EGTRRA and JGTRRA (see Box 2.1). Based on the Administration's declared preference (Bush, 2004), as well as historical experience, it is likely that the tax cuts will not expire as currently legislated but will be extended for some time. The line labelled "extend tax provisions" shows the effect of extending all expiring provisions with the exception of the special depreciation allowances.[8] Doing so increases the deficit precipitously, in particular beyond 2010, when all EGTRRA and JGTRRA provisions are scheduled to expire; by 2014, extending all provisions of these two laws increases the deficit by 1.6 percentage points of GDP. Even this estimate ignores the potentially large interaction between AMT reform and extension of the expiring provisions. As long as the AMT is not reformed, a substantial share of the income tax reductions under the regular income tax code is reversed by the expanding reach of the AMT (see Box 2.3), thus artificially reducing the cost estimates of extending the EGTRRA and JGTRRA provisions.[9]

The adjustments discussed so far all adjust the CBO's baseline for the *unified* federal budget balance including the Social Security trust funds. While the unified surplus or deficit is a useful gauge for the federal government's net borrowing

Box 2.3. The Alternative Minimum Tax

The individual alternative minimum tax (AMT) operates as a parallel tax system to the regular individual income tax code. Taxpayers who may be subject to the AMT must calculate their tax liability under both the regular income tax rules and under AMT rules. Their tax liability is determined as the higher of the two. Originally introduced to prevent a small number of high-income households from taking advantage of tax laws to eliminate their federal income tax liability, under current law the number of AMT taxpayers will rise from 2.6 million in 2002 to 35.6 million in 2010. Because the AMT adds substantially to the complexity of the tax code without achieving its original goals (OECD, 2001), and because it effectively cancels several features of the regular income tax, a reform of the AMT seems urgent. This box summarises the operation of the AMT and reports estimates of the expanding coverage of the AMT and the costs of several reform options, some of which would worsen the fiscal outlook even further.

In arriving at taxable income, many of the deductions from adjusted gross income (AGI) allowed under the regular income tax rules are not allowed under the AMT. These include personal exemptions, the standard deduction and itemized deductions for state taxes and miscellaneous expenses, notably employee business expenses. These so-called exemption preferences are one important factor why middle-income households are increasingly becoming subject to the AMT (see below). Another set of AMT rules limits the extent to which taxpayers can bring forward deductions or delay income recognition. These rules have a greater tendency to affect high-income households. Once taxable income has been calculated, the AMT exemption is subtracted – under JGTRRA, the first $58 000 for married couples or surviving spouses and the first $40 500 for single filers. A tax rate of 26 per cent applies to the first $175 000 of remaining income, and a tax rate of 28 per cent to any income above that level. However, because the AMT exemption itself phases out at a 25 per cent rate over higher income levels, marginal tax rates can be as high as 32.5 per cent or 35 per cent, respectively.

While the regular income tax has largely been indexed to inflation since 1981, the AMT is not indexed. This factor, together with the recent reductions of tax rates under EGTRRA and JGTRRA, is responsible for much of the projected increase in the number of tax filers subject to the AMT. As shown in Table 2.4, under current law the share of tax filers who either have an AMT liability or lose credits under the regular income tax is projected to rise from 1.8 per cent in 2002 to 22.4 per cent in 2010. Moreover, the composition of AMT taxpayers is projected to change greatly. At present, about half of those with incomes in the range of $200 000 to $500 000 (in 2002 dollars) are paying AMT, compared with only 10 per cent of those with incomes between $100 000 and $200 000. Hardly anyone with income below $100 000 is currently paying AMT, while at very high incomes the fraction of those paying AMT declines because the higher marginal tax rate for the top bracket under the regular income tax code more than offsets the exclusion of deductions under the AMT. By 2010, however, nearly 75 per cent of taxpayers with incomes between $75 000 and $100 000 will be paying AMT, as will practically all taxpayers with incomes between $100 000 and $500 000. As shown in the third column, about half of the increase in shares is due to the lower income tax rates under EGTRRA. As shown in the last column, the sharp rise in AMT participation has the effect of cancelling most of the tax reductions under EGTRRA for those with incomes between $100 000 and $500 000.

Box 2.3. **The Alternative Minimum Tax** (*cont.*)

Table 2.4. **AMT participation and effects**

AMT taxpayers	Current law		Pre-EGTTRA law	Percentage of EGTRRA income tax cut reversed by AMT, 2010
	2003	2010	2010	
Millions	2.4	33.1	14.4	–
As percentage of all filers	1.8	22.4	9.7	–
As percentage of filers, by AGI (thousands of 2002 dollars)				
0-30	0.0	0.2	0.2	0.0
30-50	0.1	6.9	5.0	1.2
50-75	0.5	36.6	19.7	15.3
75-100	1.1	72.9	27.0	37.2
100-200	9.3	92.0	32.2	65.0
200-500	55.3	96.2	48.3	71.8
500-1 000	28.9	49.3	12.2	15.9
1 000 +	19.3	24.1	12.1	8.2

Source: Burman *et al.* (2003b).

Because the percentage of adjusted gross income on AMT returns is projected to rise from 9 per cent in 2002 to about 55 per cent in 2010, most reform proposals that would drastically reduce the number of AMT taxpayers imply large revenue losses (Burman *et al.*, 2003*a*). For example, indexation of the AMT after 2002 would reduce the number of AMT taxpayers by 2010 from 35.6 million to 10.4 million, but the implied revenue loss over FY 2004-13, assuming that EGTRRA expires by the end of 2010, is $418 billion. If in addition personal exemptions and tax credits for child care and education were allowed under the AMT, the number of those paying AMT in 2010 would fall to 6 million, with practically nobody with income below $75 000 (in 2001 dollars) paying AMT, but the revenue loss would rise to $474 billion. By comparison, the cost over FY 2001-11 of the marginal tax reductions originally enacted in EGTRRA was estimated at $421 billion (Joint Committee on Taxation, 2001). Revenue-neutral proposals for limiting the expanding reach of the AMT without altering any other parts of the tax code would need to combine the above elements with a substantial increase in the statutory rate applied to the current 28 per cent AMT bracket, to as much as 35 per cent (Burman *et al.*, 2003a).

needs and thus the impact of fiscal policy on national saving and investment, it is potentially misleading for assessing the necessary changes that would have to be made to restore the budget to balance on a sustained basis. The so-called "off-budget" surpluses in the trust funds are projected to be on the order of 1½ per cent of GDP over the coming decade, but they are overwhelmed by the growth of Social Security liabilities in the following decades.[10] Under neither of the reform proposals for Social Security discussed below are the current surpluses accruing to the Social Security trust funds available for spending on purposes other than Social Security. The bottom line in Figure 2.3 shows the adjusted "on-budget" deficit *excluding* the trust fund surpluses. Under current policy and plausible assumptions about future policy, this deficit measure remains close to 5 per cent of GDP each year through 2014.

Implications for national income

Persistent unified budget deficits on the order of 4 per cent of GDP would be troublesome, because they would threaten to eliminate any positive effects on national income from the recent reductions in marginal tax rates. Fully phased-in, EGTRRA is estimated to reduce the average effective marginal tax rate on labour income by about 5 per cent of the current tax rate (Congressional Budget Office, 2001) and therefore raise the after-tax return to labour by about 2.8 per cent. The increase in after-tax wages should stimulate households' supply of labour, although estimates of the magnitude of the labour-supply response vary greatly. By raising exemptions for education expenses, EGTRRA may raise effective labour supply in the long run through fostering the accumulation of human capital. Finally, both EGTRRA and JGTRRA may stimulate private saving and hence accumulation of nonhuman capital, EGTRRA through a reduction in the tax on education and retirement saving and increases in after-tax income and JGTRRA through the lower taxation of capital income. To the extent that these measures reduce the cost of capital for firms, they would increase the capital stock and future productivity growth; however, empirical evidence for the link from lower capital income taxation to firms' cost of capital is inconclusive. Nonetheless, taken in isolation, the provisions of the two laws lead over time to a permanent increase in national income.

Against all these factors stands the precipitous decline in public saving over the past three years. As mentioned earlier, the provisions of EGTRRA (once fully phased in) and JGTRRA combined reduce revenues by about 1.6 per cent of GDP. Because the tax cuts are financed not through reductions in outlays, but through deficits, public saving declines by the full revenue cost. Some of this decline in public saving will be offset by an increase in private saving, principally through an increase in interest rates and possibly associated negative wealth effects. However, most estimates suggest that the increase in private saving would not exceed, and may be considerably smaller than, half of the decline in public saving. The resulting overall decline in national saving implies that, compared to a situation of unchanged national saving, the domestically owned capital stock, and hence national income from capital will ultimately be lower. Some illustrative calculations in Annex 2.1 based on a standard macroeconomic framework suggest that, under plausible parameter values the negative effect on national income of the reduction in national saving could more than outweigh the positive effects from lower marginal tax rates and other provisions of recent tax legislation. While these calculations are merely illustrative by omitting several aspects of the tax legislation, the basic result is consistent with the findings of the available studies of the likely macroeconomic effects of EGTRRA and JGTRRA (discussed in Annex 2.1), which predict at best small positive, and more often small negative, long-run effects on national income. The overall effect of recent fiscal policies on long-run national income is even more likely to be negative when account is taken of the fact that, as discussed above, recent spending legislation has raised projected deficits by on average 2½ percentage points of GDP per year between 2004 and 2011.

To allow recent tax cuts to have a positive long-term effect on national income, it is imperative to restore budget discipline as rapidly as possible, now that the removal of fiscal stimulus no longer imperils the recovery. In its FY 2005 budget the Administration has proposed to cut the deficit in half over the five years through 2009, largely by holding non-defence discretionary spending constant in nominal terms. After adjusting for projected inflation, this proposal implies five consecutive years of declines in real discretionary outlays outside of defence, which would be unprecedented since 1962, when comparable budget figures first became available. Although spending restraint is necessary, the magnitude of the projected deficits is such that revenue increases may be required as well to restore the budget to balance before the demographic stresses intensify towards the end of the 10-year projection. To the extent that revenues will have to be raised as well, one direction for doing so in an efficient manner is to broaden the tax base of personal income taxation. Broadening the base of taxation by curtailing tax expenditures to finance reductions in marginal rates has not occurred since the 1986 tax reform. If anything, much of the move towards a comprehensive income tax that occurred in that reform has been reversed since then (OECD, 2001b, Ch. III). Some major tax expenditures, notably reduced taxation of capital gains and tax-preferred savings and retirement accounts, represent a shift towards an expenditure-based tax system and are likely beneficial on efficiency grounds. Other tax expenditures however, notably the deductibility of mortgage interest (regardless of the use of the loan) and of charitable donations should be removed. Limiting the exclusion of employer health insurance premia would be desirable not only to broaden the tax base, but also to reduce the overuse of health care services (OECD, 2002).[11] Efforts to broaden the base of the corporate income tax should focus on exemptions that reduce revenues and create inefficiencies, such as sectoral tax shelters; better enforcement would also be likely to improve its revenue yield. The Treasury Department has recently adopted regulations and proposed legislation that would restrain the use of corporate tax shelters.

If the yield from broadening existing income tax bases is ultimately insufficient to restore the budget to balance, the authorities should consider a further move to a consumption-based tax system. Such a system can be implemented either through the introduction of a nation-wide value added tax (VAT) at the federal level or through exempting saving from income tax.[12] Introducing a VAT would be complicated in the US context, in which most states rely heavily on sales taxes for their revenues. However, sales taxes are currently levied mainly on goods, for which reason the trend growth rate of the tax base is slower than that of GDP. States have been willing to use federal tax bases for the taxation of income and estates and might therefore be willing to accept the introduction of a federal VAT that would establish a uniform tax base, including services. States would then be able to add their own VAT to replace the sales tax, and the consequent broadening of the states' tax base might produce substantial efficiency gains as well. The Administration's proposed Lifetime Saving Accounts and Retirement Saving Accounts, which would present an alternative move towards an expenditure-based tax system, would lead to further substantial revenue losses over the longer term instead of raising additional revenue, unless statutory income tax rates are raised.[13] Considering that only very few high-income households are currently constrained by contribution limits of existing tax-preferred retirement saving accounts, household saving would be unlikely to increase much, whereas under conservative assumptions annual revenue losses would be about 0.2 per cent of GDP by 2013 and increasing thereafter, so that the overall effect on national saving beyond the first few years is likely to be negative (Burman *et al.*, 2003c).

Sub-federal budgets and joint federal-state programmes

After deteriorating sharply during the 2001 recession and the stock-market collapse, state and local finances seem to have improved modestly since the beginning of 2003. One comprehensive measure of the fiscal condition of the state and local sector is the current account of state and local governments as defined in the national income and product accounts (NIPAs), which is current receipts (excluding capital transfer receipts) less current expenditures (excluding gross investment undertaken by state and local governments). Figure 2.4 shows the state and local current account, expressed as a share of GDP. Also shown in the figure is the same series based on data before the benchmark revisions of the NIPAs released by the Bureau of Economic Analysis on 10 December 2003. Prior to the benchmark revisions, by this measure the state and local sector appeared to be in worse financial condition during 2001 and 2002 than at any time during the past half century. The data revisions changed this picture substantially, with only the first quarter of 2003 showing a historically unprecedented deficit of about 0.4 per cent of GDP. Since then, the state and local current account has returned to surplus. Nonetheless, the factors behind the sharp downturn in state and local finances over the preceding years require policymakers' attention.

Figure 2.4. **Net state and local government saving**
Per cent of GDP

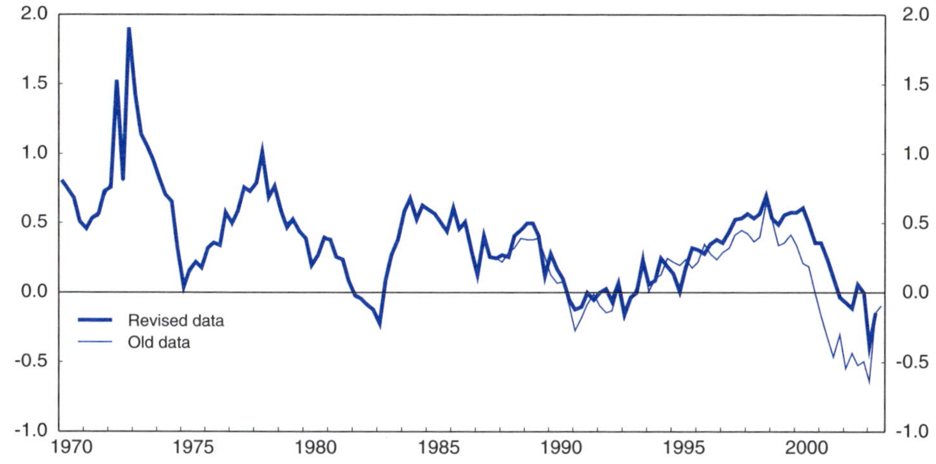

Source: Bureau of Economic Analysis and OECD.

Receipts decelerated sharply beginning in 2001, whereas expenditures continued to accelerate through that year. States were particularly hard hit, as income tax receipts, which account for about one third of state revenues but only about 5 per cent of local revenues, collapsed over the two years to mid-2003 at an annual rate of 12 per cent and sales tax receipts grew only modestly. The local sector fared much better, with property taxes, which constitute almost three quarters of its receipts, continuing to expand briskly throughout this period. Although state and local consumption expenditures, which consist mostly of wages, began to decelerate in 2001, they continued to grow at a slightly higher rate than receipts. At the same time, states faced rapid increases in payments under entitlement programmes, particularly Medicaid. A majority of the states subsequently tightened their eligibility rules for Medicaid, reducing benefits and increasing co-payments, but these measures have only recently begun to slow the growth of benefit payments. The National Association of State Budget Officers (2003) reports that state general fund spending-which represents primarily expenditure of revenues derived from general sources not earmarked for specific items and constitutes about 46 per cent of total state spending – is expected to remain roughly unchanged in FY 2004, after increasing at an average rate of 7.7 per cent in 1999-2001 but only 1 per cent in 2002-03.[14] Despite recent improvement in state revenues, most states predict large budget shortfalls for FY 2005, partly because

$20 billion in federal fiscal relief to the states paid out over 18 months will expire in mid-2004.

The Congress is currently debating legislation to renew funding for Temporary Assistance to Needy Families (TANF), a programme whose rules and funding are shared between the federal government and the States. TANF, which was originally established in 1996, operates on the basis of block grants from the federal government to the states, subject to their meeting certain requirements, notably requiring recipients to participate in work activities. The original legislation provided block grants for FY 1997-2002 of $16.5 billion each year. Since then, the grants have been renewed at FY 2002 funding levels either by quarterly appropriation laws or on a one-year basis. In February 2003 the House of Representatives passed a bill including several TANF reform provisions as well as reauthorisation of the block grants for another five years, and in September the Senate Finance Committee approved its own version. Both bills call for further tightening of the work requirements for recipients as well as substantial new resources for marriage-promotion programmes. There is concern that the proposed additional child-care funding is not sufficient to keep up with child-care cost increases and increased demand as a consequence of tighter work requirements (Parrott and Fremstad, 2003).

Longer-term challenges: imbalances in entitlement programmes

According to its most recent *Long-Term Budget Outlook* (Congressional Budget Office, 2003*e*), the CBO projects that spending on Social Security, Medicare and Medicaid combined as a share of GDP will more than double by 2050, growing from 8.3 per cent in 2003 to 17.7 per cent (Table 2.5).[15] By comparison, total federal outlays in FY 2003 were 20.2 per cent of GDP. One factor common to increased spending in all three programmes is demographic change. It is responsible for the entire increase in projected Social Security outlays, from currently 4.2 per cent of GDP to

Table 2.5. **Long-term paths for primary spending**

Per cent of GDP

	2003	2010	2030	2050
Defence[1]	3.7	3.7	2.8	2.0
Social Security[2]	4.3	4.2	5.9	6.2
Medicare and Medicaid[3]	4.0	4.8	8.4	11.5
Other	6.4	4.9	4.5	4.2
Total primary spending	18.5	17.6	21.6	24.0

1. Based on CBO's high-path assumption that defence spending follows the Administration's 2004 Future Years Defense Program.
2. Based on currently scheduled benefits.
3. Based on CBO's intermediate-path assumption that the growth rate of costs per enrolee declines to 1 per cent above the growth rate of GDP per capita.

Source: Congressional Budget Office (2003e).

6.2 per cent in 2050. However, it explains only one-third of the projected increase in Medicare and Medicaid spending combined from currently 3.9 per cent of GDP to 11.5 per cent by 2050. The remaining two-thirds of the increase in spending on these two programmes is driven by the projected growth of health care costs. Future increases in health care costs are highly uncertain; the CBO's middle-cost scenario assumes that spending per enrolee will grow 1 per cent faster than per capita GDP. By comparison, over the period 1990-2003 costs per enrolee grew 1.7 per cent in excess of per capita GDP.[16] With the retirement of the baby-boom generation and the ongoing increase in life expectancy, fewer workers (relative to the number of retirees) will be left to shoulder this rising burden, and it is widely agreed that on current policies these three entitlement programmes are unsustainable. Reforms are therefore needed to address the challenges posed by demographic changes and to contain increases in health care costs.[17]

No reforms have been implemented in recent years to address the excess spending of the Social Security trust funds relative to expected receipts that is currently projected to begin in 2018, and the eventual insolvency of the Social Security system in 2042.[18] The main challenge is how to keep the system in long-run actuarial balance without either undermining its role as a social insurance system or reducing any further the already very low returns on payroll tax contributions for middle- and high-income earners. Regarding reform of Social Security, the key questions are how much benefits should be scaled back; how much taxes should be increased; the role of (voluntary or mandatory) personal accounts; and the use of general government funding. In its December 2001 report, the President's Commission to Strengthen Social Security presented three alternative models for reforming the system, each of which included the establishment of voluntary personal accounts. Social Security benefits for workers who elect to contribute to a personal account would be reduced by the personal account contributions compounded at an inflation-adjusted interest rate that varies across models.[19] To address the remaining actuarial imbalance in the traditional defined-benefit component, one of the Commission's models proposes to index initial Social Security benefits to prices instead of wages, which would result over time in a substantial reduction of benefits compared to currently scheduled benefits.[20] Another model proposes to reduce benefits in line with increases in life expectancy. To balance the effects of this reduction for low-income earners, one of the models increases the minimum benefit payable to a 30-year minimum-wage worker from currently just over 100 per cent of the poverty line to 120 per cent. Each of these three models would require substantial transitional transfers from the general fund to the trust fund (President's Commission to Strengthen Social Security, 2001).

A potential advantage of personal accounts is that they offer a way to operate an advance funded retirement programme without the savings accumulation being reflected in the government budget, thereby avoiding the probability that such savings will be offset by increased dissaving in the rest of the government budget. However, other proposals have questioned the wisdom of converting part of what is a social insurance programme into personal accounts (Diamond and Orszag, 2004). They point out that there already exists a variety of tax-preferred individual retirement accounts outside of Social Security. These tax-preferred accounts and other alternative sources of retirement income are widely used: Social Security provides the majority of income for almost two-thirds of beneficiaries over 65, but accounts for all income for only 20 per cent of beneficiaries over 65. Moreover, there is considerable uncertainty over whether introducing *voluntary* personal accounts would generate as many contributions as the proposals assume. That said, it would not be necessary that all participants contribute up to the limit for personal accounts to improve Social Security's overall position. In its reliance on personal accounts, the Commission's proposals built on earlier recommendations by the Social Security Advisory Council (Gramlich, 1996), two of whose three proposals included personal accounts. Those two proposals, however, made participation in personal accounts mandatory. Even mandatory personal accounts would pose formidable problems. The international evidence suggests that administrative costs of personal retirement accounts are high (Whitehouse, 2000), which poses a design challenge in order for personal accounts to raise substantially the net rate of return on contributions to the programme as intended. Furthermore, if upon retirement individuals could choose between lump-sum payments and converting their balances into inflation-protected annuities, the latter might be costly due to adverse selection problems in the annuities market. A balanced combination of revenue increases and benefit reductions, for example by reducing benefits for high-income earners and adjusting the full benefit age with changes in life expectancy, would most likely succeed in strengthening Social Security's current role as a social insurance programme while returning it to long-term solvency.

The recently passed Medicare legislation has substantially worsened the spending outlook for Medicare by adding the prescription drug benefit, whereas it is uncertain to what extent the elements of competition between traditional Medicare and private plans included in the legislation will lead to substantial cost savings in the long run.[21] The legislation, like several earlier reform proposals for Medicare, is based on the notion that the programme has to move to some extent from its current defined-benefit structure to a defined-contribution system, which would rely on competition among private providers, as well as providing beneficiaries with stronger incentives to make cost-conscious decisions, in order to slow the projected rise in costs per enrolee. It is in this context that past experiences with health maintenance organisations' (HMOs) participation in Medicare and Medicare+Choice are of relevance (Newhouse, 2001). Prior to the reforms introduced by the Balanced Budget Act of 1997 (BBA), enrolment of Medicare beneficiaries in HMOs rose rapidly, from about 4 per cent of enrolees in 1991 to a peak of 17 per cent in 1999. Much of this increase was driven by HMOs' ability to select among beneficiaries, in addition to inefficiencies in health-care delivery in certain geographic areas, and thus to offer competitive plans. The BBA substantially reduced payments to private plans, with the effect that the number of participating plans fell from 346 in 1998 to 155 in November 2003, and enrolment in private plans fell from 6.4 million beneficiaries in 1999 to 4.6 million beneficiaries, or 12 per cent of the total in November 2003 (House Ways and Means Committee, 2003a). Two major challenges for reform proposals, insofar as they rely on competition among private-sector plans, are therefore how to price Medicare services in a way that private plans have an incentive to participate in Medicare while keeping costs low, and how to implement risk-adjusted payments to private plans to minimise adverse selection problems. The Centers for Medicare and Medicaid Services continue to be engaged in improving risk adjustments for Medicare payments. It remains to be seen whether the provisions regarding comparative cost adjustment under the new Medicare Advantage programme (see Box 2.2) have struck a sensible balance between the goals of raising private plan participation and cost containment.

The long-term outlook for Medicaid is likewise affected by the ageing of the population. Once the Medicare prescription drug benefit takes full effect, Medicaid will no longer provide prescription drugs to dual eligibles, although, as discussed before, the implications of the benefit for Medicaid's prescription drug expenses on other eligible persons is uncertain. Nonetheless, under CBO's middle-cost assumption the federal contribution to Medicaid is projected to rise from 1.5 per cent of GDP in 2003 to 3.2 per cent in 2050. The primary age-related component of rising Medicaid expenditures is long-term care, a benefit for which it is very difficult to cut expenditures by changing eligibility rules. More broadly, Medicaid covers many costs for low-income Medicare beneficiaries, including Medicare premiums and cost sharing as well as services, such as long-term care, not covered by Medicare. It is therefore important to recognise that some efforts to reduce growth in Medicare spending would result in faster growth in Medicaid spending; instead the focus should be on measures, such as restraining growth in prescription drug costs, that would result in savings for both programmes.

Reinforcing budget discipline

Budget windows, sunsets and transparency of the budget outlook

The preceding analysis has focused on a 10-year budget window, which is in keeping with the current CBO convention; in its FY 2003 budget the Administration reverted from its previous 10-year window to a 5-year window because it regards the longer 10-year forecast to be unreliable and therefore potentially misleading. A problem with focusing on even a 10-year window is that large, and to some extent predictable, fiscal challenges lie just beyond it. At the time that the 2001 tax cut legislation was being debated, an important argument in favour of a large-scale tax cut was that the CBO was projecting large surpluses for each of the next ten years, thus creating an opportunity for "returning unneeded funds to taxpayers". With hindsight it is questionable whether this line of argument was prudent: as argued above, trust fund surpluses should under current circumstances not be considered available for general purposes, and most of the on-budget surpluses projected in 2001 were revised away over the following three years due to economic and technical changes alone (see Figure 2.2). But the problem of the large imbalances in the entitlement programmes beyond the 10-year window was already understood at that time (Auerbach and Gale, 2001). With the retirement of the baby-boom generation as from 2010, federal outlays on Social Security, Medicare and Medicaid are projected to grow considerably faster than either GDP or the revenues that are supposed to finance these programmes. In its October 2000 *Long-Term Budget Outlook*, the CBO pointed out that extending the budget window as in the annual reports of the Trustees of the Social Security system would have turned the 10-year surplus of on average 4 per cent of GDP projected at that time into a 75-year fiscal gap of 0.7 per cent of GDP (Congressional Budget Office, 2000).[22] While the existence of a fiscal gap does not necessarily militate against a tax cut, it highlights the question of how the existing fiscal imbalance is to be addressed.

The issues surrounding the projected imbalances in the federal entitlement programmes suggest that the current 10-year window is still too short, because it has the effect of showing the trust fund surpluses, but not the corresponding accrual of liabilities. If one cares about the fiscal position in a given year, the following year ought to be of interest too. Conversely, a problem with vastly lengthening the window might be that projections too far ahead into the future are so uncertain that any policy response appears unwarranted. A very long window would also allow the authorities to "solve" existing imbalances by projecting a sufficiently large tax increase in the very far future to reduce an otherwise large fiscal gap (the related issue of sunsets is discussed below). For example, one of the proposals of the report issued by the Social Security Advisory Council in 1997 involved a payroll tax increase in 2045, 50 years into the future, a policy commitment that likely would have lacked credibility. Nonetheless, in view of the relatively predictable stresses that demographic factors will create over the next 50 years or so, it seems important that an evaluation of alternative fiscal policies takes a longer-term view than simply a fixed 10-year window. In its FY 2005 Budget, the Administration proposed that the OMB and the CBO annually report changes in long-term entitlement liabilities during the past year. Such liabilities would be measured by computing present values of outlays minus designated revenues over an infinite horizon for Social Security and over a 75-year horizon for other entitlement programmes.

A novel feature of the recent tax legislation was the large-scale use of sunsets, *i.e.* the provision that the legislation expires at a fixed date, with the effect that the tax code reverts at that date to the *status quo ante*. Temporary tax provisions have been used in the tax code for some time; one of the most-cited examples is the Research and Experimentation Tax Credit, usually referred to as the R&D tax credit. Originally enacted as part of the Economic Recovery Tax Act of 1981, it has since been extended 10 times, most recently in November 1999, and is currently scheduled to expire in June 2004. The novel aspect about the recent legislation is the revenue cost of the legislation subject to a set expiration date. For example, extension of the R&D tax credit from 2005 through 2014 would reduce revenues by $49 billion; by comparison, extending all expiring EGTRRA and JGTRRA provisions through years 2011-14 would reduce revenues by $1 030 billion (Congressional Budget Office, 2004a). In view of the historical experience that many temporary tax provisions are becoming *de facto* permanent,[23] the recent use of sunsets on such a large scale creates a problem in presenting the projections for the federal budget. By law, the CBO's baseline treats temporary provisions as expiring as scheduled (except excise taxes earmarked to trust funds and newly established entitlement programmes), but it has regularly reported the effects of extending tax legislation that is scheduled to expire before the end of the budget window. While in many cases the baseline assumption seems clearly unrealistic, assuming instead that all expiring legislation will be extended may be unrealistic too. For example, the partial capital expensing provisions enacted as part of the 2002 stimulus bill were motivated as a temporary measure to spur investment following the collapse of the technology bubble in 2001. One challenge is therefore to design budget rules that provide an incentive for using sunsets for temporary (*e.g.* countercyclical) reasons, but not for understating the true revenue costs of a measure (Auerbach, 2003).[24]

Reforming mechanisms for deficit control

Until the end of FY 2002, the Budget Enforcement Act (BEA) was the main mechanism for enforcing the rule that new legislation should not increase the budget deficit.[25] While the BEA is technically still in force, its main provisions-annual limits on discretionary appropriations and the pay-as-you-go (PAYGO) requirement that new mandatory spending and revenue laws may not increase current and projected deficits-expired in September 2002. Under those provisions, the Congress periodically established multi-year discretionary spending caps. These caps and the PAYGO requirement were enforced by sequestration: a breach of the caps for discretionary spending would trigger an executive order reducing discretionary outlays, and a breach of the PAYGO requirements would similarly trigger cuts in certain mandatory programmes. Since the BEA was first enacted in 1990, only two small sequestrations of discretionary spending have been ordered, both of which occurred in 1991. For the following six years, the spending caps were always met, largely due to defence cutbacks. However, with the emergence of unified budget surpluses in 1998, the political consensus for spending control weakened, and subsequently the BEA's restrictions were circumvented in a number of ways. In 1999 and 2000, lawmakers enacted emergency appropriations exempt from budget enforcement procedures of $34 billion and $44 billion, respectively, far above the previous annual average. Partly in response to the terrorist attacks of September 2001, emergency budget authority enacted in 2001 and 2002 was of similar magnitude as in the previous two years. Moreover, for 2001 and 2002 the caps on non-emergency discretionary spending were raised by $99 billion and $134 billion, respectively, and the use of devices such as advance appropriations led to further erosion of spending discipline. Mindful that reinstating all provisions of the BEA would make it effectively impossible to make the 2001 and 2003 tax cuts permanent, the Administration proposed in its FY 2004 budget to renew all BEA provisions, but only for two years, whereas in its FY 2005 budget it proposed to renew for five years the discretionary caps and the PAYGO requirements for mandatory programmes, but not for revenue legislation. In its FY 2005 budget the Administration also proposed a budget rule prohibiting legislation that increases the long-term liabilities of Social Security, Medicare, and other entitlement programmes. On 10 March the Senate approved an amendment to its version of the FY 2005 budget resolution reinstating the PAYGO requirements for revenue legislation as well, but it remains to be seen whether this amendment will survive negotiations between the House and the Senate over a final budget resolution.

The experience with the BEA as well as international evidence suggests above all that the effectiveness of an enforcement procedure depends critically on the existence of a political consensus for achieving the procedure's goal – in the case of the BEA, the disappearance of deficits in the unified budget. If a budget enforcement mechanism is to be adopted again, lawmakers may want to reconsider what the goal should be; for example, under the currently projected actuarial imbalances in the entitlement programmes, the goal of a balanced unified budget, or merely halving the unified budget deficit over the next five years as the Administration has proposed, may not be ambitious enough. A strength of the BEA compared to its predecessor, the Gramm-Rudman-Hollings Act of 1985, was that it held lawmakers responsible only for the budgetary consequences of their own legislation, and not for the reduction of inherited deficits or for the effects of cyclical influences outside their control. These elements should probably be retained under any future enforcement procedure in view of the difficulties experienced with the Europe's Stability and Growth Pact. The experience with the BEA once deficits disappeared and subsequently re-emerged also suggests that it is important to specify what happens once the goal is reached. For example, in light of the recent erosion of the projected surpluses for other than legislative reasons, Reischauer (2002) proposed that projected future excess revenues may not be fully at current lawmakers' disposal, but merely a fraction of them that is declining as the projection horizon lengthens. Finally, the use of emergency appropriations exempt from enforcement procedures poses the challenge of balancing the need to retain policymakers' flexibility against the effectiveness of the enforcement mechanism. The BEA exemption for emergency spending required only that the President and Congress agree on the amounts to be designated; there was for example no restriction on the use of these funds. An *a priori* definition of emergencies may be difficult to achieve. Explicit budgeting for emergency needs based on average annual amounts of emergency spending appropriated in previous years, akin to the States' rainy-day funds, raises the challenge how to prevent lawmakers from spending such funds on non-emergency purposes.

Notes

1. Figure 2.1 does not show the projections made in the CBO's annual Analysis of the President's Budget, as the revisions relative to the projections published in each January's Budget and Economic Outlook are generally small. It also omits the January 2003 projections, because the revisions relative to the August 2002 projections were small.
2. The distinction between technical and other factors is not always precise. For example, legislative changes represent CBO's best estimate of the future effects of recently enacted laws. If in later projections those estimates of the effects change, the changes are classified as technical. Similarly, changes in some factors that are related to the performance of the economy, such as capital gains realisations, are classified as technical changes because they are not driven directly by components of CBO's economic forecasts.
3. The debt-service cost of the 2001 and 2003 tax cuts are OECD calculations using CBO documents. The resulting estimates are very similar to those of Gale and Orszag (2003), Appendix Table 2. Figure 2.2 in the text is very similar to their Figure 2.
4. The CBO estimates that some of the recent weakness in personal tax receipts is related to smaller-than-expected taxable realisations of capital gains and some to lower growth of incomes that are taxed at the highest marginal rates. Even after making adjustments for these and other factors, there is a substantial unexplained residual weakness, which the CBO assumes will phase out only gradually over the projection period.
5. This estimate is based on Congressional Budget Office (2003*d*). Subsequently the Department of Health and Human Service's actuary estimated that cost of the prescription drug benefit over the same 10-year period will be $534 billion (see Office of management and Budget, 2004, Table S-13).
6. The Administration's FY 2005 budget proposes an increase in discretionary spending from $826 billion in FY 2003 to $942 billion in FY 2009, leaving the level of real discretionary spending approximately unchanged (Office of Management and Budget, 2004). The proposed defence spending reflects expenditures projected under the 2004 Future Years Defense Program, but does not include funding for operations in Afghanistan and Iraq beyond FY 2004. By contrast, the CBO baseline extends the FY 2004 supplementary appropriations over the entire 10-year window, but otherwise assumes a slower growth rate of defence outlays. Therefore, defence outlays under the Administration's proposals, assuming no additional funding for operations in Afghanistan and Iraq, are only $37 billion lower in 2006-07 than under the CBO baseline, and $15 billion lower each year in 2010-2014 (Congressional Budget Office, 2004*c*, Table 1-6). Non-defence spending would be little changed in nominal terms.
7. The cost estimates of the alternative policies discussed in this paragraph are taken from Congressional Budget Office (2004, Table 1-3). In its FY 2005 budget the Administration has proposed to extend the higher AMT exemptions, which under JGTRRA are

scheduled to expire by the end of 2004, through the end of 2005. The Administration's cost estimate for this provision of $23 billion is close to the CBO estimate.

8. There are numerous other expiring tax provisions besides those in EGTRRA and JGTRRA that have been routinely renewed in the past (see below), but past 2011 the EGTRRA and JGTRRA provisions constitute about 90 per cent of the total amount.
9. All the cost estimates reported above are based on simulations that are not fully dynamic in that they account for the effects of microeconomic responses on revenues, but not for macroeconomic feedback effects due, for example, to changes in labour supply in response to tax changes (see Council of Economic Advisers, 2004, Ch. 5 for discussion of dynamic revenue and budget estimation). While in the case of EGTRRA and JGTRRA these effects could be large, the available studies (discussed in Annex 3.1) that account for macroeconomic responses suggest that the net effect of these laws on long-run national income is likely to be small. In view of these results, the cost estimates reported in the text would presumably be little changed if they were based on fully dynamic scoring.
10. This line of argument can be taken further by noting that several trust funds are "on-budget", such as pension reserves for federal military and civilian employees, which are projected to accrue surpluses of $480 billion over the period 2004-14 (Congressional Budget Office, 2004, Table 1-6).
11. The Office of Management and Budget (2004) estimates that the exclusion of employer contributions for medical insurance premiums and medical care reduced revenues in FY 2003 by 0.94 percentage point of GDP, the deductibility of home mortgage interest reduced revenues by 0.56 percentage point, and the deductibility of charitable donations for purposes other than health and education reduced revenues by 0.28 percentage point.
12. Council of Economic Advisers (2003, Ch. 5) discusses alternative approaches to shifting to a consumption-based tax system.
13. The Administration first proposed to create Lifetime Saving Accounts (LSAs), Retirement Saving Accounts (RSAs) and Employer Retirement Saving Accounts (ERSAs) in its FY 2004 budget, and included the proposals in slightly modified form in its FY 2005 budget. While contributions to any of these accounts would not be deductible, account earnings and qualified withdrawals would be tax-free. Besides the removal of eligibility rules related to age, pension coverage, or maximum income on contributions to RSAs, the proposal would encourage consolidation of existing tax-preferred retirement accounts. Traditional (deductible) and non-deductible IRAs would no longer accept contributions, income limits on conversions of traditional IRAs would be eliminated, and taxpayers who converted IRAs into RSAs within a certain period after the proposals' enactment would be permitted to spread the tax liability from the conversion over several years. Assuming that many individuals will choose to convert existing IRAs early on, the Administration estimates that the proposal will raise revenues by about $8 billion in FY 2006, and be roughly revenue-neutral in FY 2009 before reducing revenues at an increasing rate.
14. State general fund spending comprises most of states' elementary, secondary and higher education spending, but only about one third of Medicaid spending. Most states' fiscal years run from 1 July to 30 June.
15. The long-term solvency of Social Security is also discussed in Council of Economic Advisers (2004, Ch. 6).
16. The CBO's high-cost and low-cost scenarios assume that health costs per enrolee in Medicare and Medicaid rise 2.5 per cent and 0 per cent per year in excess of the growth rate of GDP per capita, respectively. By comparison, between 1990 and 2003 costs per

enrolee in Medicare and Medicaid rose 1.7 and 2.2 per cent, respectively, in excess of the growth rate of GDP per capita. Even under its low-cost assumption regarding health costs, spending on the three big entitlement programmes is projected to reach 12.6 per cent of GDP by 2050. It should be noted, however, that under the intermediate assumption the projected growth in US age-related spending compares favourably to that in most other OECD economies (see OECD, 2001a, Chapter IV).

17. An extensive discussion of issues related to Medicare reform can be found in OECD (2002, Chapter III).

18. The year 2018 is the date at which Social Security is expected to begin running cash-flow deficits, but Social Security's interest earnings are projected to prevent the trust fund from diminishing until 2028.

19. For example, reform model 2 envisaged that workers could redirect up to 4 percentage points of their payroll taxes (up to a threshold indexed to wages of initially $1 000) to a personal account and that benefits would be reduced by the account contributions compounded at 2 per cent above inflation. Because the real interest rate assumed by the actuaries to be earned by the Social Security trust fund is 3 per cent, a rate below 3 per cent used in compounding personal account contributions implies that diverting revenue from the trust fund to personal accounts yields losses to the trust fund over the lifetime of a worker.

20. Diamond and Orszag (2004, Table 1.2) provide an illustration of the effects of the Commission's proposal to index initial benefits to prices instead of wages. An average earner who is 55 at the end of 2004 is scheduled to receive an annual benefit at full benefit age (in 2003 dollars) of $15 408, whereas a worker who is 25 at the end of 2004 is scheduled to receive an annual benefit at full benefit age of $19 400. Indexing initial benefits to prices would reduce the latter back to $15 408, or by 20 per cent.

21. Like the long-term costs of Medicare as a whole, the long-term costs of the prescription drug benefit are imprecise because of uncertainty about the future growth rate of prescription drug costs. In its long-term projections, CBO assumes that this growth rate initially continues at its recent trend of 3 percentage points above the growth rate of health care spending as a whole, but declines over the next 25 years to about 1 percentage point above it. Under this assumption, the cost of the prescription drug benefit rises from less than 0.4 per cent of GDP in 2013 to about 1 per cent of GDP in 2050. Faster annual growth in drug costs or changes to the structure of the co-payments could raise this number substantially (Holtz-Eakin, 2003b).

22. The fiscal gap is the size of the immediate and permanent increase in revenues or decrease in outlays that would be necessary to keep federal debt at its current share of GDP by the end of a given horizon. For further discussion see Auerbach (1997) and Congressional Budget Office (2000).

23. On the issue of extending temporary provisions, see Barshay (2003). That article also suggests a political economy motive for not making temporary provisions permanent, namely generating campaign contributions.

24. In the case of EGTRRA, the use of sunsets was motivated by the US Senate's so-called "Byrd rule" by which legislation with revenue effects beyond the 10-year window requires a 60-vote majority. In the case of JGTRRA, by contrast, the use of sunsets seems to have been intended to limit the calculated revenue cost of the package.

25. A more extensive description and evaluation of the BEA, together with a discussion of reform options, can be found in Congressional Budget Office (2003a), Appendix A.

Bibliography

Auerbach, A.J. (1997), "Quantifying the Current U.S. Fiscal Imbalance", *National Tax Journal*, Vol. 50, No. 3, September.

Auerbach, A.J. (2002a), "Taxation and Corporate Financial Policy", Ch. 19 in A. Auerbach and M. Feldstein (eds.), *Handbook of Public Economics*, Vol. 3, Elsevier, New York.

Auerbach, A.J. (2002b), "The Bush Tax Cut and National Saving", *National Tax Journal*, Vol. 55, No. 3, September.

Auerbach, A.J. (2003), "Budget Windows, Sunsets and Fiscal Control", mimeo, July.

Auerbach, A.J. and W.G. Gale (2001), "Tax Cuts and the Budget", mimeo, March.

Barshay, J. (2003), "Temporary Tax Breaks Usually a Permanent Reality", *Congressional Quarterly*, 15 November.

Burman, L.E., W.G. Gale and J. Rohaly (2003a), "The Expanding Reach of the Individual Alternative Minimum Tax", *Journal of Economic Perspectives*, Vol. 17, No. 2, Spring.

Burman, L.E., W.G. Gale and J. Rohaly (2003b), "The AMT: Projections and Problems", *Tax Notes*, 7 July.

Burman, L.E., W.G. Gale and P.R. Orszag (2003c), "The Administration's Savings Proposals: Preliminary Analysis", *Tax Notes*, 3 March.

Bush, George W. (2004), *State of the Union Address to Congress*, 20 January.

Congressional Budget Office (2000), *The Long-Term Budget Outlook*, October.

Congressional Budget Office (2001), *The Budget and Economic Outlook: An Update*, August.

Congressional Budget Office (2002), "The Impact of Social Security and Medicare on the Federal Budget", *Long-Range Fiscal Policy Briefs*, No. 6, 14 November.

Congressional Budget Office (2003a), *The Budget and Economic Outlook: Fiscal Years 2004-2013*, January.

Congressional Budget Office (2003b), *An Analysis of the President's Budgetary Proposals for Fiscal Year 2004*, March.

Congressional Budget Office (2003c), *The Budget and Economic Outlook: An Update*, August.

Congressional Budget Office (2003d), "Cost Estimate for H.R.1, Medicare Prescription Drug, Improvement, and Modernization Act of 2003", 20 November.

Congressional Budget Office (2003e), *The Long-Term Budget Outlook*, December.

Congressional Budget Office (2004a), *The Budget and Economic Outlook: Fiscal Years 2005 to 2014*, January.

Congressional Budget Office (2004b), "Letter to the Honorable Ron Wyden Regarding the Authority to Negotiate Prices for Single-Source Drugs for Medicare Beneficiaries", 3 March.

Congressional Budget Office (2004c), *An Analysis of the President's Budgetary Proposals for Fiscal Year* 2005, March.

Council of Economic Advisers (2003), *Economic Report of the President*, February.

Council of Economic Advisers (2004), *Economic Report of the President*, February.

Diamond, P. and P.R. Orszag (2004), *Saving Social Security*, Brookings Institution, Washington, D.C.

Elmendorf, D. and N.G. Mankiw (1999), "Government Debt", Chapter 25 in J.B. Taylor and M. Woodford (eds.), *Handbook of Macroeconomics*, Vol. 1c, Elsevier, New York.

Gale, W.G. and P.R. Orszag (2003), "The Budget Outlook: Baseline and Adjusted Projections", *Tax Notes*, 22 September.

Gale, W.G. and S.R. Potter (2002), "An Economic Evaluation of the Economic Growth and Tax Relief Reconciliation Act of 2001", *National Tax Journal*, Vol. 55, No. 1, March.

Gramlich, E.M. (1996), "Different Approaches for Dealing with Social Security", *Journal of Economic Perspectives*, Vol. 10, No. 3, Summer.

Holtz-Eakin, D. (2003a), "Prescription Drug Coverage and Medicare's Fiscal Challenges," Statement before the Committee on Ways and Means, U.S. House of Representatives, 9 April.

Holtz-Eakin, D. (2003b), "The Cost of Medicare: What the Future Holds," Heritage Lectures, No. 815, 8 December.

House Ways and Means Committee (2003a), "Medicare Prescription Drug, Improvement, and Modernization Act of 2003: Conference Agreement", November, available at *www.house.gov/medicarerx/hr1jtexplstate.pdf*.

House Ways and Means Committee (2003b), "Summary of Medicare Conference Agreement", 21 November, available at *http://waysandmeans.house.gov/media/pdf/healthdocs/confagreement.pdf*.

Joint Committee on Taxation (2001), "Estimated Budget Effects of the Conference Agreement for H.R. 1836", JCX-51-01, 26 May.

Joint Committee on Taxation (2003a), "Macroeconomic Analysis of H.R. 2, the 'Jobs and Growth Reconciliation Tax Act of 2003'", published in *Congressional Record*, 8 May.

Joint Committee on Taxation (2003b), "Estimated Budget Effects of the Conference Agreement for H.R. 2", JCX-55-03, 22 May.

Kaiser Commission on Medicaid and the Uninsured (2003), "Implications of the New Medicare Prescription Drug Benefit for State Medicaid Budgets", *Issue Brief* 4162, December.

Laubach, T. (2003), "New Evidence on the Interest Rate Effects of Budget Deficits and Debt", Board of Governors of the Federal Reserve System, Finance and Economics Discussion Series 2003-12.

National Association of State Budget Officers (2003), *The Fiscal Survey of the States*, available at *www.nasbo.org*.

Newhouse, J.P. (2001), "Medicare Policy in the 1990s", NBER Working Paper 8531, October.

OECD (2001a), *Economic Outlook*, No. 69, Paris.

OECD (2001b), *Economic Surveys: United States*, Paris.

OECD (2002), *Economic Surveys: United States*, Paris.

Office of Management and Budget (2004), *The Budget of the U.S. Government, Fiscal Year 2005*, February.

Parrott, S. and S. Fremstad (2003), "The Senate Finance Committee's TANF Reauthorization Bill", Center on Budget and Policy Priorities, 22 September.

President's Commission to Strengthen Social Security (2001), *Strengthening Social Security and Creating Personal Wealth for All Americans*, 21 December, available at *www.csss.gov*.

Reischauer, R.D. (2002), "Framing the Budget Debate for the Future", before the Committee on the Budget, U.S. Senate, 29 January.

Whitehouse, E. (2000), "Administrative Charges for Funded Pensions: An International Comparison and Assessment", World Bank, Social Protection Discussion Paper No. 16, June.

Annex 2.1

Long-run effects of fiscal policies on national income

A comprehensive analysis of the long-run effects of EGTRRA and JGTRRA on national income is complicated because of the multitude of provisions contained in these two acts. This appendix provides an illustrative calculation by focussing only on those aspects of the legislation that are most likely to have effects beyond the near-term business cycle, notably the reduction in marginal tax rates on labour income enacted in EGTRRA, the reduction in marginal tax rates on dividends included in JGTRRA, and the effects of the two acts on public debt, private saving and the domestically owned capital stock. Towards the end it discusses the results of the available comprehensive analyses of the two acts, which are Gale and Potter (2002) and Auerbach (2002b) for EGTRRA, and Congressional Budget Office (2003b) and Joint Committee on Taxation (2003a) for JGTRRA.*

The CBO estimates that, once fully phased in, EGTRRA reduces the average effective marginal tax rate on labour income by about 5 per cent of the current tax rate (Congressional Budget Office, 2001) and therefore raises the after-tax return to labour by about 2.8 per cent. Using separate estimates of the labour supply elasticity for males, full-time female workers and other female workers, Gale and Potter (2002) derive an aggregate labour supply elasticity of 0.17 and conclude that the reduction in marginal tax rates would raise labour supply by about 0.48 per cent. Moreover, EGTRRA provides various incentives for human capital accumulation, which they estimate may boost the long-run increase in labour supply to 0.69 per cent. Assessing the effects of the reduction in marginal tax rates on dividends legislated by JGTRRA is difficult because mature firms only infrequently finance new investment out of equity issuance as opposed to retained earnings. The impact of relief from dividend taxation on the cost of equity capital in the form of retentions is uncertain (see Auerbach (2002a) for a discussion of the "traditional" and "new" view of corporate equity policy). If the dividend tax cut had a sizeable effect on the cost of capital, this should have benefited the stock prices of corporations that pay dividends compared to those that do not pay dividends. By contrast, among the companies included in the S&P 500 index, the non-dividend paying stocks outperformed the dividend paying stocks by a wide margin in 2003. While various factors could be responsible for this observation, the lagging relative performance of dividend paying stocks is consistent with the view that many large investors, such as domestic tax-exempt investors like insurance companies and foreign investors, are unaffected by the change in dividend taxation. For large, widely held corporations the dividend tax cut appears therefore to have little effect on their cost of capital; for small and medium-sized enterprises, the effect

* The analysis in Congressional Budget Office (2003b) is based on the original Administration proposal, which included both much more substantial reductions in dividend income and capital gains taxation than what was included in the law, as well as the savings proposals described in the main text, which have not yet been legislated.

could be more important. For the illustrative calculation presented here, the dividend tax cut is assumed not to affect domestic capital accumulation.

EGTRRA and JGTRRA combined reduce revenues by about 1.6 per cent of GDP. Because the two laws did not feature any offsetting revenue measures or outlay reductions, this analysis assumes that the revenue losses are financed entirely through an equal-sized increase in the primary deficit. This assumption is consistent with the effects of the two laws on the CBO's deficit projections. The federal government's flow budget constraint can be written as $B_t = (1 + r) B_{t-1} + D^p_t$, where B_t denotes government debt outstanding at the end of year t, r is the nominal interest rate paid on government debt, and D^p_t denotes the primary deficit. Assuming that nominal GDP grows at rate g, so that $Y_t = (1 + g) Y_{t-1}$, the budget constraint can be expressed in terms of the ratios of debt and the primary deficit to GDP, denoted b_t and d^p_t, as $b_t = (1 + r)/(1 + g) b_{t-1} + d^p_t$. According to the CBO's latest projections, nominal GDP is expected to grow by about 4½ per cent per year in the long run, while gross interest payments are projected at about 5¼ per cent of gross federal debt. As long as the interest rate r exceeds the growth rate g, a permanent increase in the ratio of the primary deficit to GDP leads to an explosive path for the debt-to-GDP ratio. If the tax cuts were made permanent, ultimately some other deficit-reducing measures would have to be taken to stabilise the debt-to-GDP ratio. For the purpose of illustration, the tax cuts are assumed to increase the primary deficit by 1.6 per cent of GDP for 10 years, after which corrective measures are taken to offset their effect on the primary deficit. Using the above values for interest and growth rates, the debt-to-GDP ratio at the end of the ten-year period would be 16.5 percentage points higher than without the revenue reductions.

To calculate the effect of this increase in government debt on the domestically owned capital stock and therefore national income, about 30 per cent of the decline in public saving, or ½ per cent of annual GDP, is assumed to be offset by an increase in private saving. This offset is caused in part by a rise in interest rates due to the larger stock of government debt. Recent evidence presented in Laubach (2003) suggests that interest rates would rise by roughly 60 basis points in anticipation of a 16.5 per cent increase in the debt-to-GDP ratio. Combined with the reduction in the effective marginal tax rate on interest income from 25.3 per cent to 23.2 per cent (Congressional Budget Office, 2001) and an aggregate saving elasticity with respect to the after-tax return on saving of 0.2 (Gale and Potter, 2002), the increase in interest rates raises private saving by roughly 0.1 per cent of GDP. A probably more important channel, which is difficult to quantify, is the decline in household net wealth caused by the increase in interest rates, which will cause households to save in order to rebuild their wealth. In total, the 30 per cent offset implies that the domestically owned capital stock declines by 11.5 per cent of GDP. Following the calculation in Elmendorf and Mankiw (1999), which is based on an estimated gross marginal product of capital of 9.5 per cent, this decline in the capital stock leads to a reduction of gross national income by about 1.1 per cent. Using a labour share in income of 0.65, the overall long-run effect of the two tax laws on national income would by this calculation be $0.65 * 0.69 - 1.1 = -0.65$ per cent. It is worth noting that this result holds regardless of the degree to which the shortfall in national saving and capital accumulation is compensated by foreign capital inflows. Even in the extreme case that foreign capital inflows make up the entire 11.5 per cent decline in the domestically owned capital stock, the income earned by this capital inflow does not accrue to domestic residents.

Although the calculations above are merely illustrative and abstract from many details of the tax legislation, the result that the beneficial effects of the marginal tax rate reductions on the long-run level of national income are more than offset by the negative effects of the decline in national saving is consistent with the findings of the more comprehensive analyses of EGTRRA presented in Gale and Potter (2002) and Auerbach (2002b). Gale and Potter find that after 10 years the level of GNP is reduced by 0.68 per cent (Gale and Potter, 2002,

Table 7). Auerbach reports long-run declines in the level of output relative to baseline of between 0.4 per cent and 2.4 per cent, depending on how and when revenues are being raised to restore the budget to balance. The results concerning the long-run effects of JGTRRA reported in Joint Committee on Taxation (2003a) vary depending on the type of economic model used, with all models showing increases in real GDP relative to baseline during the early years of the analysis (2003-08), but unchanged or lower real GDP relative to baseline in the later years (2009-13). Thus real GDP grows faster during the earlier years, but this if offset by slower growth later on. The level of GNP under these simulations is likely to be reduced further because the share of the domestically employed capital stock owned by foreigners presumably rises as national saving declines.

III. Maintaining price stability

Over the period since the end of 2001 monetary policy has maintained an accommodative stance, with the real federal funds rate fluctuating in a narrow band around zero.[1] Nonetheless the recovery gained momentum only around the middle of 2003. Earlier last year, with GDP growth faltering and core price measures continuing to decelerate, the Federal Reserve was facing the risk of inflation turning into deflation with little room left for conventional monetary policy measures. As the pace of economic activity has picked up markedly since mid-2003, this risk is now much diminished. Whereas in the earlier episode the challenge for the Federal Reserve was to reduce long-term interest rates further without additional large reductions in the federal funds rate, more recently it has turned to fostering the recovery by limiting market expectations of an early policy response to faster output growth. In either case, effective Federal Reserve communication with the public has been of critical importance. After reviewing recent developments in Federal Reserve policy, this Chapter discusses issues related to Federal Reserve communication. Finally, it argues that some clarification of the Federal Reserve's price stability objective could further enhance the effectiveness of monetary policy.

Avoiding deflation

Fears that the currently low rates of inflation would turn into deflation have receded since the middle of 2003 in view of the substantial strengthening in output growth and, to a lesser extent, employment increases (Figure 3.1). With the recovery increasingly firmly established, disinflationary pressures are likely to subside even if in the meantime inflation declines somewhat further. The risk of deflation appeared more acute in the spring of last year when, despite the massive monetary and fiscal stimulus since 2001, the recovery was still relatively weak. At the time of the May Federal Open Market Committee (FOMC) meeting, GDP was estimated to have grown at a 1.6 per cent annual rate in the first quarter of 2003 after having grown 1.4 per cent in the previous quarter. The momentum toward disinflation was magnified by ongoing robust productivity growth, a side effect of which was that payroll employment continued to contract (Kohn, 2003a). At its May meeting, the FOMC changed the balance of risks assessment in its statement by separating for the first time its assessment for output growth from

Figure 3.1. **Total and core inflation**[1]
Year-on-year per cent change

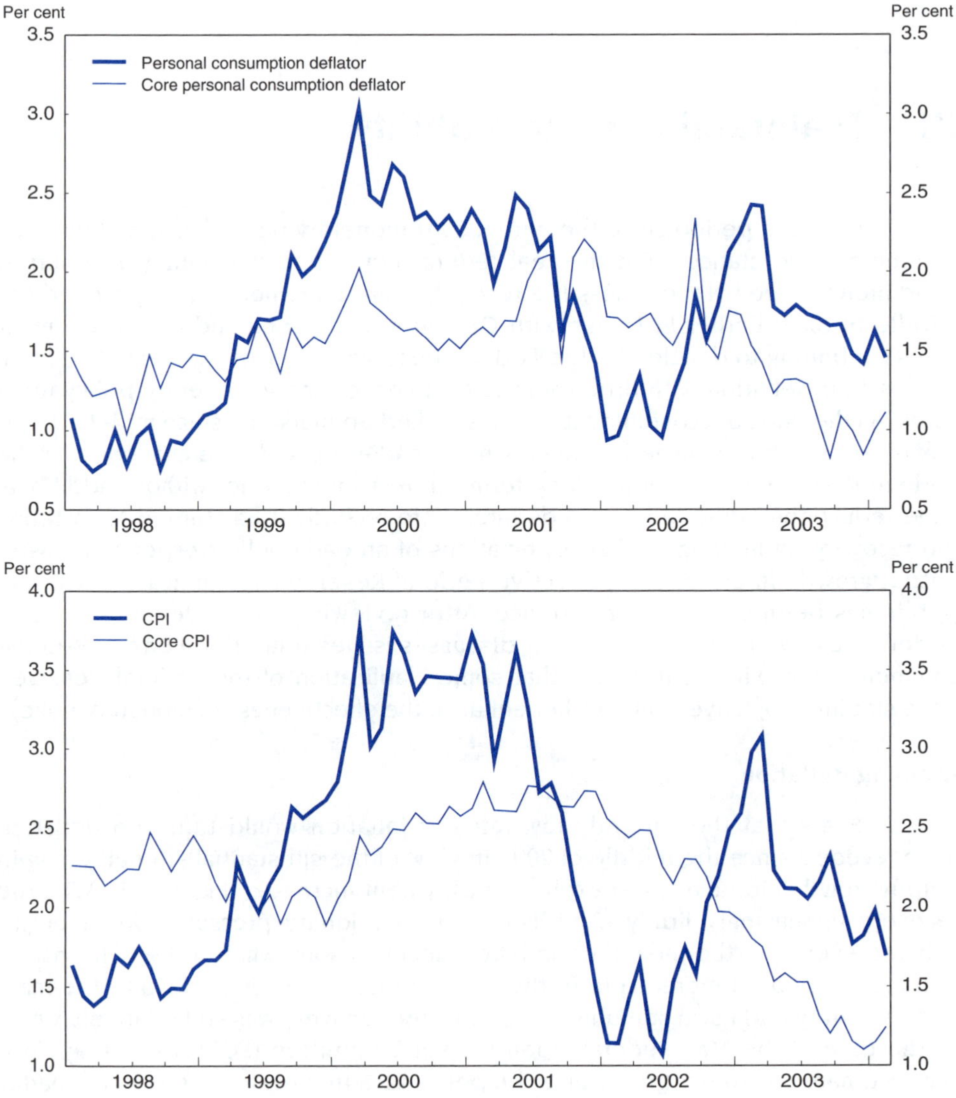

1. Core inflation is the rate of increase over one year of the consumption deflator and CPI, respectively, excluding food and energy products and services.

Source: Bureau of Economic Analysis and Bureau of Labor Statistics.

that for inflation, thereby making clear that even though it expected growth to pick up, inflation was likely to decline further. Moreover, it indicated its concern about the risk of further disinflation by noting that "the probability of an unwelcome substantial fall in inflation, though minor, exceeds that of a pickup in inflation from its already low level".

Already well before the May meeting, FOMC members had made clear that outright deflation would be undesirable and had discussed non-traditional policy measures that the Federal Reserve could take in the event that deflation occurred with the federal funds rate close to or at zero (see *e.g.* Bernanke, 2002). As will be discussed below, market expectations of future short-term interest rates are a critical determinant of current long-term interest rates, and hence the central bank can ease financial conditions by affecting long-term interest rates to the extent that it can reduce expectations of future short-term interest rates, even if the current short-term interest rate cannot be reduced further. A complementary channel for influencing long-term interest rates is through changes in the composition of the central bank's balance sheet or outright balance sheet expansion through purchases of long-term securities (Bernanke and Reinhart, 2004). Market participants interpreted the May FOMCstatement as signalling that the Federal Reserve might need to engage in some of these non-traditional measures, and bond markets rallied sharply over the weeks prior to the next FOMC meeting (Figure 3.2). Over the period between the May and June FOMC meetings, the yield on the ten-year Treasury note declined by about 60 basis points. Over the same period inflation expectations at the one-year horizon as measured by household survey responses declined sharply, but this decline may have reflected to a large extent falling energy prices (Figure 3.3). Moreover, federal funds futures prices indicated that markets placed a higher than 50 per cent probability on a 50 basis-point cut in the federal funds target at the June FOMC meeting. In the event, although the FOMC devoted considerable attention to the subjects of deflation and non-traditional monetary policy measures at its June meeting, it did not engage in any such policy measures and reduced the federal funds target by only 25 basis points (Figure 3.4). Over the next four weeks, the ten-year yield rose 90 basis points, a development presumably unwelcome to the FOMC. Misunderstandings between the Federal Reserve and the markets probably contributed to this temporary episode of extraordinary volatility in financial markets (Kohn, 2003b). However, interpreting the sharp rise in nominal yields as a sign that financial markets considered monetary policy excessively tight is at odds with the fact that about 40 basis points of the increase in nominal ten-year yields was accounted for by a rise in expected inflation as measured by the difference between nominal and inflation-indexed yields (Figure 3.3). A more plausible interpretation of the simultaneous upward revision of expected future real interest rates *and* inflation is that the FOMC's decision and statement shifted the focus of attention from the risk of deflation to the risk of rising inflation. This arguably excessive reaction of inflation expectations will be discussed further below.

Figure 3.2. **Rates on selected Treasury securities**

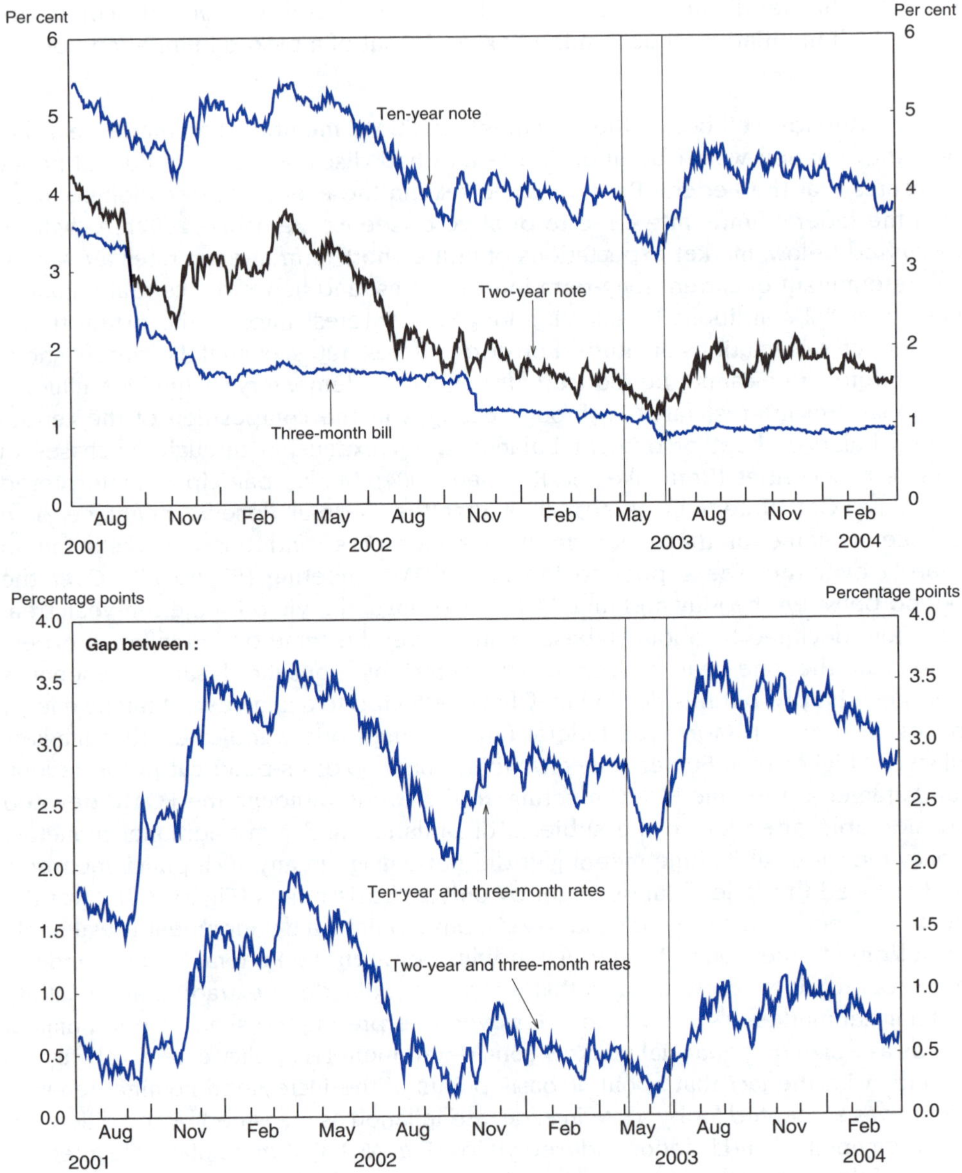

Note: Vertical lines indicate FOMC meetings (6th May and 24/25th June 2003).
Source: Board of Governors of the Federal Reserve System.

Figure 3.3. **Inflation expectations**

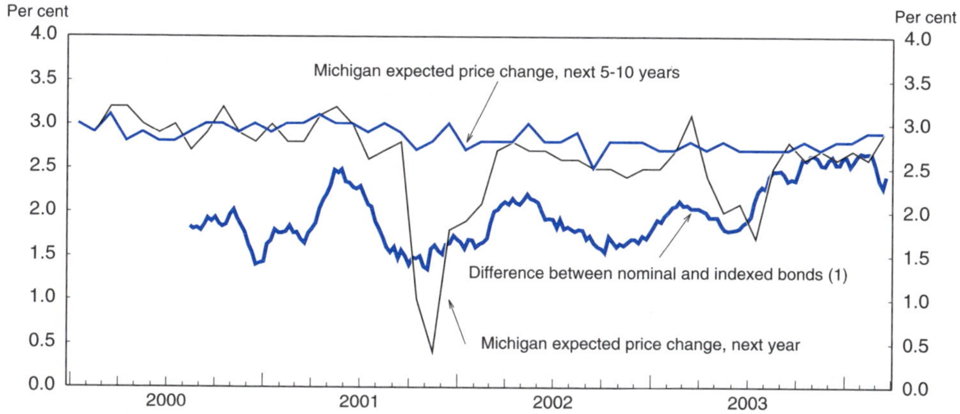

1. Difference between the 10-year constant-maturity Treasury bond and Merrill Lynch Treasury index-linked bond. The indexed bond used in the calculation changes in January each year to maintain a constant maturity.
Source: Board of Governors of the Federal Reserve System; Thomson Financial and University of Michigan.

The possibility that the swings in long-term yields reflected difficulties in the communication between the Federal Reserve and financial markets during May to July was likely an important factor behind subsequent efforts by the FOMC

Figure 3.4. **Nominal and real federal funds rate**

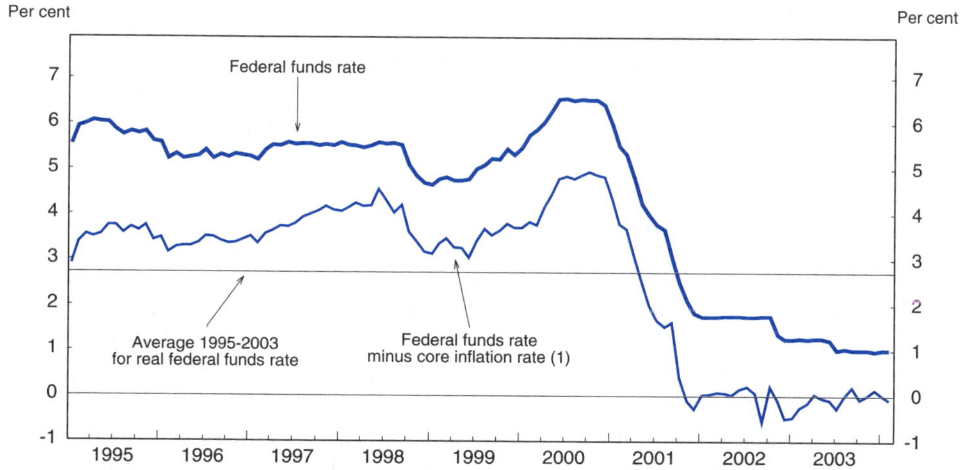

1. Based on the deflator for personal consumption expenditures, excluding food and energy.
Source: Board of Governors of the Federal Reserve System and Bureau of Economic Analysis.

to be more explicit in communicating its intentions going forward. Already before the August 2003 meeting, FOMC members emphasised that an important aspect of the May statement was an implicit commitment that monetary policy would maintain an easy stance as long as the risk of a substantial fall in inflation remained (Bernanke, 2003b). In its August statement, the FOMC made this commitment explicit by adding to the balance of risks statement that under the circumstances at the time, "policy accommodation can be maintained for a considerable period". At the time of the August meeting, GDP was estimated to have grown by 2.4 per cent at annual rate in the second quarter, and there were indications that third-quarter growth would be substantially stronger, partly because of personal income tax cuts and rebates. In these circumstances, the FOMC needed to communicate to markets that, because of the extremely low level of inflation as well as the continued robust productivity growth, a firming in output growth did not pose any inflationary risks over the foreseeable future and would therefore elicit a different monetary policy response than during previous recoveries. By the late autumn, data confirmed that the recovery was widespread and firmly established, GDP, productivity and profits were surging, and the labour market at last showed signs of improvement. At the time of its December meeting, the risk of deflation seemed much diminished, and the FOMC viewed the balance of risks with regard to inflation as almost neutral, despite further deceleration in both core prices and wages over previous months. Measured by the yield on ten-year Treasury notes, which has fallen of late below its level of mid-July, the FOMC has apparently succeeded in communicating that policy will remain accommodative for some time to come, despite substantially more upbeat economic news as well as ongoing fiscal deterioration. After its January 2004 meeting, the FOMC replaced its "considerable period" language by the statement that it believes that it can be "patient in removing its policy accommodation", which was understood as signalling that it was moving closer to raising the funds rate target. Nonetheless, as the time at which monetary stimulus will need to be withdrawn inevitably draws closer, a challenge for the Federal Reserve remains to communicate effectively its likely future policy stance.

Challenges in communicating the policy stance

The recent experience with low and declining inflation at a time when the federal funds rate has been close to its zero lower bound has imposed new demands on Federal Reserve communications which, considering the uncertainty surrounding the effects of monetary policy in this environment, have been met to a considerable extent. The latest episode has emphasised the critical role played by market expectations about the future path of short-term interest rates in determining current long-term interest rates.[2] As discussed above, this mechanism was potentially at work when, following the FOMC's expression of concern about further disinflation at its May 2003 meeting, long-term Treasury yields fell sharply to their lowest level since the late 1950s on expectations that the federal funds rate might be reduced further before being eventually raised, and that the Federal Reserve could even begin to purchase long-term securities. In addition to raising the Federal Reserve's control over *nominal* long-term interest rates, particularly relevant in a situation in which the federal funds rate is close to zero, it is also critical that the FOMC communicates clearly its outlook for inflation because the extent of stimulus transmitted from monetary policy to the economy is determined by *real* long-term interest rates. The behaviour of the spread between nominal and inflation-index Treasury yields during the recent episode suggests that long-term inflation expectations may remain somewhat unstable, an issue discussed further below. Consequently, a challenge for the FOMC is to communicate not only its assessment of current economic conditions, but also to inform markets as thoroughly as possible about its views of both prospective economic developments and monetary policy responses.

One complication in communicating the FOMC's outlook for the economy and its expectation of future policy decisions is that often there are widely different views on these issues held by the 19 Committee members. The only channel through which any quantitative information has been communicated in the past are the ranges and central tendencies of FOMC members' projections for nominal and real GDP growth, PCE inflation and the unemployment rate published in the semi-annual *Monetary Policy Report* to the Congress. The width of the reported ranges for these variables provides an indication of the dispersion of individual members' views.[3] From this information market participants can draw only vague inferences about the FOMC's outlook for the economy. Communicating the FOMC's expectation for its own future policy decisions is even more difficult lest doing so would create credibility problems. The additional complication is that the future path of monetary policy is largely determined by information becoming available only in the future, and therefore any statement about the FOMC's likely future policy decisions is conditional on a particular set of economic developments. The FOMC therefore cannot commit to a particular value of the federal funds rate at a particular date in the future, but merely to how it expects to respond to the news that it expects to receive. The difficulty of communicating the conditional nature of this commitment has been demonstrated by the repeated clarifications that FOMC members have made since the adoption of the "considerable period" clause in the statement following the August 2003 meeting (Greenspan, 2003).

Despite these difficulties, further steps by the FOMC might be helpful to reduce information asymmetries between the Committee and the public. Besides the issue of clarifying the objectives of policy, which will be discussed below, the minutes of the FOMC meetings could be released in a timelier manner, instead of after the following meeting as under current practice. Going further, the FOMC might release forecasts like those in the *Monetary Policy Report* more frequently, for a larger number of variables and for a longer horizon (Bernanke, 2003a and 2004).

The discussion accompanying these forecasts would provide a vehicle for communicating the underlying deliberations and reasoning, including the diversity of views among the Committee members as well as analysis of the risks surrounding the forecast. Importantly, increasing in this manner the amount of information released by the FOMC might also make it more feasible to communicate its own (conditional) expectations for the future path for the federal funds rate because it would make transparent that this funds rate path is just one element of, and thus contingent on, a comprehensive view of future economic developments. If the future turned out differently than anticipated, the risk should be minimal that a departure from the previously predicted path would be perceived as reneging on a prior commitment.

Strengthening the policy framework

The Federal Reserve's incremental adjustments to its communication with the public, notably the changes over time to the FOMC statements, has probably helped to improve the effectiveness of monetary policy by reducing information asymmetries between the Fed and the public. However, Gurkaynak *et al.* (2003) provide evidence of remaining information asymmetries, most likely reflecting uncertainty about long-run inflation. These authors show that forward rates far into the future react strongly to unexpected components of both monetary policy decisions and a variety of economic data releases. They do not find the same result for inflation-indexed Treasury bonds, suggesting that inflation expectations are not well anchored.[4] Such uncertainty can have large welfare costs in an environment in which agents learn adaptively about long-run inflation (Orphanides and Williams, 2003). Much debate has therefore evolved around the question whether the Federal Reserve should adopt an inflation-targeting framework. Indeed, there is evidence to suggest that inflation expectations are better anchored in inflation-targeting countries than in countries without inflation targets (Levin *et al.*, 2003). This debate is complicated by the fact that most countries that have adopted inflation targets have done so as part of a fairly comprehensive reform of their framework for monetary policy.[5] Given the success of US monetary policy in achieving price stability over the past two decades, while at the same time stabilising output and coping with a number of new shocks such as the productivity acceleration, the stock market collapse and the terrorist attacks, arguably there is no need for drastic changes to the current framework. While scepticism towards a move in the direction of a more rigidly rules-based regime thus seems well-founded (Ferguson, 2003), this is not to say that *no* element of inflation targeting could improve the US policy framework.

One argument that has been advanced against inflation targeting in the United States is the concern whether an inflation target would be consistent with the existing multiple, non-hierarchical objectives of the Federal Reserve, or alternatively that monetary policy decisions could become more skewed towards inflation stabilisation instead of full employment.[6] Even if not intended, the fact that a numerical value is attached to one, but not the other objectives of policy, may lead to an elevation of this objective above the others (Kohn, 2003b). Also, accountability towards the Congress and the public may become focussed on achieving the inflation target at the expense of the other objectives. Another argument made against inflation targeting is that it may unduly restrict the flexibility to respond to events whose implications for future inflation are unclear, in particular financial crises such as the one of September 1998 following the Russian default or the terrorist attacks of September 2001. More generally, there are circumstances in which monetary policy may have to aim at avoiding some particularly bad outcomes, such as the recent possibility of deflation, even if doing so implies that the stance of policy is unusually easy, and hence the *mean* expectation of future inflation may be higher than desired (Kohn, 2003b; Greenspan, 2004). A framework in which the central bank was aiming to ensure that at all times the mean (or mode) of inflation expected at some specific horizon was equal to some particular target might find such a response difficult to justify.

While the recent excellent performance of US monetary policy may provide no reason for undertaking a shift to inflation targeting along all the dimensions of the framework as implemented in other countries, a quantification of the FOMC's interpretation of the price stability objective mandated by the Federal Reserve Act would likely improve the effectiveness of monetary policy. In a situation of sustained low inflation such as in recent years it is particularly important that inflation expectations be firmly anchored, so that unavoidable temporary declines of inflation below the desired range do not engender expectations of deflation which might become self-fulfilling. Equally important, in a situation of rapid output growth (as at present) but substantial remaining spare capacity, preventing a sharp rise in inflation expectations is critical to avoid turning a policy of fostering the recovery into an "inflation scare" such as occurred frequently during earlier recoveries (Goodfriend, 1993). The evidence that a numerical objective seems to help anchor inflation expectations combined with evidence that long-run inflation expectations in the United States are apparently excessively sensitive to the unexpected component of economic news suggests that such a quantification could reap many of the benefits that inflation targeting has yielded for other countries, while avoiding the criticisms made above.

Specifically, quantification of the price-stability objective would require the specification of both a price index and an optimal long-run inflation rate (or range) for this index which would presumably be greater than zero (Bernanke, 2003c; Gramlich, 2003). It would be desirable that this quantification have the approval of the relevant Congressional committees to clarify that the quantification is in fact consistent with the existing mandate of the Federal Reserve Act, and that it does not constitute an elevation of this mandate over the others. Through communications with the Congress and the public the FOMC could presumably dispel any impression that it was insufficiently focussing on objectives other than price stability, especially if it chose to go beyond its current convention of releasing its statements and minutes by publishing a document more similar to inflation-targeting central banks' *Inflation Reports*. Emphasising the long-run nature of this inflation rate would facilitate private-sector decisions that have long-term consequences without reducing the Federal Reserve's flexibility of responding to unforeseen events whose near-term effects on output and inflation may be highly uncertain. Nor would it be necessary to specify an exact horizon by which inflation should have returned to the objective. Providing a specific anchor for long-term inflation expectations would nonetheless be far from a vacuous commitment. Doing so would not limit but rather enhance the Federal Reserve's ability to respond flexibly to current events, even if a given response implies deviating from the price-stability objective for some period, because the observation of deviations from the objective would be less likely to adversely affect inflation expectations. Finally, reduced uncertainty about long-run inflation should lead to lower long-term interest rates *via* a decline in risk premia.

Notes

1. This statement holds if the real federal funds rate is defined as the nominal federal funds rate less the 4-quarter moving average of core personal consumption expenditure (PCE) inflation. If that measure of inflation is replaced by core CPI inflation or by consumer-survey or indexed bond-based measures of inflation expectations, the real funds rate has been well below zero over the past two years.
2. In dealing with the zero bound on nominal interest rates, the recent literature has emphasised the importance of affecting current long-term interest rates through expectations of future short-term rates. See Krugman (1998), Reifschneider and Williams (2000), and Eggertson and Woodford (2003).
3. The same challenge is faced by other central banks that publish their forecasts for variables such as inflation and GDP growth, notably central banks with inflation targets. For example, the Bank of England's Monetary Policy Committee (MPC) uses the confidence bands in its fan charts to convey not only individual members' uncertainty around a particular point forecast, but also dispersion of views among Committee members about the point forecast itself (Britton *et al.*, 1998). Presumably, the MPC's situation is easier than the FOMC's because the MPC has only 9 members.
4. See Bernanke (2004) for a discussion of related work. However, from Figure 3.3 it is evident that survey-based measures of long-term inflation expectations are much less volatile than measures of inflation expectations derived from the yields of nominal and inflation-indexed bonds.
5. For example, New Zealand's adoption of an inflation target coincided with new legislation making the Reserve Bank independent from the Treasury, whereas in the United Kingdom and Sweden adoption followed their exit from the exchange rate mechanism and hence the reorientation of monetary policy towards a different framework. Besides changes to the objectives of monetary policy, the adoption of inflation targeting was often accompanied by changes in the procedures for reporting to the public and accountability more generally. See Bernanke *et al.* (1999).
6. Section 2A of the Federal Reserve Act states that "The Board of Governors of the Federal Reserve System and the Federal Open Market Committee shall maintain long run growth of the monetary and credit aggregates commensurate with the economy's long run potential to increase production, so as to promote effectively the goals of maximum employment, stable prices, and moderate long-term interest rates".

Bibliography

Bernanke, B.S. (2002), "Deflation: Making Sure 'It' Doesn't Happen Here", before the National Economists Club, Washington, D.C., 21 November.

Bernanke, B.S. (2003a), "A Perspective on Inflation Targeting", at the Annual Washington Policy Conference of the National Association of Business Economists, 25 March.

Bernanke, B.S. (2003b), "An Unwelcome Fall in Inflation?", before the Economics Roundtable, University of California, San Diego, 23 July.

Bernanke, B.S. (2003c), "Panel Discussion", at the 28th Annual Policy Conference, Federal Reserve Bank of St. Louis, 17 October.

Bernanke, B.S. (2004), "Fedspeak", at the Meetings of the American Economic Association, San Diego, 3 January.

Bernanke, B.S., T. Laubach, F.S. Mishkin and A.S. Posen (1999), *Inflation Targeting: Lessons from the International Experience*, Princeton: Princeton University Press.

Bernanke, B.S. and V. Reinhart (2004), "Conducting Monetary Policy at Very Low Short-Term Interest Rates", at the Meetings of the American Economic Association, San Diego, 3 January.

Britton, E., P. Fisher and J. Whitley (1998), "The Inflation Report Projections: Understanding the Fan Chart", Bank of England, *Quarterly Bulletin*, February.

Eggertson, G. and M. Woodford (2003), "The Zero Bound on Interest Rates and Optimal Monetary Policy", mimeo, Princeton University, 26 June.

Ferguson, R.W. Jr. (2003), "Rules and Flexibility in Monetary Policy", at the University of Georgia, 12 February.

Goodfriend, M. (1993), "Interest Rate Policy and the Inflation Scare Problem: 1979-1992", Federal Reserve Bank of Richmond, *Economic Quarterly*, Vol. 79.

Gramlich, E.M. (2003), "Maintaining Price Stability", before the Economic Club of Toronto, 1 October.

Greenspan, A. (2003), "Remarks", at the Securities Industry Association annual meetings, Boca Raton, 6 November.

Greenspan, A. (2004), "Risk and Uncertainty in Monetary Policy", at the Meetings of the American Economic Association, San Diego, 3 January.

Gurkaynak, R., B. Sack and E. Swanson (2003), "The Excess Sensitivity of Long-Term Interest Rates: Evidence and Implications for Macroeconomic Models", Board of Governors of the Federal Reserve System, Finance and Economics Discussion Series 2003-50.

Kohn, D.L. (2003a), "Productivity and Monetary Policy", at the Federal Reserve Bank of Philadelphia Monetary Seminar, 24 September.

Kohn, D.L. (2003b), "Panel Discussion", at the 28th Annual Policy Conference, Federal Reserve Bank of St. Louis, 17 October.

Krugman, P. (1998), "It's Baaack! Japan's Slump and the Return of the Liquidity Trap", *Brookings Papers on Economic Activity*, 1998:2.

Levin, A.T., F.M. Natalucci and J.M. Piger (2003), "The Macroeconomic Effects of Inflation Targeting", at the 28th Annual Policy Conference, Federal Reserve Bank of St. Louis, 16 October.

Orphanides, A. and J.C. Williams (2003), "Imperfect Knowledge, Inflation Expectations, and Monetary Policy", forthcoming in B. Bernanke and M. Woodford (eds.), *Inflation Targeting*, Chicago: University of Chicago Press.

Reifschneider, D.L. and J.C. Williams (2000), "Three Lessons for Monetary Policy in a Low-Inflation Era", *Journal of Money, Credit, and Banking*, Vol. 32, No. 4, November.

IV. Improving confidence in financial markets

In recent years, financial-market confidence has been harmed by a number of influences such as the bursting of the stock-market bubble and geopolitical uncertainties. But corporate governance and accounting scandals have also played a role and could well be one factor behind the uneven pace of the recovery from the 2001 recession (Ferguson, 2003b). Continued reforms in this area, focusing on transparency and accountability, would bolster financial-market confidence and thereby contribute both to sustaining strong economic growth and to a less fragile external adjustment process. Against the backdrop of recent developments in foreign-exchange and stock markets, this Chapter reviews recent corporate-governance and accounting reforms and their effects so far. It also deals with other issues relevant in this context, notably the systemic risks surrounding private pension plans and government-sponsored enterprises as well as the Basel II Accord still under negotiation.

Exchange-rate and stock-market developments

Investor concerns regarding the magnitude and trend in the US external imbalance, prospects for a deeper fiscal shortfall, unfavourable interest-rate differentials and the plethora of corporate governance problems have weighed on the dollar since early 2002 (Figure 4.1, Panel A). Although, at around 28 per cent, the depreciation has been dramatic against the euro, in effective terms the dollar has weakened by only around 12 per cent, since it has remained strong against Latin American and Asian currencies. This has followed upon an effective appreciation of around 34 per cent from 1995 to 2001, which contributed to the rise in the external deficit. As a result, the exchange rate is still above its long-term average and estimates of purchasing power parity. Model simulations suggest that, in the absence of other adjustments, considerable further currency depreciation would be necessary to bring the external deficit back to more sustainable levels, although a scenario based solely on exchange-rate depreciation is not likely to work very well because of repercussions on foreign growth and hence US exports. Current account adjustment would seem to require both lower domestic absorption through appropriate domestic policies (in particular, fiscal restraint) and an improvement in growth prospects abroad. The potential for dollar depreciation to

Figure 4.1. **Exchange-rate and stock-market developments**

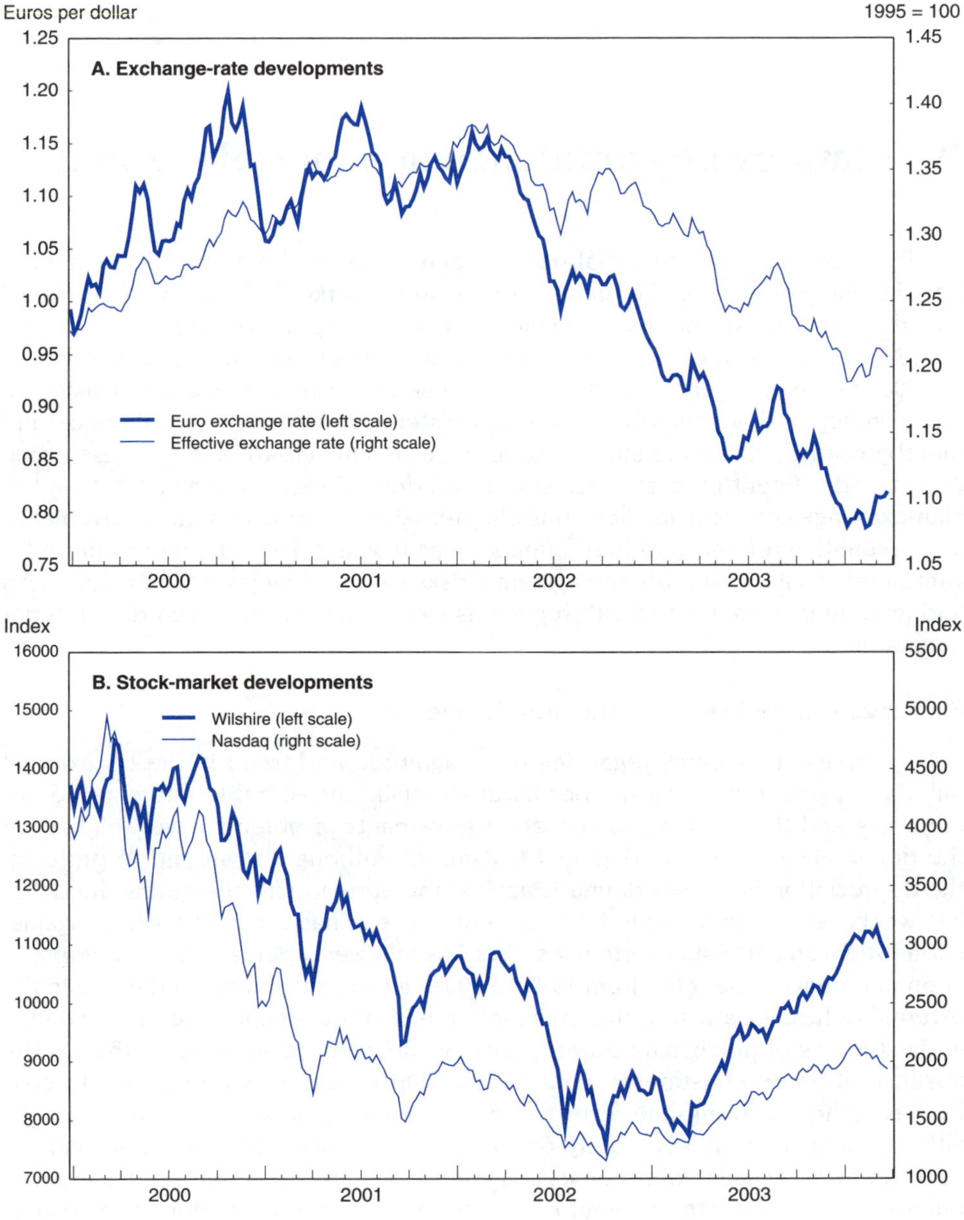

Source: Thomson Financial and OECD.

become disorderly or to overshoot would increase if the policy response to corporate scandals were to be inadequate (Horne and Merlin, 2002). In this case, international investors might further reduce acquisition of dollar assets until they were persuaded that the situation was correcting satisfactorily. However, there are also other factors at work, such as the lack of investment alternatives and some features of the US economy – deep capital markets, flexible factor markets, a strong investment climate and robust productivity and profit growth. Indeed, so far the fall in the dollar has not spilled over to stock or bond markets.

The increased risk aversion that weighed on equity markets in the first few years of the decade appears to have lifted (Figure 4.1, Panel B). All major stock-market indices have risen considerably since their lows in March 2003, reflecting improved earnings prospects. In the two years before, stock prices had reacted sharply to news of a scaling back of profit forecasts and various corporate scandals. While shares have recuperated only part of the losses suffered since their peak in 2000, volatility of all major equity indices has declined significantly over the past year. While earlier studies revealed a relationship between corporate governance and firm value (Gompers *et al.*, 2001), a recent survey of corporate governance standards among the S&P 500 firms (Hooper, 2003) finds that volatility in share prices is negatively correlated with such standards and especially their changes over time. The criteria taken into account include board structure, shareholder treatment, information disclosure and executive compensation. The survey also finds that, even into 2003, standards still differed widely across firms and that improvements in corporate governance have not been universal.

Corporate governance and accounting reforms

As noted, corporate scandals exacerbated the stock-market decline in the early part of the decade. Starting with the collapse of Enron in 2001, it became clear that the preceding boom years had been accompanied by instances of fraud, other misconduct and a serious erosion in business principles. Important factors explaining the corporate malfeasance seem to have included declining audit quality and weaknesses in governance structures, compounded by executive compensation schemes that provided undue incentives to boost short-term company earnings and by questionable accounting practices.[1] During the boom years, many corporations developed a short-term focus, fuelled by an obsession with quarter-to-quarter earnings and the temptation that inherently resulted from the massive amount of stock options granted to insiders, often outweighing their positive incentive effects. In 2001, for example, the ten most highly rewarded chief executive officers in the S&P 500 were granted option packages with an estimated average value of $170 million per person[2] (Holmstrom and Kaplan, 2004). Analysts, some tainted by conflicts of interest, contributed to creating an atmosphere in which "hitting the numbers" became the objective rather than sound, long-term strength and performance (Donaldson, 2003). This environment made it irresistible for many managers to make adjustments – fraudulent or otherwise – in financial reports in order to meet targeted results. It also led many gatekeepers (accounting firms and legal and financial advisers) to get into the game and enhance their compensation by offering "value added" services that tested professional and ethical standards.

To address the widespread decline in investor confidence and perceived weaknesses in corporate governance structures, Congress passed the Sarbanes-Oxley Act (SOA), which took effect 30 July 2002. This is arguably the most important securities legislation since the 1930s. Self-regulatory organisations, such as the New York Stock Exchange (NYSE) and National Association of Securities Dealers (NASD), have established basic corporate governance standards as part of their listing requirements and other organisations (*e.g.* the Conference Board) have proposed a number of voluntary corporate governance codes. Among other things (see Annex IX of the 2002 *Survey* for more details) the SOA:

- created a new Public Company Accounting Oversight Board (PCAOB);
- promoted auditor independence;
- added new disclosure requirements for public companies;
- strengthened the oversight role of corporate audit committees and established their independence;
- documented the responsibility of chief executive and chief financial officers (CEOs and CFOs) for corporate reporting and internal controls;
- authorised the Securities and Exchange Commission (SEC) to set minimum standards of professional conduct for attorneys practicing before it; and
- enhanced civil and criminal penalties for securities fraud.

The rules mandated by the SOA are now in place, but their implementation is still underway. Thus, it is still too early to draw firm conclusions. Nonetheless, it appears that the reforms' impact has been largely positive. Concerns that some provisions of the SOA (such as requirements for CEOs to certify financial statements) could adversely affect business behaviour are as yet unproven. On the other hand, new scandals involving the NYSE and, most recently, in the mutual fund industry have shown that there is still unfinished business in the area of corporate reform.

Accounting and auditor independence

The creation of a special, national board (the PCAOB) to oversee the auditing of public companies' financial reports is perhaps the most visible reform under the SOA. In establishing the PCAOB, the Act introduces a new check on the quality of audit services supplied to public corporations whose securities are listed on US exchanges. The role of the board is to strengthen the auditors' incentives to do their job properly, even in the face of pressure from managers who might in some instances prefer not to accurately report their companies' performance. To increase the chance of detecting any future misconduct by auditors, each public accounting firm must register with the board (paying registration and annual fees) and must submit to periodic reviews of its performance. If there is evidence of misconduct, the board has the power to impose sanctions, including barring auditors from supplying their services to a US-listed corporation. The PCAOB, which is overseen by the SEC, began its work a year ago. Its staff is expected to increase from over 100 in late 2003 to around 300 people. More than 700 firms have already registered with the board, and foreign companies have to do so by mid-2004. Inspections have commenced, with annual reviews scheduled for firms auditing more than 100 public companies.

The SOA goes beyond direct oversight of auditing firms, however, to address the conditions under which external auditors are chosen and employed. To limit the influence of managers who prepare financial reports, a corporation's choice of auditor must be made by a committee of independent directors. For each of its clients, the accounting firm that does the audit must periodically assign a new person as the lead audit partner. Both provisions are intended to reduce the opportunities for collusion between auditors and managers. Moreover, in order to avoid potential levers for managerial influence over auditors, registered public accounting firms are no longer permitted to sell certain non-audit services to their customers. Any exceptions to this as well as the fees paid to auditors must be disclosed to investors. In January 2003, the SEC strengthened its rules regarding auditor independence accordingly. In particular, it defined more precisely the non-audit services that must not be provided to a client and the auditor rotation frequency (every five or seven years, depending on the partner's role in the audit). In April 2003, as directed by the SOA, the SEC adopted a provision prohibiting managers from taking any action to influence the auditor in a way that could result in rendering the audited financial statements materially misleading. These measures should help restore investors' confidence in the audit process and the integrity of financial information, although it remains to be seen whether rotating certain partners on audit teams, rather than auditing firms themselves, will be sufficient to avoid periodic capture.

The SOA also sets forth criteria that must be met by an accounting standard setting body if its rules should be "generally accepted". In April 2003, the SEC decided that the Financial Accounting Standards Board (FASB) meets these criteria and that the Board's pronouncements must continue to be followed in the preparation of financial statements. In enacting the SOA, Congress recognised that accounting standards that involve too many exceptions and interpretations might have contributed to efforts by managements and accountants to structure transactions in a way that provides a desired result and yet allows the company to avoid clear disclosure of their economic consequences in financial statements. Congress therefore mandated the SEC to examine whether a system of "principles-based" accounting standards should be adopted in the United States. After studying the issue, the SEC considered that the best approach would be to develop an accounting system that provides sufficient detail and structure so that the standard may be applied on a consistent basis, while minimising exceptions from the standard. In December 2003, the FASB proposed changes that are in line with these recommendations. Moreover, there is now a process in place to encourage convergence of the standards of the International Accounting Standards Board (IASB), which are to be adopted by the EU, amongst others, and of the United States. One difficult issue is the proper accounting for the cost of stock options. The FASB has proposed to require companies to treat stock options as expenses from 2005 to provide better information to investors – at present they are only required to disclose their effect on earnings in footnotes on financial statements – but there is some industry as well as Congressional reticence to impose such a requirement. In any case, several large companies have already moved to expensing stock options while making more use of share grants.[3]

Strengthening corporate governance

Recent events confirm that, prior to the SOA, the boards of US companies were exhibiting less than the optimal amount of independence from and oversight of management (Holmstrom and Kaplan, 2004). Many of the recent corporate scandals were the consequence of shifting power in favour of CEOs, who are usually also the Chairman of the board, and away from the boards of directors over the past decade or more (Donaldson, 2003). "Imperial" CEO/Chairs came to dominate boards through strong influence over direction nominations. This was particularly the case with compensation committees where conflicted directors appointed by the CEO decided bonuses and pay with the aid of consultants hired by management. Moreover, it was natural for internal audit functions to report to the board *via* the CEO who has, in some cases, also had direct dealings with the external auditors. The ensuing intense discussion of corporate governance and increased scrutiny of business led to the growing recognition that, for the protection of investors, this situation needed to be reversed. Duties of corporate board members are generally established by state statute, but the SOA and the SEC rules implementing it now outline additional specific responsibilities of a company's board, primarily pertaining to its audit committee. The above-mentioned mandate of independence for the latter is essential to the new central role of the board. There is evidence that audit committees are meeting more often and for longer periods and have become more inquisitive. On the other hand, compensation committees still need to reassert control and demand more executive pay be tied to specific performance measures. The November 2003 NYSE listing requirement that compensation committees (as well as audit and nomination committees) be made up entirely of independent directors is welcome but will need some time to have an effect. Requiring the expensing of stock options would make compensation more transparent and avoid inappropriate incentives facing managers, such as boosting earnings in the short term at the expense of long-term outcomes. Perhaps most critically, the director nomination process needs to be reformed so as to offset the CEO's control over it, and the recent moves by the NYSE and NASD in this direction (see also below) are welcome. Finally, an unresolved question for the United States remains the practice of combining the CEO and Chairman positions, although this approach may be appropriate at particular points in the development of a corporation (Donaldson, 2003).

Another crucial issue in this regard is the strengthening of management accountability. Managers of public corporations oversee the preparation of the financial reports that their companies have to file periodically under existing securities regulations. Holding them accountable for the quality of those reports can thus serve as a further check on their accuracy and completeness. Managers who expect their companies' actual performance to become known also face more powerful incentives to serve the investors' interests. The SOA promotes management accountability by clarifying the roles and responsibilities of various corporate officers, by introducing sanctions for those who fail to live up to those obligations, and by requiring that corporations adjust their internal governance structures so that outside investors can more readily verify the management's incentive to serve the shareholders' interests. In particular, the Act demands that CEOs and CFOs certify the accuracy and completeness of financial statements contained in quarterly and annual reports. It makes false certification a Federal criminal offence, subject to fines of up $5 million, imprisonment of up to 20 years, and the eventual loss of bonuses, incentive compensation or other gains that offenders have received from their company during the year after the issuance of a false report. Moreover, a corporation's attorneys are expressly held responsible for reporting any evidence they might receive of a violation of the Act or other duties. The certification provision was very controversial because of concerns that it could make managers more risk-averse and stifle innovation in addition to the considerable SOA compliance costs. A positive effect has been that more issues are apparently both raised and resolved even before the auditing process begins.

Apart from increasing focus on executive responsibility, recent corporate governance reform seeks to promote investors' access to information about the performance and operation of public companies. Recognising that investors need accurate, reliable and timely reports to make informed investment and voting decisions, the SOA introduces new disclosure requirements. In particular, directors, officers and principal investors now have to disclose their transactions in company stock more quickly than before so that shareholders can react more rapidly to such information. Indeed, faster disclosure strengthens the capacity of outsiders generally to act on news of insider transactions. To facilitate compliance with the new rules, the SEC has created an on-line filing system for insider transaction reports, which are accessible on the Internet. The Act also stipulates that corporations make more information available about the quality of their internal control structures. A PCAOB rule adopted in May 2003 calls for an annual evaluation of internal control over financial reporting with a view to encouraging companies to devote sufficient resources and attention to this issue. For many companies, the internal control reports will represent the most significant single obligation associated with the SOA reforms. In view of the substantial time and resources needed to properly prepare the reports, they will be due only after a transition period. One of the revelations of the recent accounting failures was the abuse of off-balance-sheet transactions. All such transactions, arrangements and obligations now have to be revealed in quarterly and annual reports filed with the SEC. Financial analysts and auditors, too, must publicly disclose to investors whether any conflicts of interest might exist to limit their independence from influences other than the desire to serve the interest of shareholders. This provides an additional check against any conflicts that might remain after the other reforms are taken into account. Finally, the SOA aims to improve the effectiveness of the securities disclosure regulations by dramatically increasing some of the sanctions for violating them (providing for prison terms of up to 25 years).

Reinforcing the SEC

Restoring investor confidence also requires strengthening the enforcement of the federal securities laws and regulations. To this end, the SOA calls for an increase in SEC funding and staff which is to expand by about 25 per cent (from around 3 000 in 2002). The SEC has been criticised for reacting to market problems rather than anticipating them. Indeed, the number of initiated enforcement actions remained largely unchanged at around 500 per year from 1994 to 2001 before jumping towards 700 as corporate scandals unfolded. In part this reflected insufficient SEC funding by Congress, which adversely affected the frequency and scope of examinations. However, an internal report, produced by SEC staff and consultants in 2003, depicts an overly cautious agency, hampered by bureaucratic inefficiencies and problems in monitoring a rapidly changing market.[4] Chief among the flaws is a reactive culture that often fails to identify danger ahead of time, leaving the agency to respond after others expose problems. The report found that the SEC used to generate just one-third of its enforcement cases internally, the rest being spurred by external sources (including "whistleblowers"). The SEC is already taking steps to fix these shortcomings. It aims to complete a review of the financial statements of one-third of reporting companies each year, focusing on the largest companies, as mandated by the SOA.[5] It is enhancing its enforcement programme so that it can carry out more investigations and complete them sooner, emphasising "real-time" enforcement in major cases.[6] And it is establishing an Office of Risk Assessment to identify and prioritise current risks.

Besides stepping up enforcement efforts and implementing the SOA, the SEC has moved on other fronts, addressing such critical areas as shareholder access to the director nomination process. At the moment, shareholders are generally given an opportunity to vote only on those candidates nominated by the company. In addition, many companies use plurality rather than majority voting for board elections, the result being a "rubber stamping" of company choices. The business community, in particular, has argued that strengthening shareholder rights could turn every election of directors into a contest, which would be costly and disruptive to companies and discourage some qualified board candidates from agreeing to appear on a company's slate. On the other hand, proponents of such a move have emphasised that it would make corporate boards more responsive and accountable to shareholders as well as, in many instances, more diverse. After studying the issue, the SEC adopted new rules to improve disclosure related to the nomination process and proposed a requirement for companies to incorporate in the election materials the names of nominees for directorship submitted by shareholders. However, these rules can apply as proposed only in those cases where state law allows security holders to nominate a candidate for election as a director. Although limited, this initiative is welcome and is in line with the proposed revisions to the OECD corporate governance principles that call for a more forceful role for shareholders (OECD, 2004).

The need for the SEC to become more pro-active has been illustrated by renewed scandals in recent months, involving the NYSE and the mutual funds industry in particular. As noted, in 2002, self-regulatory organisations (SROs) such as the NYSE and NASD also submitted proposals designed to strengthen the corporate governance of their listed firms, requiring *inter alia* shareholder approval of most equity compensation plans and a larger role for independent directors. These proposals were approved by the SEC in November 2003. However, recent developments have revealed severe problems at the NYSE itself, both as to its own governance and as to the fundamental question whether it can regulate and police itself effectively. According to the SEC, regulatory conflicts arose due to the concentration of power in the hands of the NYSE's chairman and CEO, and the NYSE has been criticised for failing to expose and discipline misconduct by specialists and exchange members. A new management adopted, and the SEC recently approved, governance changes at the NYSE, which enhance the independence of the board and split the positions of chairman and CEO. Moreover, they aim to better insulate the NYSE's self-regulatory staff from pressure and influence exerted by both the CEO and business interests. It remains to be seen whether these initiatives are sufficient and whether it will not be necessary to create a separate SRO. Alternatives would be a complete structural separation of regulation from the business of being a market or an on-site presence of the SEC at the NYSE (and perhaps other exchanges), an approach that has served regulators in other industries. The SEC has announced that it will examine the effectiveness of self-regulatory organisations more generally in the context of a review of overall market structure.

The risks of ineffective regulation and weak governance have also been highlighted by evidence of widespread abusive activity in the mutual funds industry, although the recent scandal encompasses a great deal of wrongdoing by intermediaries and brokers. This is all the more important since mutual funds are financial intermediaries that occupy a major place in the US economy, providing financial resources to fund business growth and job creation. Over 90 million Americans have invested around $7½ trillion (about one-fifth of total household financial assets) in mutual funds, which are entrusted with more than one-fifth of the retirement savings market and are hence crucial to the financial well-being of the population. The industry has been exempted from some of the SOA reforms: for instance, the law's requirement to have outside auditors evaluate its internal controls. Although the SEC was already investigating some of the mutual fund abuses that involved broker-dealers, it realised their full extent only after a widening state investigation that began last summer. Abusive practices included late trading, abusive market timing, selective portfolio disclosure and undisclosed payments to gain placements on brokers' preferred lists, with fund insiders facilitating or participating in this irregular activity. "Late trading", that is allowing favoured investors to submit orders after the stock market shuts, is illegal but in its recent investigations, the SEC has found that many fund managers let intermediaries send orders after the official deadline, which allowed the latter to hide illegal, late trades among legitimate transactions. Another practice, "market timing", – the rapid trading in and out of the fund to exploit the difference in the fund's daily fixed price and the fluctuating value of its underlying shares – is not illegal, but many funds had stated that they would preclude the behaviour, and so were committing fraud when they failed to do so. More fundamentally, both practices breach the basic obligation of fund managers to treat all their investors equally. In December, the SEC proposed new rules that would address late trading, market timing and related abuses by closing loopholes, reinforcing compliance rules and enhancing disclosure requirements. More recently, the agency has made proposals to require mutual funds to adopt better governance practices, focusing on board independence. While some new rules are certainly needed, better enforcement of both existing and new ones as well as more active monitoring of the mutual funds industry are crucial to assure that funds operate in the interest of all investors.

Bankruptcy and private pensions

Although the importance of defined-benefit (DB) corporate pension plans has declined steadily and defined-contribution plans, which pose less financial risk to employers, have become predominant since the mid-1990s, the emergence of substantial DB plan funding gaps in recent years has significant macroeconomic and policy implications. DB plans remain an important source of retirement security for 44 million American workers and retirees. Their assets still amount to almost 15 per cent of GDP, accounting for more than two-fifths of those in private pension plans. Given the long lives of such plans, they will continue to affect corporate costs and profits for decades. Under-funded pension obligations have already acted as a drag on corporate profits and credit ratings for a number of major US corporations. The failure of several large companies with significantly under-funded plans has also weakened the finances of the Pension Benefit Guaranty Corporation (PBGC), which has partially insured private pensions since 1975. Given the adverse impact on corporate finance and potential risks to financial-market stability, policymakers need to address the weaknesses of the regulatory framework, which has been tested by the emergence of the funding gaps. Some improvements in the situation due to the economic recovery should not lead to complacency, since to a considerable extent the problems facing the system are not cyclical but structural.

With rising life expectancies, the average number of years spent in retirement has continued to grow. These demographic pressures have been compounded by more recent financial-market developments. The stock-market decline has severely weakened the value of plan portfolios, given that a significant proportion of assets – more than half in the late 1990s – are invested in equities. In addition, the sharp drop in long-term interest rates has substantially increased the discounted present value of future liabilities. As a result, total under-funding for under-funded plans in the single-employer DB system, which was less than $50 billion at the end of 2000, rose sharply to around $400 billion at the end of 2002 (Figure 4.2, Panel A). Against this backdrop, rating agencies began to scrutinise pension obligations more closely in their assessments of firms' credit worthiness and downgraded many companies with particularly large liabilities, causing their stock prices to fall and their credit spreads to widen. Since then, rises in the stock market and higher contributions of firms have significantly reduced under-funding to an estimated $350 billion by the end of 2003, and this trend is likely to continue as the economy recovers and long-term interest rates pick up. In a longer-term perspective, it is difficult to argue that excessive investment in equities *per se* is responsible for the pension system's financial problems, given the substantial capital gains realised in the late 1990s. However, it has had some adverse indirect effects, which ultimately affected investor confidence. Recent research (Coronado and Sharpe, 2003) suggests that insufficiently transparent accounting practices led investors to place an unjustifiably high valuation on firms with high pension plan earnings from equity investments. The stock-market boom also contributed to insufficient employer contributions to their DB pension plans in the face of long-standing demographic pressures. While a recent FASB ruling requires enhanced disclosure of pension plan contributions and asset allocation,

Figure 4.2. **Private pension under-funding and PBGC financial position**
Single-employer programme, fiscal year

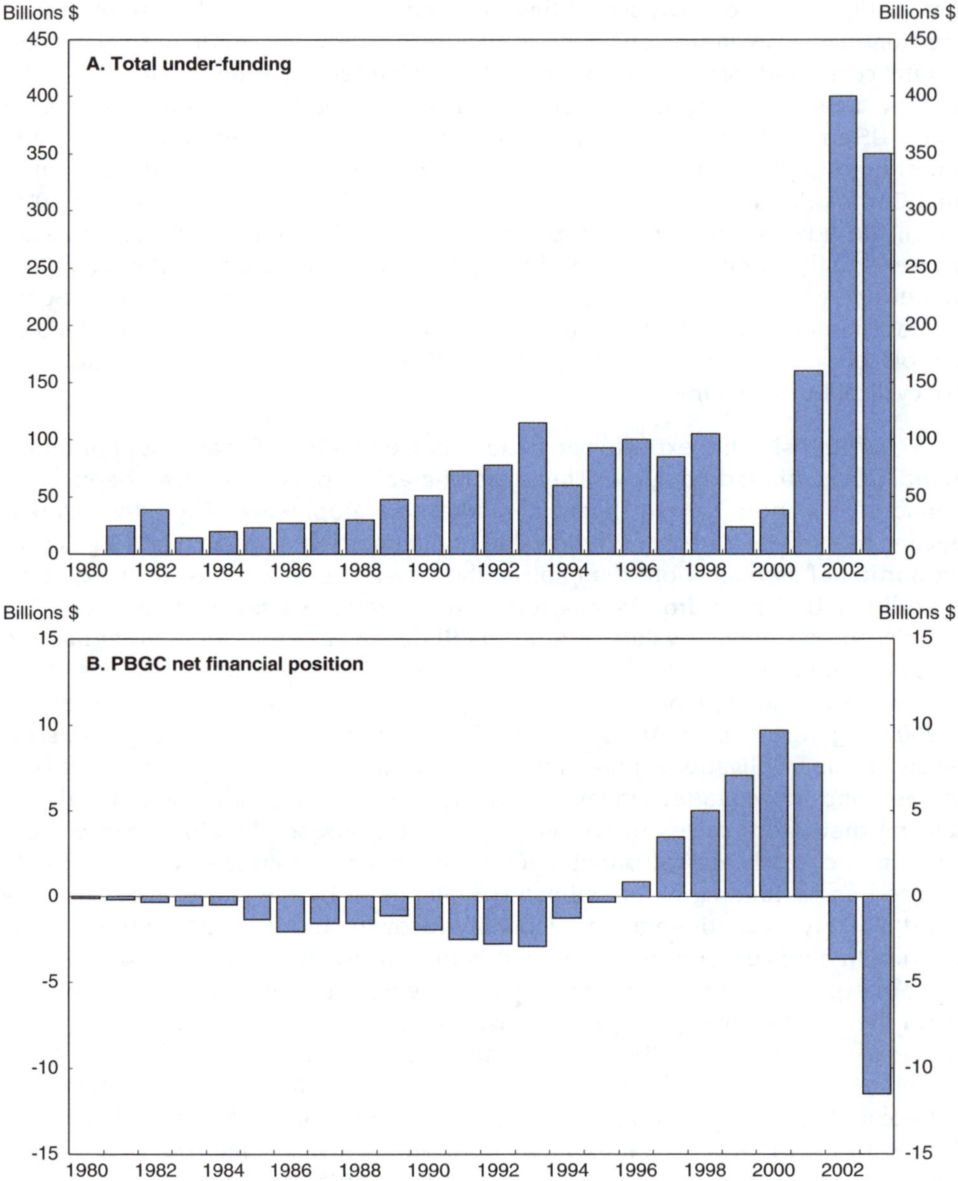

Source: Pension Benefit Guaranty Corporation.

it does not alter the potentially problematic calculations of pension cost that are included in corporate income statements.

As a result of record pension under-funding and the failure of a number of major plan sponsors in mature industries, PBGC finances deteriorated sharply in the last two years, with the single-employer insurance programme moving from a surplus of $7.7 billion in FY 2001 to a deficit of around $11 billion in FY 2003 (Figure 4.2, Panel B). During the economic downturn in the early 1990s, the pension insurance programme already had to absorb what were then the largest claims in history. But these claims appear modest compared to those it has had to cover recently (Table 4.1). Terminations of insured plans have mainly concerned the steel and airline industries, which now account for 56 per cent and 17 per cent, respectively, of historic PBGC claims. By comparison, these two industries have historically represented less than 3 per cent and less than 2 per cent, respectively, of participants covered by the PBGC. Pension claims against PBGC for 2002 alone were greater than the total since its inception in 1975, and, at current premium levels, it would take about 12 years to cover just the claims for 2002. Stochastic simulations carried out by the PBGC suggest that, in the absence of corrective measures, there is only a 19 per cent probability that it would be in a surplus position by 2013 (Pension Benefit Guaranty Corporation, 2003). The General Accounting Office (GAO) has found that the health of the PBGC single-employer insurance programme – the multi-employer programme is relatively small – requires the attention of policymakers. Because of the extraordinary recent losses, the dramatic increase in pension under-funding and the risk of additional large claims, the GAO has placed the programme on its "high risk" list.

Table 4.1. **Top 10 firms presenting claims since 1975**

Top 10 firms	Fiscal year of plan termination	Claims (billions $)	Covered participants	Funded ratio[1] (per cent)
Bethlehem Steel	2003	3.6	95 000	49
LTV Steel	2002	1.9	79 600	50
National Steel	2003	1.3	35 400	54
Pan American Airways	1991, 1992	0.8	37 500	31
Trans World Airlines	2001	0.7	34 300	47
US Airways Pilots	2003	0.6	6 000	71
Eastern Air Lines	1991	0.6	51 200	65
Wheeling Pittsburg Steel	1986	0.5	22 100	27
Polaroid	2002	0.4	11 400	67
Sharon Steel	1994	0.3	6 900	21

1. Funded ratio at termination for PBGC benefits; participants lose additional benefits not covered by PBGC.
Source: Pension Benefit Guaranty Corporation (PBGC).

In mid-2003, the Administration issued a set of proposals to deal with these problems, which are consistent with the principles promoted by the OECD for the regulation of private pensions. *First*, as a necessary initial step toward comprehensive reform of the pension plan funding rules, the accuracy of liability measurement is to be improved to reflect the time structure of each plan's benefit payments. This would be accomplished by measuring a plan's liabilities using a yield curve of highly-rated corporate bonds to calculate the present value of future payments. In 2002, Congress passed legislation that temporarily changed the pension discount rate from 105 per cent to 120 per cent of the 30-year Treasury bond interest rate in order to provide funding relief to plan sponsors. A bill currently under consideration in Congress would replace the Treasury bond rate with a corporate bond rate for a two-year period before moving to the proposed yield-curve approach for discounting pension liabilities. To grant such further funding relief[7] with no offsetting action to address systemic under-funding would seem to be ill-advised. Moreover, it would be prudent to use a conservatively low discount rate to calculate pension obligations while aiming at greater accuracy and transparency.

Second, in order to improve incentives for adequate funding, better disclosure to workers, retirees, investors and creditors is to be ensured. It is clear that current liability disclosure methods are inadequate to inform workers about the funded status of their benefits. For example, in its last filing prior to termination, the US Airways pilots' plan reported that it was 94 per cent funded on a current liability basis; at termination, however, it turned out that it was only 35 per cent funded on a termination basis, resulting in $1.6 billion of pilot losses, given legal limits on PBGC benefit guarantees. The fact that, under current law, firms are not obliged to provide timely and transparent information about the funding of corporate pension plans can also have a distortionary impact on the stock prices of plan sponsors. The Administration proposes appropriately to increase the timeliness and accuracy of disclosure by obliging firms to make public each year the value of their pension plans' assets and liabilities measured on both an ongoing and a termination basis.

Third, new safeguards against under-funding would be provided by requiring financially troubled companies with highly under-funded plans to immediately fund or secure any plan improvements in the form of new benefits or lump-sum payments. Similarly, unfunded benefit increases by severely under-funded plans sponsored by corporations with below investment-grade debt ratings would be prohibited. The urgency of such measures is highlighted by the fact that, according to the PBGC,[8] under-funding in financially troubled companies is estimated to have exceeded $80 billion at the end of FY 2003, up from $35 billion a year earlier.

Fourth, the Administration calls for, and is currently examining, additional reforms to protect workers' retirement security by improving the funded status of DB plans. There are many weaknesses with funding rules, which would be only partially addressed by the above proposals. In particular, funding targets are clearly set too low, and amortisation periods for plan improvements are relatively long. Employers can stop making contributions when a pension plan is funded at 90 per cent of "current liability", which does not recognise the full cost of providing annuities as measured by prices in the private market and the possible additional cost involved in an early termination of the plan. As long as this "full funding limit" is respected, companies do not have to pay the variable-rate PBGC annual premium of 0.9 per cent of the dollar amount of a plan's under-funding that is due in addition to the annual flat-rate charge of $19 per participant. Moreover, the funding rules often act to disguise market conditions and allow "contribution holidays" even as plans are in reality becoming increasingly under-funded. Thus, Bethlehem Steel, the largest claim in the history of the PBGC (Table 4.1), was able to pay no variable-rate premium and make no cash contributions to its plan for five and three years, respectively, prior to termination. The current funding rules are particularly lax for flat benefit plans, where benefits can be increased regularly for past service, creating sudden jumps in liabilities that are amortised over long periods. The structural under-funding of many steel companies' pension plans is due to such benefits. Linking amortisation periods to the expected future period of service of active plan members would help solve this problem. There is also a need to further reduce the risk shifting and moral hazard in the current system, which implies that sound, well-funded plans – and potentially taxpayers – bear the burden of unsound, under-funded plans. If these transfers become too large, then over time strong companies with well-funded plans may choose to terminate them by switching to defined-contribution plans. While care must be taken to avoid encouraging adverse selection and creating disincentives to employer participation through excessive premium increases, the PBGC should have greater flexibility so as to charge higher premiums to firms generating more risk to the system.

Distortions from government-sponsored enterprises

A number of government-sponsored agencies, later to become enterprises, were created in the 1930s in order to overcome perceived problems of the financial system. In particular, they were charged with developing the market for housing and agricultural finance. These now privately owned institutions benefit from some advantages denied to other private firms. Even though no explicit guarantees exist, the market appears to believe that the federal government will not allow these institutions to default on their debt. In addition, they enjoy a line of credit with the Treasury and a number of other privileges, such as being exempt from SEC registration and disclosure requirements faced by other private institutions (see Annex I of the 2000 *Survey* for more details). These government-sponsored enterprises (GSEs) have expanded strongly in recent years and are now major players in the financial markets (Figure 4.3). This primarily reflects the rapid growth of the housing-finance GSEs, in particular Fannie Mae (Federal National Mortgage Association) and Freddie Mac (Federal Home Loan Mortgage Corporation), the

Figure 4.3. **Rapid expansion of government-sponsored enterprises**
Billions of dollars; end of period

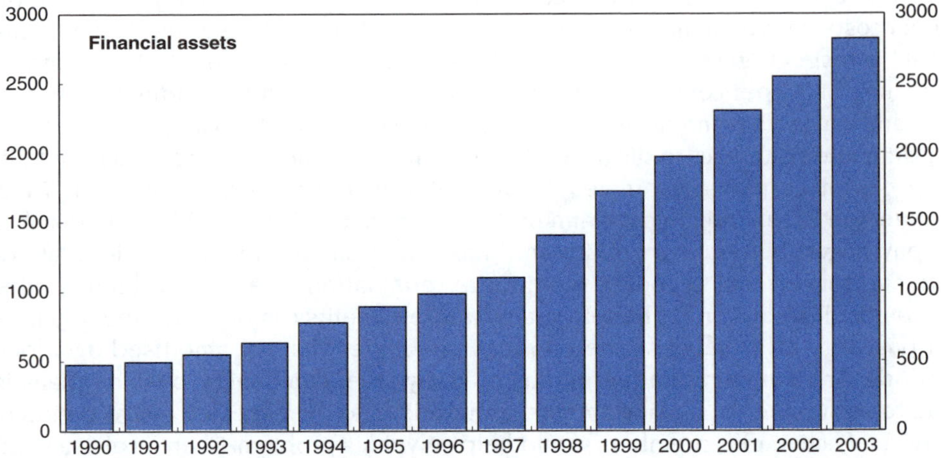

Source: Board of Governors of the Federal Reserve System.

two enterprises chartered by the federal government to support the secondary market for residential mortgages, which have grown into two of the largest financial institutions in the world, as well as the Federal Home Loan Bank system (FHLB), which as a group is as large as Freddie Mac.

Although the direct statutory benefits of the various charter privileges are relatively modest, the privileges signal a special relationship between the federal government and the GSEs, feeding market perceptions that, if necessary, the former would bail out the latter. Indeed, when one GSE – the Farm Credit System – suffered threatening losses in the 1980s, the Congress authorised financial assistance to avoid a default, so that, in that case at least, the implied federal guarantee became real. Given this perception, investors are willing to accept a lower yield on GSE debt than on the debt of other private companies. This funding advantage has allowed the GSEs to dominate the market for certain types of mortgage securities. The Congressional Budget Office tried to gauge this implicit subsidy and concluded that the average interest-rate gain, across all types of housing GSE securities was around 40 basis points in 1998-2000, which translated into $10 to $15 billion per year (Congressional Budget Office, 2001). Adjusted for the growth of the enterprises, the implied current annual subsidy is, at the minimum, above the upper end of that range (Holtz-Eakin, 2003). The CBO estimates that only about half of the funding advantage gets passed on to homebuyers, the rest going to executive compensation and to shareholder profits. On the basis of similar interest-rate assumptions, a recent study (Passmore, 2003) puts the discounted present value of the gross implicit subsidy to GSE shareholders and homeowners at $119 to $164 billion, with the former retaining more than half of the gains, and estimates that the implicit subsidy accounts for more than half of the market value of Fannie Mae and Freddie Mac. Moreover, it finds that, if they were purely private, these enterprises would hold far fewer of their mortgage-backed securities in portfolio (see below) and as a consequence would be much smaller, while their capital-to-assets ratios would double. Finally, the implicit subsidy does not appear to have substantially increased homeownership or homebuilding because the estimated damping effect of the GSEs on mortgage rates is minor (7 basis points, according to Passmore).

These findings raise concerns over fairness and economic efficiency, but also over the potential destabilising effect of the implicit subsidy on the financial system. Given their funding advantage, the debt issued by housing GSEs has tripled since 1995 (to reach $2.2 trillion at end-2002) and, if recent trends continue, could soon exceed the privately held debt of the federal government. The GSEs have used the proceeds from issuing debt to amass enormous portfolios of mortgages and mortgage-backed securities. Given that they are now also in the asset-management business – which is not their mandate – their financial health depends heavily on the performance of those portfolios. While the credit risk associated with mortgages has been low so far, the housing GSEs have increasingly become exposed to interest-rate and prepayment risks, which means that they are vulnerable to losses from both increases and decreases in interest rates. A year ago, OFHEO, the regulator of Fannie Mae and Freddie Mac, published a comprehensive report (Office of Federal Housing Enterprise Oversight, 2003a), which concluded that the likelihood that the two enterprises will pose a systemic risk is quite low. The report acknowledged, however, that the economy could be seriously impaired if one of them were unable to meet its obligations. This is not surprising, since almost all banks and other financial institutions hold substantial portions of their capital in the securities of the two GSEs. Thus, even a small mistake in GSE risk management could have ripple effects throughout the financial system.

This highlights the importance of effective regulation. OFHEO introduced risk-control mechanisms only in 2002, ten years after its inception. A special examination of Freddie Mac was undertaken only after a new auditor replaced the company's long-term auditor Anderson LLC in 2002 and detected significant irregularities, which necessitated a $4.5 billion accounting restatement. The recently published report (Office of Federal Housing Oversight, 2003b) found that Freddie Mac disregarded accounting rules, internal controls and disclosure standards, while the incentive compensation plans of senior executives contributed to improper accounting and management practices. It recommended that OFHEO require the enterprise to hold a capital surplus and limit the growth of the retained portfolio until it produces timely and certified financial statements. Most recently, OFHEO announced a special review of Fannie Mae, which had also admitted significant accounting errors.

Against this backdrop, the Administration has proposed legislation to create a new regulatory agency for housing GSEs that would be able to deal with their size and complexity and have sufficient strength and credibility to reduce systemic risk. The new regulator would be granted permanent funding mechanisms and have authority to set both risk-based and minimum capital standards and to reject new GSE activities and receivership powers necessary to wind down the affairs of a troubled GSE. While these are steps in the right direction, the distortions created by the implicit government subsidy and the risks to taxpayers from the GSEs could remain. Without reducing the size of the GSEs portfolios, investors may still perceive them as "too big to fail".[9]

The impact of Basel II

The health of the banking system is crucial to investor confidence. The 1988 Basel Capital Accord, the current international framework on commercial bank capital adequacy, aims at promoting the soundness and stability of the international banking system and providing an equitable basis for international competition among banks. Although it was intended specifically for internationally active banks, the Accord has, in practice been applied beyond these institutions. Views differ as to whether the Accord has achieved its objectives (for a negative assessment, see Rodriguez, 2003). There is agreement, however, that it appears to have outlived its usefulness for some institutions. From the perspective of US supervisors, it needs to be replaced, at least for the largest, most complex banks, for three major reasons: it has serious shortcomings as it applies to these large entities; the art of risk management has evolved; and the banking system has become increasingly concentrated all over the world (Board of Governors of the Federal Reserve System, 2003). In particular, the 1988 Accord specifies only a few levels of credit risk, even though the credit quality can vary greatly. This limited differentiation among degrees of risk provides incentives for regulatory capital arbitrage,[10] so that minimum capital ratios of larger banks become less meaningful and creditors and investors are hampered in evaluating the strength of these institutions.

Over the past several years, the Basel Committee on Banking Supervision has been working on a new Accord to reflect changes in the structure and practices of banking and financial markets and to make, in particular, minimum regulatory capital requirements more sensitive to an institution's risk profile. Furthermore, it aims to strengthen market discipline by requiring banks to publicly disclose related key information. The most recent version of the new Accord, now known as Basel II, was released in a consultative paper in April 2003. The Basel Committee is developing important modifications to its proposal that it hopes to have available as an agreement by mid-2004, with a view to implementing the new regime by the end of 2006. The US banking agencies have proposed to implement Basel II somewhat differently from other nations (Ferguson, 2003a). Most banks would not be required to adopt Basel II, although they may do so if they wish; rather they would remain under the existing Accord. This is because the agencies consider that, in general, their banks have relatively straightforward balance sheets, already hold considerable capital in excess of the Basel I minima and have long been subject to comprehensive supervision. In these circumstances, the costs of imposing a new capital regime on thousands of US banks would not seem worthwhile. Only large, internationally active banks would be required to adopt Basel II. Initially, this would mean that only about ten banks would be concerned, although market expectations are that a similar number of other large banks would find it advantageous to adopt the new system voluntarily.

The proposed bifurcated application of Basel II in the United States has raised a number of concerns. Although the banks remaining under the current regime avoid the costs of adopting the new one, some have argued that Basel II would give the largest banks, if not a lower overall capital requirement, then lower capital charges on certain credits and hence a competitive advantage. Focus has been placed on residential mortgages, small business loans and credit cards. The Federal Reserve is currently conducting empirical research on these issues, which might lead to modifications to the proposed bifurcated application of Basel II or to changes to the current capital regime in the United States (Ferguson, 2003c). A solution to these problems and endorsement by the United States, with the world's biggest banking system, is crucial to the success of any proposed new Accord.

Notes

1. Erickson *et al.* (2003) provide evidence that the probability of accounting fraud increases with the share of corporate compensation that is stock based. Erickson *et al.* (2004) show that firms charged with accounting fraud went so far as to pay income taxes on their overstated earnings.
2. In the same year, the median value of total compensation for CEOs of S&P 500 companies was about $7 million.
3. There has been a trend towards replacing options with "restricted" stock. Restricted shares must be held for a fixed period before they can be sold. They are favoured by experts because they encourage a focus on the company's long-term growth and profitability.
4. According to a report in the Wall Street Journal on 24 December 2003.
5. The SEC is mandated by the SOA to review the disclosures, including financial statements, made by each reporting issuer that is listed on a US stock exchange or trades on NASDAQ at least once every three years.
6. It has also increased its extra-territorial activity, in line with its standard that if companies want access to US capital markets, they have to submit to SEC oversight. It has, however, been willing to accommodate foreign regulatory schemes where there have been conflicts between foreign and US law in implementing the SOA.
7. The legislation under consideration would also, during a two-year period, allow companies in specific sectors to pay only part of the amount in principle required to shore up their under-funded plans.
8. Testimony of S.A. Kandarian, Executive Director, before the Special Committee on Aging, United States Senate, 14 October 2003.
9. Some observers consider that fully privatising and eventually breaking up the housing GSEs is the only solution (Wallison, 2003).
10. This entails "gaming" the system through selling, securitising or otherwise avoiding exposures for which the regulatory capital requirement is higher.

Bibliography

Board of Governors of the Federal Reserve System (2003), "Capital Standards for Banks: The Evolving Basel Accord", *Federal Reserve Bulletin*, Vol. 89, No. 9, September.

Congressional Budget Office (2001), *Federal Subsidies and the Housing GSEs*, Washington, D.C., May.

Coronado, J.L. and S.A. Sharpe (2003), "Did Pension Plan Accounting Contribute to a Stock Market Bubble?", *Brookings Papers on Economic Activity*, No. 1.

Donaldson, W.H. (2003), "Corporate Governance", *Business Economics*, Vol. XXXVIII, No. 3, July.

Erickson, M., M. Hanlon and E. Maydew (2003), "Is There a Link Between Executive Compensation and Accounting Fraud?", xerox, 3 October.

Erickson, M., M. Hanlon and E. Maydew (2004), "How Much Will Firms Pay For Earnings That Do Not Exist? Evidence of Taxes Paid or Allegedly Fraudulent Earnings", *Accounting Review*, April.

Ferguson, R.W., Jr. (2003a), "The Proposed U.S. Approach to Regulatory Capital: An Update", The Federal Reserve Board, Washington, D.C., 13 November.

Ferguson, R.W., Jr. (2003b), "Economic Outlook", The Federal Reserve Board, Washington, D.C., 21 November.

Ferguson, R.W., Jr. (2003c), "Concerns and Considerations for the Practical Implementation of the New Basel Accord", The Federal Reserve Board, Washington, D.C., 2 December.

Gompers, P.A., J.L. Ishii and A. Metrick (2001), "Corporate Governance and Equity Prices", NBER Working Paper No. 8449, August.

Holmstrom, B. and S.N. Kaplan (2004), "The State of US Corporate Governance 2004", AEI – Brookings Joint Center for Regulatory Studies and University of Chicago George J. Stigler Center for the Study of the Economy and the State, Related Publication 04-02, January.

Holtz-Eakin, D. (2003), "Regulation of the Housing Government-Sponsored Enterprises", CBO Testimony before the Committee on Banking, Housing and Urban Affairs, US Senate, 23 October.

Hooper, P. (2003), "Corporate Governance for Analysts and Investors", Deutsche Bank US *Economics Weekly*, 21 November.

Horne, P. and A. Merlin (2002), "Does Enronitis Threaten the Dollar and the Economy?", *Business Economics*, Vol. XXXVII, No. 4, October.

OECD (2004), OECD *Principles of Corporate Governance*, draft revised text, January.

Office of Federal Housing Enterprise Oversight (2003a), "Systemic Risk: Fannie Mae, Freddie Mac and the Role of OFHEO", Washington, D.C., February.

Office of Federal Housing Enterprise Oversight (2003b), "Report of the Special Examination of Freddie Mac", Washington, D.C., December.

Passmore, W. (2003), "The GSE Implicit Subsidy and Value of Government Ambiguity", Board of Governors of the Federal Reserve System, December.

Pension Benefit Guaranty Corporation (2003), 2002 *Annual Report*, Washington, D.C.

Rodriguez, L.J. (2003), "Banking Stability and the Basel Capital Standards", *Cato Journal*, Vol. 23, No. 1 (Spring/Summer).

Wallison, P.J. (2003), "Are Fannie and Freddie Safe and Sound?", *The International Economy*, Summer.

V. Product market competition and economic performance

Overview

The state of product market competition in the United States has changed significantly over the past several decades, reflecting several concurrent developments. Antitrust policy has moved beyond strict reliance on market concentration measures, designed to broadly link industry structure to conduct and performance, to adopt a more nuanced approach using modern industrial organisation analysis. Regulatory reform efforts in a broad range of industries began in the 1970s and accelerated over the course of the 1980s, resulting in (partial) deregulation in many sectors and an increased reliance on competitive forces as a means to improve efficiency. With a view to boosting incentives for innovation, intellectual property rights were strengthened by a series of court decisions in the 1980s and 1990s, increasing the short-run market power of firms developing new products; this has raised the question of how to balance the long-run benefits from the dynamic process of creative destruction against the short-run losses in efficiency arising from innovators' temporary monopoly positions. The growing importance of knowledge-based industries (*e.g.* pharmaceuticals and semiconductors) and network industries (*e.g.* telecommunications services including the Internet and software) has interacted with these other developments to raise new challenges for efforts to ensure dynamic efficiency. And, last but not least, the increased integration of the global economy has exerted greater pressure for efficiency through foreign competition. The aim of this chapter is to assess the role that policies that bear on product market competition have played in the performance of the US economy and to recommend changes in areas where further improvements are possible.

The institutional framework governing competition legislation and enforcement is the focus of the first section. As the basic legislation has not changed for decades, antitrust policy has evolved through the interaction of academic analysis, court decisions and agency guidance. In terms of sanctions imposed, enforcement appears unusually energetic, and private litigation is also extraordinarily important. The high risks of sanction and damages for violation have encouraged claims for, and sometimes entailed, exemptions, special treatment or anti-competitive state regulation; these should be removed in the areas where they exist. Another anomaly that ought to be corrected is the partial exemption of non-profit enterprises and government-related firms from competition enforcement.

The following two sections step back from the institutional details[1] and discuss economic performance over the past decade, and more especially the contribution to growth of policies promoting competition, both from the internal market and foreign sector. Indicators of the extent of barriers to trade and of administrative and economic regulations highlight the pro-competitive orientation of economic policies, and such conditions have spurred gains in productivity, investment and innovation. Most of the economy is also open to competition from foreign producers through international trade, resulting in low prices (relative to other Member countries) and hence higher consumer welfare. Nonetheless, there are some serious barriers to such competition, and policy initiatives that lessen reliance on anti-dumping or safeguard actions (such as the softwood lumber and steel cases discussed in Chapter I) should be pursued.

Moreover, an international price comparison reveals that domestic prices for drugs are high by international standards. This reflects a combination of trade restraints and intellectual property rights (IPRs), which are the topic of the fourth section. High drug prices have led to calls for reforms to state purchasing programmes and to the rules governing patent protection for pharmaceuticals. Such efforts, if successful, would likely reduce innovation, with an uncertain net impact. Nonetheless, some reforms, notably limitations on agreements between generic-producing firms and branded-drug manufacturers that have the effect of limiting generic entry, should be considered. More generally, the strengthening of intellectual property rights since the early 1980s has been accompanied by a surge in patents, though the evidence linking this to increased innovation is slight. And some problems have resulted from the shift to stronger IPRs, most notably related to patent challenges. Some patents issued are questionable. This, combined with the rising costs of patent litigation, indicates that a post-grant opposition system that eases the process of challenging patents (and raises patent quality) could boost welfare.

The generally pro-competitive direction of regulatory policies has contributed to the strong US economic performance, but a number of challenges remain. The final topic addressed here is a review of the experience with regulatory reforms that have placed even greater emphasis on market forces. While these efforts have been very successful in most industries, issues have arisen in telecommunications and electricity – and hence these sectors are discussed in some detail. Within telecommunications, the beginning of competition for voice services in local markets following the 1996 Telecommunications Act has started to bear fruit, but policies are still needed to ensure that competitive entry in local voice services and in broadband are not thwarted by dominant carriers. At the same time, however, policy formulation must strike an appropriate balance between fostering new competition and maintaining incentives for both incumbents and new entrants to invest in and modernise telecommunication infrastructure. Technological convergence between telecommunications and information services will also require a reconsideration of universal service fees and network access charges, which is now underway. In particular, careful consideration will have to be given to as to whether the application of these legacy regulatory mechanisms might in fact inhibit technological convergence and the growth of new services.

Introducing competition into electricity markets has also proved difficult, and restructuring has stalled in the wake of the California meltdown in 2000-01. This failure reflected flaws in the regulatory framework, not the impact of competition in wholesale and retail markets. The urgency of structural reform – in addition to increased investment – has been more widely recognised since the August 2003 blackout in the northeast (see Chapter I). Policies to increase regional transmission integration and encourage investment in transmission, and in some regions generation, are needed to improve security and efficiency. Programmes extending competition to the retail sector could benefit from domestic and international experience.

Competition legislation and enforcement

The basic antitrust statutes have remained unchanged for 50 years – the Sherman Act, for over 100 years – so that policy has evolved not through changes in the law but through court decisions interpreting their general terms. Implementation has been restated over the last 30 years in terms of price theory. Since the late 1970s enforcers have emphasised strong action against horizontal price fixing coupled with close economic analysis of other restraints, monopolisation and mergers. The level of sophistication has increased, as the enforcement agencies (the Antitrust Division of the Department of Justice (DOJ), and the Federal Trade Commission (FTC)) now apply econometric tools and game theory concepts to measuring market reactions and explaining oligopoly and strategic behaviour. The federal courts generally support the price-theoretic approach, but novel economic concepts in government cases may fail to persuade them. Recent decisions have resisted agency efforts to define predation in terms of opportunity cost and to bar a distribution system because of its tendency to exclusivity.

By treating agreements among competitors about price and output or market division as crimes, US law demands that competitors actually compete. The law presumes that such agreements lead to higher prices, lower quality and/or reduced innovation. By contrast to this "*per se*" approach to obvious collusion, determining whether horizontal agreements of other kinds are illegal depends on applying a "rule of reasonableness", which means evaluating their net competitive effects in particular cases. These "rule-of-reason" cases are complex and time consuming. To speed up enforcement, the agencies have suggested intermediate standards for assessing the economic effects of horizontal agreements – more nuanced than *per se* condemnation, but less costly than full rule-of-reason analysis. The courts have not rejected the concept, but they have been sceptical of most of the tests suggested. Agreements in the vertical dimension, along the supply chain, are nearly all subject to rule-of-reason analysis, because of the stronger likelihood that they serve some efficient purpose.In theory, purely vertical agreements about minimum resale prices are illegal *per se*, but there is very little public enforcement at the federal level in the absence of a clear horizontal effect, and the law permits a significant degree of upstream control over resellers' sales tactics. In general, for all conduct except horizontal price fixing, US enforcement authorities do not intervene, absent some showing of economic power or market impact.

Merger policy tries to prevent market power while supporting entry and capital mobility. Policy about horizontal mergers was systematically elaborated in the regulatory agencies' 1992 Guidelines, which codify concerns about how mergers could facilitate co-ordination or increase a firm's unilateral market power. The enforcement stance is tolerant. Mergers are not challenged if there is no barrier to entering the market, and the agencies will listen to claims that mergers increase efficiency. Acquisitions of "failing firms" are treated leniently, which facilitates exit (and hence entry). The threshold at which pre-merger notice is required has been increased substantially. This change had the intended effect of greatly reducing the number of filings. Congress has insisted that special rules remain in place to control concentration in broadcasting and media.[2]

US law regarding monopolies threatens sanctions and even divestiture against exclusionary conduct. But unlike the law of most Member countries, otherwise it tolerates the exploitation of market power. The Sherman Act of 1890 does not prohibit a dominant firm from charging high prices or reducing output, as long as its market position is not due to improper conduct. The rationale is that permitting a firm to retain the profit from its market power would advertise an entry opportunity and avoid the contradiction of punishing vigorous competition when it succeeds. Rather, what is forbidden is conduct that achieves or maintains a monopoly by unfair means, principally by excluding other efficient competitors. Although simple exploitation is not a violation, the law strongly presumes the value of low prices, and hence it is sceptical about claims of price predation. "Predatory" prices violate the law only if the alleged predator could recoup its losses in conditions of post-predation monopoly unthreatened by entry. The courts continue to resist the agencies' efforts to relax this scepticism.

Measured by the range and magnitude of sanctions imposed, US enforcement appears unusually energetic. In monopolisation cases, divestiture is possible, but rare. The Antitrust Division retreated from demanding divestiture in the recent *Microsoft* litigation after an appellate court expressed scepticism about the appropriateness of such a remedy (in light of its revision of the district court's liability findings). Against hard-core cartels, criminal fines and imprisonment are now standard practice. The basic fine against a corporation can be up to $10 million (and for an individual, up to $350 000), but that may be increased to twice the gain from the illegal conduct or twice the loss to the victims. This calculus is broadly consistent with economic models of deterrence, being based on the gain from the violation corrected for the likelihood of detection. Justifying the higher fines requires making a detailed demonstration to the sentencing judge about actual effects. Unusually, the United States prosecutes the individuals who are responsible for corporate violations and sends them to jail. The maximum prison term is three years. In 2002, sentences imposed on individuals totalled nearly 30 years, a record (Figure 5.1). The credible threat of tough sanctions makes the government's offer of leniency an effective tool for discouraging and discovering cartels. Insights from game theory motivated key changes that have made the leniency programme more productive. There are some concerns, though, that the motivation to confess and thus avoid fines may be undermined by the threat of treble damages in civil litigation. A bill is pending in Congress to amend the Clayton Act of 1914 so a firm that benefits from criminal leniency would be exposed only to claims for single damages; in addition, it would raise the basic corporate fine to $100 million and increase the maximum prison term to 10 years.[3]

Private litigation is unusually important in the United States. About 800 antitrust cases are filed each year (723 in 2001, 830 in 2002), of which only about 10 per cent are US government enforcement actions. These are not all trivial disputes: a recent case awarded over $1 billion (and this award was confirmed on appeal). In these private suits, the courts deal with issues such as price discrimination and vertical restraints that are not high priorities in the agencies' enforcement programmes. The original Sherman Act, and later the Clayton Act, promise treble damages and attorneys' fees to promote deterrence and compensate for the difficulty of detecting covert unlawful activity. But now that class actions facilitate aggregating claims and criminal fines have greatly increased, the incremental value of awarding exemplary damages ought to be reconsidered, particularly if they undermine the effectiveness of the leniency programme.

The two federal agencies commit about 1 275 staff (FTE) to competition enforcement. Because of the law's strong economic content and the analytic demands of complex cases, each keeps scores of PhD economists on staff. The agencies' functions and powers are broadly similar, the principal differences being that only the DOJ deals with criminal cases and only the FTC has responsibility for consumer protection and advertising. Outright conflicts, duplication and forum shopping have been avoided, but the redundancy imposes some costs on each agency to co-ordinate policies and actions with the other. The roles of

Figure 5.1. **Competition law enforcement**

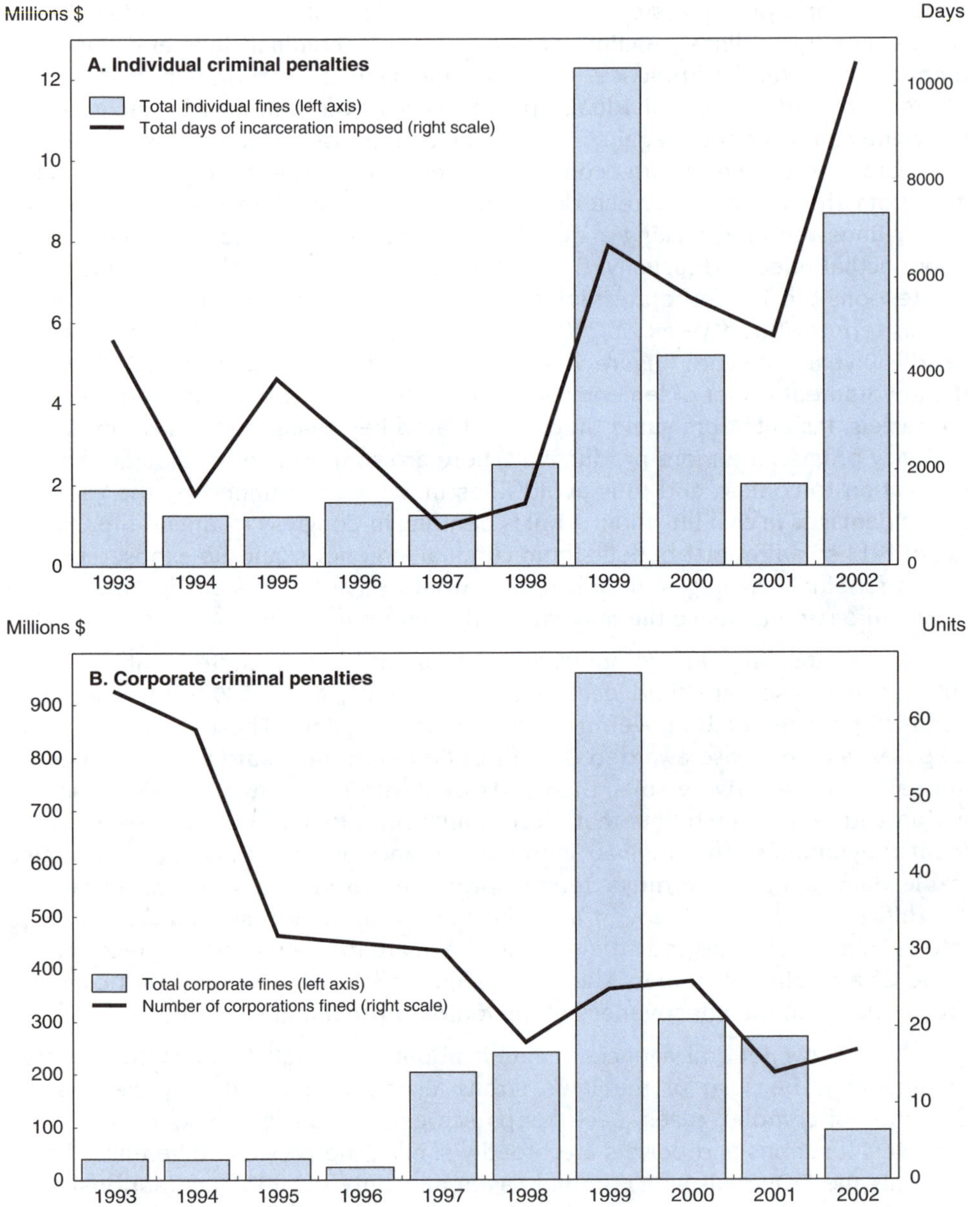

Source: US Department of Justice.

state officials must also be considered. State enforcers have tried to block some mergers and vertical restraints that the federal enforcers did not challenge. In recent years, the federal agencies and state enforcers have developed better means of co-operation to reduce direct conflicts, but disagreements persist. Notably, a group of states rejected the government's settlement of the *Microsoft* case, and one persisted in seeking stronger relief.

The serious consequences of violating the law encourage claims for exemption, special treatment or even regulation as a substitute for competition law enforcement. There are few sectors in the US economy from which competition policy and law are completely excluded. But in many sectors, the policy is implemented through special rules or enforcement structures. Some of these make no practical difference, but others look like special-interest protections, and many were obviously enacted to undo enforcement. Separate enforcement systems for meat packing and agricultural co-operatives date from the 1920s, prompted by early FTC monopolisation cases against these organisations. Other laws have reversed findings against pooling of sports broadcast rights, against manufacturing and distribution agreements in the soft drink industry, against price-fixing in the insurance industry, and against agreements among universities about financial aid awards. Many non-profit enterprises are exempt from Section 5 of the FTC Act of 1914, a historical oddity that impairs action against their commercial misconduct.

Sector-specific agencies have competition policy roles. Their performance of these roles varies. Some apply competition policies reasonably consistently with the competition agencies. Where antitrust laws and regulation co-exist, convergence is most obvious. In gas and oil pipelines, for example, "regulation" typically amounts to a hands-off decision to allow market forces to work, as long as the market is not too concentrated. In electric power, though, this is complicated by deference to state regulation at retail level. In telecoms, divestitures following an antitrust suit launched restructuring 20 years ago, but changes have stalled due to compromises in the settlement and in Congress's 1996 legislative intervention (see below). In transport, the experience with separate agencies has been disappointing, as they have permitted mergers that led to market power and have sustained exemptions and anti-competitive practices that should be reined in. For example, in ocean shipping, the regulatory scheme permits cartel conduct that would be illegal in other sectors, while the Federal Maritime Commission has taken only a few tentative actions under its mandate to protect competition; and in surface transport, motor freight rate bureaux still have antitrust immunity for agreements about some subjects.

The "state action doctrine" is an important gap in US antitrust policy. A clear, affirmative, and actively supervised state government policy to displace competition immunises private anti-competitive conduct from liability under federal law. Embodying the US commitment to federalism, the doctrine stems from a 1943 Supreme Court decision that permitted a state to sponsor a cartel. Later decisions have permitted anti-competitive state regulation of transportation, hospitals, health care and other professional services, retail distribution, utilities, residential and commercial rent, and other subjects. Congress could override such decisions, and it did so when it voided widespread anti-competitive state regulation of local trucking. The extent of deference to states' sovereignty risks embarrassing the national commitment to competition. Yet a September 2003 FTC study of the issue treated only technical issues about the interpretation of doctrine and did not examine market effects or identify sectors where state-level constraints on product market competition should be removed.

Another gap involves government entities, which are generally beyond the reach of competition law enforcement or private litigation even if they are involved in commercial operations. Entities that are owned and operated by the US government are immune by federal law, while the state action doctrine shields those of state and local governments. The immunity may be particularly significant for electric power systems, hospitals and port authorities, where private competitors have complained that the government entities enjoy unfair competitive advantages.

Strong competitive forces have contributed to good economic performance

The US economy has performed comparatively well since 1990, despite the recent recession (Table 5.1). At the aggregate level, average GDP growth between 1990 and 2002 was the highest of the G7 countries, and above the OECD and European Union averages. The level of GDP per capita remains the highest among the G7, and GDP per hour worked has continued to be near the top. The good performance has reflected both productivity and employment growth over the period. Moreover, productivity growth accelerated markedly over the second half of the 1990s, and there has been a further acceleration more recently. While the relationship between policies affecting competition at the microeconomic level and aggregate performance remains somewhat tenuous, a number of recent studies have documented important linkages.

One set of indicators used to document links between competition policies (broadly defined) and aggregate economic performance has been developed at the OECD to provide a quantitative summary of the extent of regulation affecting competition.[4] Such measures of the extent of barriers to trade and of administrative and economic regulations generally show that the United States is quite open to competitive pressures, although some OECD countries (the United Kingdom in particular) have even lower obstacles to product market competition (Figure 5.2). It is also important to note that such indicators show that competitive forces have been stronger in the United States than in most other Member countries for some time.

Table 5.1. **Recent trends in output, employment and productivity**

	United States	Japan	Germany	France	Italy	United Kingdom	Canada	OECD	European Union
Average GDP growth, 1990-2002[1]	**2.9**	**1.5**	**1.4**	**1.9**	**1.5**	**2.2**	**2.7**	**2.6**	**2.1**
of which:									
Labour productivity	1.7	1.3	1.3	1.2	1.2	1.9	1.3	1.1	1.0
Employment	1.2	0.3	0.1	0.7	0.3	0.3	1.3	1.5	1.0
of which:									
Unemployment[2]	0.0	–0.2	–0.3	0.0	0.1	0.1	0.0	–0.1	0.0
Labour force	1.2	0.5	0.3	0.7	0.2	0.2	1.3	1.6	1.0
Demographics[3]	1.2	0.6	0.2	0.8	0.2	0.2	1.4	1.7	0.7
Participation rates[4]	0.0	–0.1	0.2	–0.1	0.0	0.0	0.0	–0.1	0.3
Average GDP growth, 1995-2002	**3.2**	**1.1**	**1.5**	**2.4**	**1.8**	**2.8**	**3.6**	**2.7**	**2.3**
of which:									
Labour productivity	1.9	1.4	1.0	1.1	0.8	1.7	1.5	1.7	1.1
Employment	1.3	–0.2	0.5	1.3	1.0	1.1	2.0	1.1	1.2
of which:									
Unemployment[2]	0.0	–0.3	0.0	0.4	0.3	0.6	0.4	0.1	0.4
Labour force	1.3	0.1	0.5	0.8	0.7	0.5	1.7	1.0	0.9
Demographics[3]	1.0	–0.5	–0.5	0.4	0.3	0.2	1.0	0.8	0.2
Participation rates[4]	0.3	0.6	0.9	0.5	0.4	0.3	0.7	0.2	0.6
Memorandum items:									
MFP growth,[5] 1991-2002	0.9	0.1	0.6	0.5	0.7	1.1	0.9	n.a.	n.a.
MFP growth,[5] 1995-2002	1.1	0.3	0.2	0.7	0.1	0.7	1.2	n.a.	n.a.
GDP per capita[6]	100.0	74.0	73.4	74.2	72.0	73.8	83.8	71.3	71.7
GDP per hour worked[6]	100.0	73.2	93.2	110.1	94.6	85.5	86.5	81.8	92.3

1. Except Germany: 1992-2002.
2. A positive sign indicates that unemployment has declined and contributed to boost output growth.
3. The contribution from demographics comprises changes in the size and age composition of the working-age population.
4. This measures the effect from changes in age-specific participation rates.
5. Total economy.
6. 2002 levels, PPP based, USA = 100.

Source: OECD.

By these measures, restrictions on product market competition are inversely related to multifactor productivity growth, suggesting that the low barriers in the United States have contributed to its good performance relative to continental Europe (Nicoletti and Scarpetta, 2003). Similar stimulative effects have been found on investment (Alesina *et al.*, 2003). Thus, low barriers to entry in the United States have likely played a part in generating strong labour productivity growth through both increased multifactor productivity and greater capital deepening. And product market competition has probably helped maintain policies conducive to labour market competition, as low rents decrease the incentives for workers to engage in "rent seeking" by lobbying for employment protection

Figure 5.2. **Indices of regulations affecting product market competition**
0-6 indicator from least to most restrictive

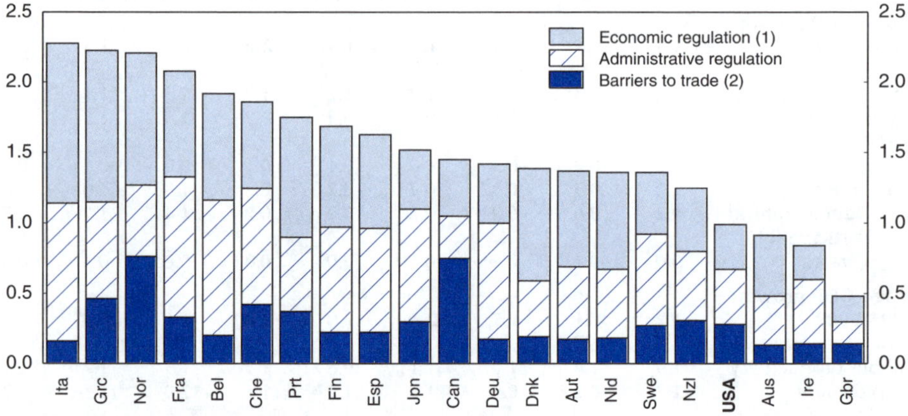

1. Includes barriers to competition and state control.
2. Includes trade and FDI restrictions.
Source: Nicoletti and Scarpetta (2003).

policies (Blanchard and Giavazzi, 2002). A liberal labour market in the United States has ensured that productivity-enhancing technologies – which by definition imply weaker employment growth than otherwise or labour-shedding, at least from existing activities – are adopted quickly (Feldstein, 2003). This channel has been quantitatively important in explaining the diffusion and productivity impact of information and communications technologies (ICT) in the United States, and hence relatively strong growth performance after 1995 (Gust and Marquez, 2002).

A competitive environment also boosts research and development and the diffusion of technologies, among the primary factors contributing to long-run economic growth (Ahn, 2002; OECD, 2003). Firms are forced to make such knowledge investments to avoid losing market share in the longer run. The United States has one of the highest rates of investment in R&D and is a world leader in development (if not production) in a number of leading knowledge-based industries – notably computer hardware and semiconductors, software, pharmaceuticals and biotechnology (Figure 5.3). In addition to the impetus from competition and the favourable effect of market size, such innovative activity may have been boosted by strong intellectual property rights (IPRs), which increase the returns received (see below).

Barriers to foreign trade are relatively low

The importance of foreign competition[5] in US (and other) markets is difficult to assess. Complications arise because domestic markets can be insulated in

Figure 5.3. **Gross domestic expenditure on R&D as a percentage of GDP**

2001[1]

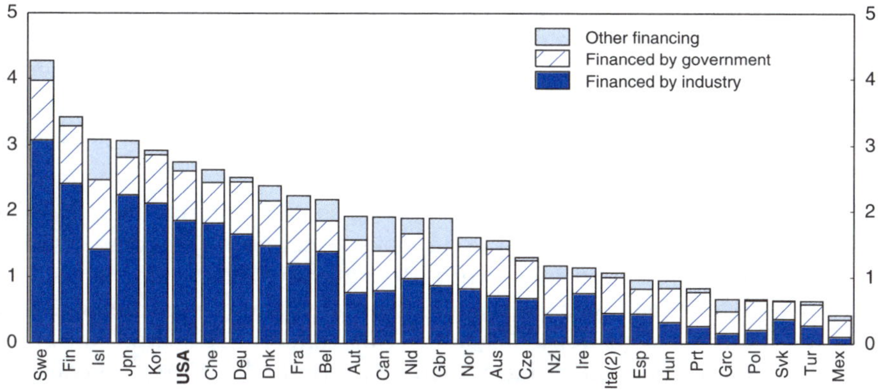

1. Australia, Ireland, Italy, Switzerland, Turkey: 2000; Greece, Mexico: 1999.
2. The breakdown between private and public expenditure for Italy was unavailable. The 2000 figure was estimated using weights from 1996, which was the latest year for which the breakdown is available.

Source: OECD, *Main Science and Technology Indicators* (2003/2).

many ways: tariffs; explicit non-tariff barriers such as quotas and voluntary export restraints; policies that indirectly discriminate against foreign products such as health, safety, labelling and certification requirements (although such standards often serve legitimate welfare objectives); government procurement policies; heavy-handed customs procedures; and threatened or levied anti-dumping and countervailing duties that cannot be justified (see below). Indeed, such measures should be held to the same standards as on domestic markets. An empirical analysis for a panel of 21 OECD countries, which uses a crude country-size-adjusted measure of trade exposure to capture competitive pressures, suggests that an increase in trade exposure by 10 percentage points raises output per capita by 4 per cent (OECD, 2003). According to this measure, the United States has become more open to foreign competition over the past two decades, like many other OECD countries.

Given the many possible methods to prevent foreign access to domestic markets and the difficulty of summarising such effects in an empirical model, the information conveyed by prices provides a metric whereby the strength of arbitrage across national boundaries that disciplines domestic firms' price-setting behaviour can be assessed. Such comparisons must compare similar goods and adjust for net indirect taxes and transportation costs.[6] A recent study develops comparisons of domestic prices to world prices for 124 goods based on the prices collected by the OECD to compute purchasing power parities, which are converted to producer prices and adjusted for transport costs (Bradford, 2003). Unfortunately, data availability (and the labour intensity of such calculations) limited the statistics to eight countries covering price quotes from 1991 to 1993. Although these measures are not perfect, the results, summarised for 29 industries in Table 5.2, indicate that the United States (with an "effective tariff", *i.e.* the percentage differential between domestic and world price, of under 12 per cent) was a decade ago easily the most open of the countries considered. In 18 sectors its price was the lowest of the eight countries and in a further eight sectors it ranked second.

The sectoral breakdown of the results is also informative. US relative prices were nearly uniformly low with one major exception. The comparison indicates that drugs and medicines were dramatically more expensive in the United States than in the low-price country (Australia) and more expensive than in most other countries considered as well.[7] This differential is well known – for example, it is not uncommon to find newspaper reports describing US consumers' trips to Canada (or Mexico) for cheaper prescription drugs. This partially reflects US safety-based restrictions on parallel importing to prevent counterfeit and untested products. Although the European Union (EU) permits parallel importing (internally), it also restricts imports from third countries due to concerns over counterfeit and defective medicinal products. The interaction between IPRs and competition, especially in pharmaceuticals, is discussed at the end of this section.

Leadership to successfully conclude the Doha round is needed

In addition to its openness to foreign competition, the United States has also continued to pursue further trade liberalisation. Beside bilateral free-trade negotiations (Chapter I), the Administration has continued to hold talks on a Free Trade Area of the Americas, which would open trade within the Western hemisphere. Most importantly, negotiations regarding the Doha round are underway. The US proposal to eliminate export subsidies in agriculture and reduce other trade distortions in that area is welcome – as is the proposed elimination of industrial and consumer goods tariffs by 2015. However, progress has still to be forthcoming.

Despite the relative openness of the economy and the positive set of proposals for the Doha round, a stronger push to conclude the negotiations would be welcome. One area where a renewed focus may lead to significant welfare gains is on efforts to reduce global anti-dumping and safeguard actions – starting with a curtailment of domestic use of these tools. The United States (along with the European Union) has been a major user of such measures; the experience in the last several years with anti-dumping and countervailing duty sanctions against Canadian softwood lumber and the safeguard measures regarding steel, both discussed in Chapter I, are only the latest examples. From a pure welfare economics

Table 5.2. **Ratio of the domestic to the world price, 1991-93**

Industry	Australia	Belgium	Canada	Germany	Japan	Netherlands	United Kingdom	**United States**
Agriculture, fisheries and forestry	1.067	1.157	1.112	1.529	1.584	1.080	1.648	**1.158**
Processed food	1.086	1.372	1.192	1.447	2.099	1.299	1.202	**1.090**
Beverages	1.447	1.444	1.535	1.765	1.540	1.328	1.694	**1.061**
Tobacco	1.472	1.947	1.955	3.531	1.000	1.385	2.217	**1.060**
Textiles	1.111	1.218	1.163	1.101	1.478	1.140	1.237	**1.051**
Apparel	1.264	1.569	1.175	1.457	1.384	1.280	1.074	**1.158**
Leather and products	2.944	1.777	1.236	1.437	1.329	1.658	1.168	**1.143**
Footwear	1.657	1.823	1.415	1.328	2.289	2.239	1.027	**1.111**
Furniture and fixtures	1.299	1.958	1.558	1.392	2.707	1.471	2.172	**1.020**
Paper and products	1.438	1.659	1.060	1.606	1.804	1.965	1.783	**1.050**
Printing and publishing	1.120	1.310	1.205	1.024	1.186	1.342	1.029	**1.005**
Drugs and medicines	1.001	1.692	2.680	2.643	1.217	3.349	1.845	**3.105**
Chemical products	1.092	1.137	1.064	1.107	1.555	1.075	1.064	**1.037**
Petroleum and coal products	2.127	3.375	1.320	2.847	3.359	4.335	4.067	**1.007**
Rubber products	1.219	1.680	1.015	1.711	2.016	1.655	1.566	**1.032**
Pottery, china, etc.	1.727	1.007	1.145	1.511	2.383	1.016	1.082	**1.070**
Metal products	1.430	1.622	1.328	1.770	1.977	1.837	1.602	**1.165**
Office and computing machinery	1.008	1.513	1.234	1.446	1.000	2.101	1.666	**1.015**
Machinery and equipment, nec	1.343	1.682	1.297	1.325	1.559	1.527	1.388	**1.175**
Radio, TV and communication equipment	1.178	1.558	1.204	1.298	1.226	1.432	1.236	**1.034**
Electrical apparatus, nec	1.536	1.936	1.316	1.713	2.106	1.556	1.320	**1.073**
Shipbuilding and repairing	1.278	1.267	1.107	1.354	1.200	1.545	1.536	**1.000**
Railroad equipment	1.374	1.314	1.093	1.404	1.238	1.509	1.503	**1.016**
Motor vehicles	1.224	1.351	1.197	1.315	1.000	1.648	1.680	**1.106**
Motorcycles and bicycles	1.231	1.761	1.252	1.599	1.000	1.385	2.002	**1.057**
Aircraft	1.191	1.199	1.082	1.282	1.020	1.462	1.454	**1.001**
Transport equipment, nec	1.516	2.034	1.109	1.888	1.315	2.065	1.924	**1.057**
Professional goods	1.125	1.571	1.082	1.379	1.077	1.369	1.586	**1.074**
Other manufacturing, nec	1.237	1.807	1.209	1.863	2.348	1.636	1.416	**1.030**
Weighted geometric means	1.266	1.555	1.270	1.539	1.567	1.541	1.480	**1.118**

Source: Bradford (2003).

perspective, neither tool is easy to justify; rather, both result in higher prices for consumers and impede necessary adjustments that would lead to a superior (long-run) allocation of resources.[8] For example, a study of the cost of anti-dumping orders in place as of 1993 found that these lowered welfare by $2 to $4 billion annually, making anti-dumping actions one of the costliest US trade protection measures (Gallaway *et al.*, 1999).

Nonetheless, the creation of the World Trade Organisation (WTO) solidified the international standing of anti-dumping and safeguard actions, in part to lower reliance on "extra-legal" forms of protectionism such as voluntary export restraints. Two after-effects are now apparent. *First*, the use of anti-dumping and safeguard measures by countries that are not OECD members (who traditionally have been the major users, except Japan) has surged; while OECD members accounted for more than 95 per cent of anti-dumping actions in the late 1980s, this proportion had fallen to about 50 per cent by the second half of the 1990s. *Second*, the WTO has taken a tough stand regarding whether such actions fall within permissible boundaries since its inception in 1995. In the twelve anti-dumping cases decided by May 2003, the challengers prevailed on at least one significant issue (Tarullo, 2003), and each of the six US safeguard actions has had some aspect deemed in violation of WTO obligations (Irwin, 2003). Some analysts have suggested that this set of WTO decisions does not accord well with the deference to national authorities regarding anti-dumping determinations that rest on "permissible interpretations" under Article 17.6 of the Anti-Dumping Agreement.[9] Perhaps as a result, the Congress has established a principal negotiating objective for the Doha round that negotiators seek to preserve the ability of the United States to enforce its trade laws, including anti-dumping law. This set of developments has taken the issue beyond simple welfare economics; while the static efficiency gains from tight standards of review at the WTO could be used to justify its decisions, a number of commentators (*e.g.* Sykes, 2003 and Tarullo, 2003) have emphasised the political cost of rigid enforcement, and hence possible long-run damage to the trading system.

The best outcome would involve US leadership to maintain a strong dispute resolution system that encourages less reliance on anti-dumping and safeguard actions. This could start by stepping back from the tariffs levied recently (as in the case of steel products) and by refraining from further protectionist measures. It may also be useful to strengthen the economic analysis used in making safeguard determinations. The current standard comes dangerously close to a "correlation equals causation" argument; *i.e.* the finding of serious harm from imports necessary for a safeguard action does not usually reflect a careful evaluation of the exogenous changes in supply and demand conditions in the industry (Sykes, 2003; Irwin, 2003), and improved efforts in this regard appear possible (Irwin, 2003).

Intellectual property rights

The relatively higher level of domestic drug prices noted above reflects the interaction of several factors, including adherence to a free-market policy, concerns about untested foreign products, a belief in the future benefits of technological innovation and the strong enforcement of intellectual property rights (IPRs). But the importance of IPRs is far greater – particularly in assessing the strength of competitive forces in the economy. They are a building block of the modern knowledge economy, playing a central role in information technology, life sciences (such as pharmaceuticals and biotechnology) and beyond. They provide incentives to research and to disclose information. Well-defined rights to the returns from discoveries may promote technology transfer to rivals at home and abroad. But these potential benefits must be weighed against the social costs stemming from the temporary monopoly power they provide to protected innovations. Moreover, IPR policies have been changed significantly over the past two decades, and an assessment of the benefits and costs of these reforms is overdue.[10] The following sections discuss, in turn, the recent evolution of patent rights and their impact on research and innovation, and the role of patent protection in the pharmaceutical industry and especially on drug prices – in each case with an eye to possible modifications to current practices.

Lessons from patent reforms

Patenting has risen sharply since the early 1980s, more than tripling by 2001 (Figure 5.4). This increase occurred in the wake of several significant changes that resulted in stronger patent rights. A series of court decisions from 1980 to 1998 extended (or affirmed) patentability of genetically engineered bacteria, software and business methods and financial services products. In 1982, the Court of Appeals of the Federal Circuit (CAFC) was established as the central forum for patent cases; prior to this, cases were heard in federal circuit courts around the country, leading to "forum shopping" for patent-friendly or patent-sceptical courts. The CAFC brought consistency to patent decisions, but was also accompanied by a significant broadening in patent-holders' rights (Lerner, 2002). On top of these changes, the US Patent and Trademark Office (PTO) became solely funded by fees in 1999, and compensation for patent examiners has lagged those of comparable private-sector positions. Critics have suggested that the threshold for patent issuance has fallen as a result. Finally, the global Trade-Related Aspects of Intellectual Property (TRIPS) agreement of 1994 led to a change in US patent length from 17 years following patent issuance to 20 years from patent application (with some important exceptions related to pharmaceuticals). While research has linked the surge in patenting to these changes (Hall, 2003), other factors, such as improved management and more focus on applied research, have perhaps been more important (Kortum and Lerner, 1998).

Figure 5.4. **Domestic patent grants**
1970-2001

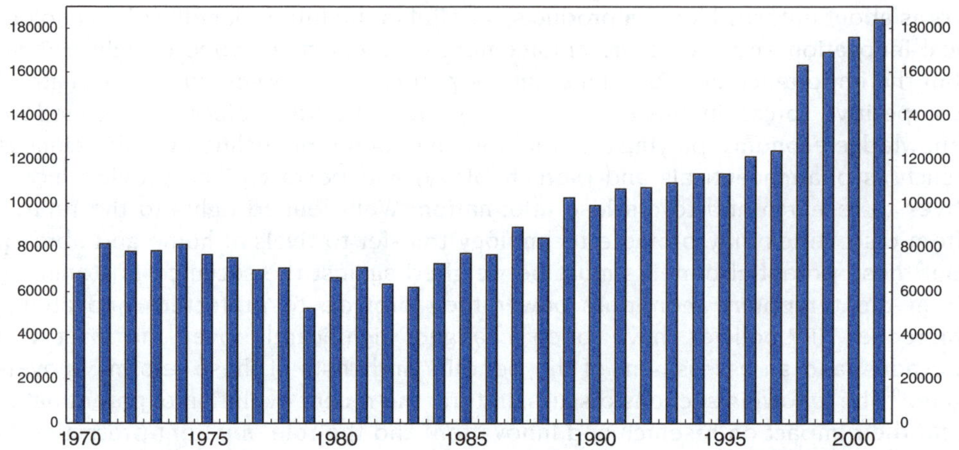

Source: US Patent and Trademark Office.

Although the surge in patents has coincided with an expansion in R&D expenditure, there is not much evidence that innovation has increased as a result of a patent reform (Jaffe, 2000; Gallini, 2002). One factor may be that patents are not the most effective way to protect intellectual assets: surveys of companies suggest that superior sales and service, lead time and secrecy are far more important in securing returns to innovation than patents (Cohen *et al.*, 2000; Arundel, 2001) – except in the pharmaceutical industry (and perhaps some others), a point returned to below. In assessing whether the strength of patent rights in the United States has moved beyond the optimal level, the question is whether too much current income and output is sacrificed for the additional innovation generated.

The upturn in patenting has nevertheless facilitated some positive developments. Perhaps most importantly, strong patent protections facilitate vertical specialisation and entry of firms specialising in intellectual assets by allowing them to attract financial capital and by lowering the transaction costs associated with negotiating contracts (Lerner, 1994). Studies have demonstrated the importance of these channels in industries where patent rights are easy to define, such as biotechnology and chemicals (*e.g.* Arora and Fosfuri, 2000; Anand and Khanna, 2000). And the growth of design-only firms in the semiconductor industry has owed significantly to the strengthening of patent protections since 1980 (Hall and Ziedonis, 2001). However, even this positive development has been accompanied by negative side-effects in some cases, most notably a rise in patent litigation. Agreements regarding patent licensing can also lead to anticompetitive behaviour; the Department of Justice and Federal Trade Commission's Antitrust Guidelines for the Licensing of Intellectual Property attempt to balance the potentially pro- and anti-competitive aspects of licensing (Gilbert and Tom, 2001). Patent pooling by rival firms can either contribute to the exercise of market power – for example, when the patented items are potential substitutes – or aid the development of essential standards for complementary innovations (Shapiro, 2001).[11]

The discussion has highlighted concerns regarding the strength of patent protections. Of course, property rights are likely to be a more effective means to spur innovation than alternatives such as prizes or auctions when the value and cost of projects are not easily discernible because those firms with superior information are provided with incentives under IPRs (Gallini and Scotchmer, 2001). Nonetheless, some changes to current practices would lead to a better balance between these incentives and the negative distortions created under the existing system. The "litigation tax" associated with the current patent right system has become significant, with patent litigation *per patent* increasing by 50 per cent from the early 1980s to the late 1990s (Hall *et al.*, 2003). While it is difficult to quantify exactly, Lerner (1995) estimated that the cost of litigation associated with patents issued in one year (1991) would exceed one-quarter of total expenditures on basic research by private firms in that year. Two aspects of the current system contribute to the high level of litigation: first, the fall in the quality of patent application reviews at the PTO that has accompanied an expansion in the breadth of patentable material and the relative decline in examiners' compensation, and then the limited nature of third-party review of what are called prior-art searches. The current re-examination procedure allows a patent holder or any other party to request that the PTO reconsider the grounds on which a patent was issued by presenting prior art that is previously unknown to the PTO and relevant. The prior art must have been printed in an earlier patent or publication. Challengers are (essentially) not involved in the re-examination beyond notifying the PTO of the prior art. In Europe, challenges to patents issued by the European Patent Office can be brought by a third party within nine months of the patent grant by presenting evidence that the patent is not valid. Moreover, the challenger has the right to appeal the patent office's decision. The European system has led to a much larger number of successful administrative challenges to patents: the *ex post* probability that a patent will be revoked via a challenge has been about 3 per cent in Europe but essentially zero in the United States (0.02 per cent) (Hall *et al.*, 2003). A move to an opposition system in the United States would reduce patent litigation but might lead to more opposition of cases that should not be challenged. Nonetheless, on balance, an opposition system is likely to be cheaper and lead to better outcomes according to a number of experts.[12]

Two other areas where reforms should be considered are the scope of business method patents and the degree to which firms or researchers can use information provided in a patent to develop new innovations, especially related to software. A recent summary of research (Hall, 2003) finds that most scholars view the standards for patent issuance in the business methods area to be too low and recommends a tightening in the "non-obviousness" requirement in this area. (A trivial example of this problem is the recent issuance of a patent on a method to cut hair with scissors using two hands simultaneously). With regard to "reverse-engineering" of patented material in order to facilitate invention, current policies that (potentially) award treble damages if wilful infringement of a patent is found may limit progress in software development. An exception for software that allows duplication of non-patented elements and use of components necessary for interoperability and interface should be considered.[13]

Intellectual property rights and pharmaceuticals

While patent protections may not be among the most important methods used to reap the profits from innovation in many industries, they are vital in the pharmaceutical industry (Cohen *et al.*, 2000; Arundel, 2001). US pharmaceutical patents receive special treatment because the process regulating drug introductions can take a long time. The Drug Price Competition and Patent Restoration Act of 1984 (known as the Hatch-Waxman Act) was designed to address this issue, promoting innovation and easing generic drug approval. It restored up to five years of patent time lost to pre-market clinical testing and the Food and Drug Administration (FDA) approval process and allowed generic entry without the duplication of certain testing. The original statute also provided for a 180-day exclusivity period to the first applicant to apply to manufacture a generic and challenge an existing patent of the innovation. Branded drug manufacturers were entitled to a 30-month postponement of FDA approval of a generic application when the generic might have infringed on a patent related to the drug.[14]

The interaction of the 30-month delay in approval and the 180-day exclusivity had raised concerns about anticompetitive effects. In certain agreements, generic firms agree not to market the drug for which they have requested generic drug approval and the branded drug company consents to making payments to the generic firm. Because of the 180-day exclusivity provision of the Hatch-Waxman Act, these agreements prevented generic entry for some time for certain drugs. The Federal Trade Commission (FTC) and private plaintiffs have challenged a number of these agreements as violations of antitrust laws; to date, the FTC and the courts have limited their arguments to the facts associated with any one agreement and have not acted to make them *per se* illegal. Agreements regarding patent disputes should not be discouraged, as they may resolve conflicting claims in an efficient matter. But two reforms should be considered:[15] since the purpose of the

180-day exclusivity period is to strengthen the entry incentive (because, for example, the generic may face a cost disadvantage relative to the incumbent), agreements that delay entry should provoke revocation of the exclusivity period; there should also be limits on the ability of incumbents to pay new entrants. Legislation enacted in December 2003, which contains provisions to discourage agreements that may be anti-competitive while encouraging early patent resolution, may help cure these problems.

More broadly, the strong protection afforded IPRs in the United States is one factor contributing to high domestic branded drug prices and the significantly higher level of health care expenditure in the United States relative to other countries (a focus of the previous *Survey*). Several aspects of this situation are noteworthy. Drug prices are lower in other member countries largely because of differences in regulations (Vernon, 2002). As a result, US sales are responsible for recovery of a disproportionate share of drug development costs (Danzon, 1997), which are rising rapidly and exceeded $800 million (on average, per drug) in recent years, double the levels a decade earlier (Tufts Center for the Study of Drug Development, 2003).[16] Recent studies have also shown that the return on capital approximately equals the cost of capital in the industry (Grabowski *et al.*, 2002), although earlier studies found excess returns in previous decades, suggesting that more research is needed (Berndt, 2002). The prices paid by US customers vary substantially, with federal government programmes typically facing the lowest prices and individual households paying the highest, although most drug purchases are made by insurers, which negotiate prices with drug companies. This has led to increased efforts, especially among states, to enact programmes that ensure they receive the lowest prices; there have also been proposals to open up the US market to imports from Canada.[17]

Given the set of factors just mentioned, it seems quite likely that successful efforts to lower US drug prices would decrease the supply of new drugs in the long run, as prices are unlikely to rise materially in other countries. Whether this would prove welfare-improving thus depends upon whether the long-run loss from foregone drug development would exceed the gain from increased current consumption of pharmaceuticals or other goods.[18] Also, studies have suggested substantial gains from new drug development through improved health (*e.g.* Lichtenberg and Virabhak, 2002) and through lower expenditures on other treatments (*e.g.* Lichtenberg, 2002). One study (Finkelstein, 2003) has argued that for a few kinds of treatments the dynamic gains from new drug development exceeded the static benefits that would have occurred from treating a greater number of individuals with then-current drugs. But a comprehensive analysis of the potential benefits of increased consumption of current drugs relative to the costs from foregone pharmaceutical development has not been undertaken, probably because such an evaluation would be very difficult. Although it is not conclusively known whether policies that alter investment incentives through changes in government purchasing programmes would have positive or negative long-run effects, the predominant view in the United States is that such effects would be negative.

Regulatory policies and competition

While the summary approach linking indices of economic policies to macroeconomic outcomes discussed earlier in this chapter can yield some aggregate perspective, the direct – and often large – effects of regulatory policies on prices and efficiency within individual markets is both easier to measure and more illustrative when considering how future efforts at regulatory reform may play out. Early views held that regulation increased welfare by offsetting monopoly power; but there is now consensus that regulations often serve to preserve monopoly status, protect inefficiencies in production and impede adjustments to shifting market conditions (*e.g.* Winston, 1998). As a result, efforts to increase competition in regulated industries through (partial) deregulation or regulatory reform were considerable in both the United States and the rest of the OECD between the mid-1970s and the mid-1990s. The transportation sector (airlines, trucking, intercity buses and railroads) was largely deregulated in the United States by the mid-1980s; banking services were liberalised in the early 1980s, although limitations on interstate banking were lifted only in the late 1990s; and regulations in the natural gas sector have been substantially eased (OECD, 1999).

The effects of liberalisation in these areas have been consistently positive. Operating costs have fallen across the board, and load factors have risen in the transportation sector. Prices for consumers have also dropped significantly – while the quality and range of services offered has tended to increase. Innovations in marketing and product offerings have been substantial. Airlines have developed a broad selection of price/features packages; the introduction of the airline hub-and-spoke system generated an unexpected increase in flight frequency; rail and truck lines have developed price/service combinations to meet customers' production and inventory management plans; and banks have expanded their financial-service offerings, improving risk management opportunities (Winston, 1998). Nonetheless, a number of policy distortions affecting competition in air services remain. The United States has bilateral "open skies" arrangements with a number of European countries, but the largest market (the US-UK market) does not have an agreement, and those currently in place severely limit competition (with restrictions on ownership, market share and landing rights). There are also limits to foreign competition on US domestic routes and to foreign ownership of domestic carriers. There would be substantial benefits to consumers from further liberalisation.

The favourable experiences with deregulation, together with technological advances in both telecommunication services and electricity generation, combined to create pressure for regulatory reform in these sectors over the course of the 1990s. Progress has been made in both cases. But these gains have been accompanied by a number of setbacks, that have highlighted difficulties in ensuring competition in network industries, as well as by some policy mistakes. There is now a solid body of cross-country evidence that liberalisation policies in network industries have led to higher productivity and, in some cases, better quality and lower prices.[19] However, close attention needs to be paid to the design of reforms (Gonenc *et al.*, 2001).

Before turning to the details of each sector, it is noteworthy that the division of regulatory responsibilities between federal and state agencies is quite similar in both areas.[20] The institutional structure of regulatory policy has been largely unchanged since before World War II. For telecommunication services, the Federal Communications Commission (FCC) has exclusive jurisdiction over interstate matters and intra-state issues where legislation pre-empts state authority. FCC rules are subject to appeal through the judicial system, which has figured prominently in the FCC's most controversial decisions. Each of the 50 states and the District of Columbia have Public Utility Commissions (PUCs), which generally have jurisdiction over intra-state concerns such as local and within-state long-distance prices and entry into local markets. For electricity markets, the Federal Energy Regulatory Commission (FERC) regulates wholesale electric power sales and the prices charged for transmission services across states, while the state PUCs regulate distribution and retail sales, oversee construction of facilities and determine prices in their local markets.[21] The joint federal-state system has both costs and benefits: individual state discretion can promote the development of innovative policies, but it can also lead to conflict over priorities and jurisdiction, uncertainty regarding policy direction and increased opportunities for regulatory capture.[22]

Telecommunications

The telecommunications industry has changed significantly in the last 20 years in response to regulatory reform and, perhaps more importantly, rapid technological progress.[23] Competition for long-distance voice services entered a new phase in 1984, when, among other things, seven independent Regional Bell Operating Companies (RBOCs) were spun off from AT&T as part of the settlement of the antitrust case against it.[24] While AT&T provided the bulk of long-distance service in 1984 (with a market share of nearly 70 per cent, Figure 5.5, Panel A), competitive pressures eroded this position, and its market share had fallen to about 33 per cent by 2002. The effects of widespread competition (together with technological change) in long-distance service on prices were readily apparent. Since 1984, real prices for interstate and intra-state long-distance have dropped 64 per cent and 54 per cent, respectively (Panel B), although an indeterminate

Figure 5.5. **Market shares and prices in long-distance telephone services**

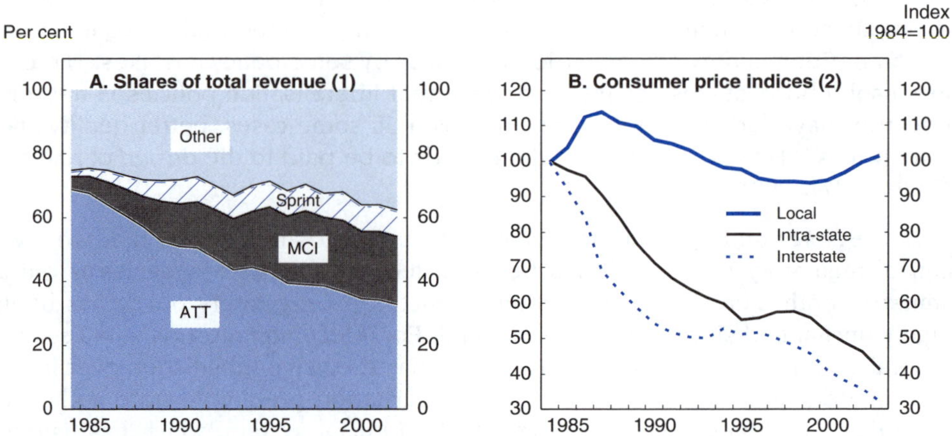

1. Including incumbent local exchange carriers, competitive local exchange carriers and wireless toll service revenues.
2. Relative to all items.

Source: Federal Communications Commission and Bureau of Labor Statistics.

amount of that drop can be attributed to falling access charges. Relative prices for local service rose for the first few years following divestiture; this probably reflected a rebalancing of implicit subsidies for local prices from long-distance prices prior to the creation of a competitive long-distance market. It is also apparent from Figure 5.5 that the fall in AT&T's market share was quite gradual; AT&T still held over 65 per cent of the long-distance market in 1990 – six years after its break-up. This moderate pace should provide perspective when considering the spread of local competition.

The policy changes that accompanied AT&T's break-up continued to be based on the view that local service was a natural monopoly. However, technological changes and experience with competition in some local areas generated interest in furthering local service competition.[25] By 1995, at least 23 states had certified one or more competitors. Competition initially occurred through competitive access providers; these firms provided dedicated access for large business customers to the inter-exchange market, by-passing portions of the local incumbent's exchange network and offering few, if any, local services. Some states, notably New York, also experimented with competition in local services by allowing voluntary unbundling arrangements between local network operators and firms planning to offer local services through licensing of the unbundled network elements – but this never fully blossomed. In particular, there was little incentive for local operators, *e.g.* RBOCs, to provide unbundled services.

The Telecommunications Act of 1996 began the national effort to spur local service competition. The central idea embedded in the legislation was that competition could be generated with a *carrot-and-stick* approach. The *carrot* allowed the Bell operating companies entry into long-distance service outside their local service area and within their region if local service was found to be open to competition. The *stick*, as implemented in the FCC rules, mandated that incumbent local exchange carriers (including Bell companies) allow requesting carriers to: interconnect to their local networks where feasible with charges based on Total Element Long-Run Incremental Cost (TELRIC); unbundle network elements and provide requesting carriers access to these at TELRIC prices; and resell telecommunications services provided at the retail level to requesting carriers at a wholesale price based on retail prices minus avoidable costs. Bell company participation in the long-distance market was aimed at increasing competition there further, and local service competition was desired as a means to lower prices, improve services and, particularly, spur innovation. While these two goals are distinct, the *carrot-and-stick* approach linked them because of concerns that the technical support from RBOCs necessary for local competition (such as physical modifications to switches, processing of competing carriers' requests for access to network elements and other operational services required to facilitate sharing of the local loop) would not be forthcoming without some incentive for their co-operation; Bell company entry in long-distance services was used as an enticing carrot. In the event, legislation was slow to apply, in part because of court challenges to FCC implementation of the Act.

The development of local-service competition was halting, at best, after 1996. Uncertainty regarding the outcomes of legal challenges was one factor, and through 1998 all five Bell company applications to enter in-region long-distance markets were rejected for lack of open local markets. The first approval came in New York in late 1999. But the situation has now changed, and some degree of local competition has now spread through much of the country. In recent data (mid-2003), at least one competitive local exchange carrier provided local service to customers in zip codes containing 95 per cent of the US population; the median household had seven such carriers in its zip code; 39 per cent had 10 or more. Entry has been greatest in more populated areas (Figure 5.6); an exception to this is Texas, where competitive carriers have been very aggressive – in part reflecting the early support to local competition from the Texas public utility commission. Bell company applications to provide long-distance services now have been approved in all applicable states and the District of Columbia. While the period over which Bell company competition in long-distance services and substantial entry in local services has occurred is quite short, there is some evidence that prices have fallen (Hausman *et al.*, 2002).[26] Moreover, the delay of Bell company entry into long-distance services probably came at some cost to consumers (Crandall and Hazlett, 2000), although in recent years wireless, Internet and cable telephony offers have put downward pressure on prices.

Figure 5.6. **Number of competitive local exchange carriers across the United States**

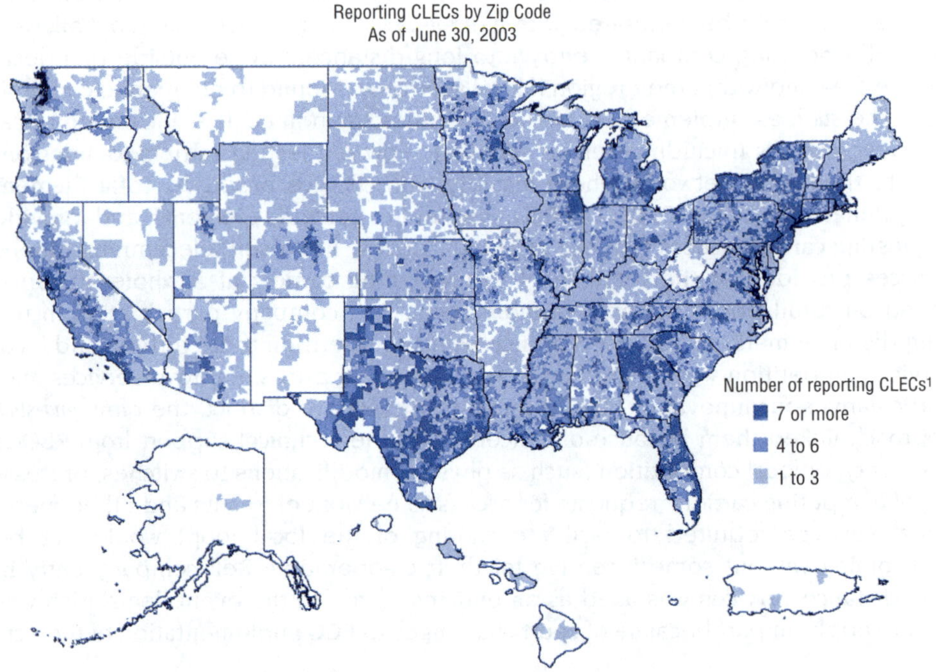

1. CLEC has at least one customer in Zip Code.
Source: Federal Communications Commission (2003), *Local Telephone Competition: Status as of June 30, 2003*, Industry Analysis and Technology Division, Wireline Competition Bureau, December.

Government policies were one factor slowing the emergence of local competition…

Competitive entrants have achieved only modest market shares; 14.7 per cent of local access lines were provided by competitive carriers at mid-2003, seven years after the Telecommunications Act, though their share rose more than 3 percentage points over the previous year and is the second highest for new entrants across OECD countries. The faster penetration of new competitors among large customers – where their market share was 23 per cent most recently – indicates that this submarket has responded more quickly to competitive forces, while the small business and residential submarkets, where competitive providers held 12 per cent of lines, has been less affected. Some of this differential probably reflects a lower incentive to switch for small customers, as their local service prices were already low before competition.[27] In particular, universal service goals had resulted in a severely distorted set of prices for residential and business customers. The 1996 Act aimed to restructure and increase the transparency of the subsidies from business to residential, and from urban to rural, customers in a manner that facilitated competition. (Such changes would be necessary in a purely competitive market to prevent cream-skimming by competitive entrants of business customers paying high regulated rates). However, these changes have been slow to materialise, leading some researchers to conclude that the limited development of competition in local residential services occurred until recently because competitors have had difficulty offering rates below the subsidised rates faced by these customers (Crandall and Waverman, 2000).

The data also show that local competition has developed primarily through entrants' use of the incumbents' facilities, either through purchase of unbundled network elements (UNEs) or resale of services purchased at a wholesale discount. At mid-2003, 58 per cent of competitive carriers' lines were based on UNEs and 18 per cent were based on reselling. Critics of UNE prices have focused on several issues. One has been that unbundling of network elements at TELRIC prices would lower incentives for investments in facilities to provide advanced services: incumbents' incentives would be lower if TELRIC prices do not account for the risk associated with new investments, and entrants might wait to invest until after they had the opportunity to develop experience with the successful investments of incumbents through purchase of unbundled elements.[28] Another concern has been the implementation of TELRIC prices by state regulatory agencies. It has been common for such prices not to distinguish sufficiently between rural and urban areas, despite the cost differences, and UNE prices for similar services have varied widely across states (Crandall and Hazlett, 2000), suggesting an inconsistent application of the methodology. States have also suffered from a lack of guidance from the FCC regarding performance criteria to judge whether an incumbent local exchange carrier (LEC) has provided interconnection and access to UNEs in a non-discriminatory manner. On the other hand, defenders of TELRIC state that properly implemented TELRIC prices compensate Bell companies for the risk of new investments, and lower UNE prices should boost demand and stimulate entry.[29]

In its February 2003 Triennial Review decision, the FCC amended the guidelines for unbundling network elements partly in response to previous court rulings that found the Commission's earlier unbundling regime too broad. As a result, Bell companies must continue providing wholesale service to their competitors as they have in the past while reviews by state regulators are conducted to see if this should be changed. The key focus of the state reviews will be to determine if competitors need access to Bell company switches in order not to be "impaired" as a competitor, where impairment covers both availability of switching from an alternate source and an economic criterion for whether a competitor can utilise its own switch. The Triennial Review seeks to refine the imposition of unbundling rules to target market segments where third-party alternatives exist on self-deployment by competitors is feasible, while de-regulating those segments where competition is self-sustaining. For example, tThere is a presumption in the

FCC order that there is no impairment to competitors seeking to serve businesses using T1 lines[30] or higher. If a state review determines that certain network elements need not be unbundled, then the competitive carriers currently employing these elements have three years to switch to another platform, presumably their own facilities. This set of decisions is intended to spur investment in facilities-based competition, although the outcome of state reviews will be important in determining the incentives facing the industry. While experience with UNEs has been limited to recent years, there has been empirical evidence that unbundling boosts investment (Willig *et al.*, 2002), consistent with the view that competition lowers prices, increases demand and hence generates higher capital requirements. Nevertheless, experience is also consistent with arguments that the UNEs deter investment by reducing ILEC returns from investment and deter CLEC investment by providing free option to use ILEC equipment. A move to eliminate unbundling may not result in investment in facilities in the near term by competitive carriers currently serving a large customer base, given their financial problems.

The Review also amended the rules governing advanced (broadband) services, again in an effort to spur deployment. Previous rules allowed line sharing, under which competitive digital subscriber line (DSL) carriers (a form of high-speed internet connection) buy only the high-frequency portion of a copper loop from an incumbent carrier, when the incumbent already offers voice service over the same line. This unbundling requirement will be phased-out over the next three years; new customers can be added for one year using line sharing. Only one company uses this service, and its phase-out will see the company fall back to purchasing the entire copper loop. The FCC is, however, maintaining its line-splitting rules, which facilitate joint use of an unbundled loop by voice and data competitors. New investments in fibre-to-the-home need not be shared with competitors. Hybrid deployments of fibre/copper wire are subject to lesser unbundling requirements. The relaxation of unbundling requirements on broadband services may affect competition, as it would result in only Bell companies and cable providers offering the service in a local area (as satellite services are currently only a marginal part of the market, as discussed below). However, the authorities point to the potential trade-off between promoting investment and promoting competition. An alternative would have been to preserve unbundling requirements for existing services (while noting that at some point facilities-based competition would be expected to be the standard) and clarify that investment in advanced services (*i.e.* moving fibre closer to the home) would be exempt from unbundling for some time.

... and will need amendment in response to emerging technologies

The 1996 Act preserved the view that local fixed-line telephone service was not a close substitute for alternative telecommunications services and hence required a set of regulatory rules to facilitate competition over the local loop. This view is increasingly, but not totally, outdated as a result of new technologies. Mobile phone service is the most direct narrow band competitor; 148 million mobile lines were held at mid-2003 (45 per cent of the total). This represented an increase of 85 per cent from the end of 1999 – a period over which the number of total fixed lines fell 6.4 per cent.[31] It is still the case that the substantial preponderance of mobile phone subscribers also subscribe to fixed-line telephone services. Cable and internet telephony is still limited, but it is growing fast and could further blur the distinction between telecommunications and information services. This emerging competitive fringe will create challenges for the current framework of access charges and fees that fund universal service.

In particular, universal service goals were expanded as part of the 1996 Act. There are currently four government support programmes for: high-cost carriers (which are often in rural areas); low-income households; rural health-care providers; and schools and libraries. These are funded by fees (*i.e.* taxes) on interstate and international revenues of carriers providing telecommunications services and are difficult to defend on economic efficiency grounds. With regard to the goal of universal service, there is little evidence that the subsidies are of much benefit, as demand for basic local fixed-line telephone service is relatively price-inelastic (*e.g.* Wolak, 1996; Hausman, 1997, 1998*b* and 1999). Pursuing legitimate equity goals through cross-subsidisation is very costly. The fees have a high efficiency cost, because interstate and international calling is price-sensitive and priced above marginal cost, implying that any boost to prices from fees yields a large deadweight loss. For example, Hausman (1997) estimates that the efficiency loss for each extra dollar of revenue from fees on interstate and international calls slightly exceeds one dollar; in 2001, universal service fund contributions by carriers were slightly more than $5 billion dollars, implying a similar deadweight loss. (Other taxes on services with lower price elasticities, such as income taxes, have efficiency losses that are an order of magnitude smaller.) A final problem arises because universal service fees are levied on carriers providing telecommunications services, and technological change has begun to blur the line between telecommunications and information services. For example, internet telephony is not subject to universal service fees because it is deemed an information service; as technological advances make this service more attractive, the current fee structure will make even less economic sense. Access charges create a similar distortion: because internet telephony has been classified as an information service, it pays access charges only to enter the local loop and not for inter-exchange traffic – creating strong incentives to develop services to avoid higher access charges for inter- or intra-state connections for traditional voice services.[32] Access charge reform should be high on the policy agenda. The FCC is currently seeking comments on the appropriate regulatory treatment of Internet telephony. This inquiry will address the issues raised in the preceding discussion, including the applicability of access charges.

Broadband deployment poses challenges beyond those associated with the development of new voice services. Approximately 16 per cent of the adult population – about 30 million people – had residential broadband connections in March 2003 – a six-fold increase over the level in mid-2000 (Pew Internet and American Life Project, 2003). Provision is dominated by cable (67 per cent of lines) and DSL provided by incumbent telephone carriers or other firms using UNEs purchased from incumbents (30 per cent of lines). Cable firms have not been subject to unbundling requirements, and these will be removed for incumbent telephone carriers under the most recent Triennial Review. This asymmetric treatment reflects the legacy of Bell company dominance in local phone service, which has led to the designation of Bell companies as dominant providers for services over their lines and hence subject to extra regulation. In broadband service, the market facts clearly do not support the view that Bell companies are dominant (and more detailed empirical work backs up this claim, *e.g.* Crandall *et al.*, 2002; Hausman *et al.*, 2001a and 2001b). But, as noted, removal of their unbundling requirements will lead to a duopoly between a cable firm and incumbent telephone carrier in each market, limiting competition further. Although some cable operators voluntarily provide access to independent Internet providers because of service imperatives as well as broader competitive considerations, for the time being it would seem preferable to maintain Bell companies' unbundling requirements and require that cable firms allow open access to independent ISPs. Technological developments may at some point obviate the need for such policies.[33]

Electricity

Regulatory reform in the electricity sector was driven, in part, by many of the same factors that had influenced efforts in telecommunications: successful liberalisation in many other industries; a new perspective on the technical feasibility of separating transmission and distribution from generation and retailing; technological progress in the form of economically efficient smaller-scale generating plants; and dissatisfaction with the distortions to prices across states and different customers induced by regulation (especially in states with high prices).[34] Unlike in other areas where the United States has often been a leader in reform, the US experiments followed those in a number of other Member countries, most notably that in the early 1990s in England and Wales. Although the recent blackout in the northeast has highlighted the need for change, the spectacular failure of the California experiment in 2000-01 has chilled enthusiasm for reform throughout the country, and the lessons from this experience are a focus of what follows.

Regulation contributed to wide variation in electricity prices across states

While regulatory reform should be expected to improve efficiency, it is notable that the US electric power industry performed very well for a long time under the traditional regulated-monopoly model in terms of international standards for productivity, costs, reliability and prices (Joskow, 2003). Problems began to arise in the 1970s, as fossil fuel prices surged. In 1978, the Public Utilities Regulatory Policies Act (PURPA) created a class of qualifying facilities (QFs) including generators using non-fossil fuel and renewable energy sources and co-generators, which supply electricity as a by-product of industrial processes. PURPA required utilities to connect QFs to the transmission networks and purchase power from them at avoided costs; these provisions were designed to stimulate investment in generation that was less dependent on fossil fuels and more environmentally friendly. A number of states, particularly California and several in the northeast, embraced this requirement wholeheartedly, sometimes requiring utilities to enter 20- to 30-year contracts with QFs. In addition, these states also turned to nuclear power to a greater extent. Both decisions turned out to be costly (in part because fossil fuel prices retreated in the second half of 1980s and because of technological developments), resulting in much higher regulated retail electricity prices in these regions than elsewhere in the country (Table 5.3). Retail prices in New York, California and New England have been more than double those in low-cost states in the west and south (such as Idaho, Kentucky, Washington and Wyoming) in recent years.

A positive side-effect of PURPA was the demonstration that independent generators could supply power to a vertically integrated generation, transmission and distribution system without disruption. This combined with technological change in the form of compact, reliable and relatively low-emission gas turbines to spur interest in developing a competitive generation sector. The 1992 Energy Policy Act (EPAct)

Table 5.3. **Retail electricity rates**
(Cents/KWh)

Census division	Residential		Commercial		Industrial		All sectors	
	2002	2001	2002	2001	2002	2001	2002	2001
New England	11.1	11.6	9.5	10.1	7.9	7.7	9.9	10.2
Mid Atlantic	10.7	10.8	9.9	9.8	5.7	5.8	9.2	9.1
East North Central	7.6	7.7	7.2	7.0	4.7	4.6	6.4	6.3
West North Central	6.7	6.8	5.4	5.5	4.0	4.2	5.5	5.6
South Atlantic	7.4	7.8	6.3	6.4	4.1	4.2	6.3	6.5
East South Central	6.3	6.5	6.3	6.3	3.6	3.7	5.2	5.3
West South Central	7.6	7.6	6.8	7.1	4.4	4.5	6.2	6.4
Mountain	7.5	7.5	6.4	6.4	4.7	4.5	6.3	6.2
Pacific Contiguous	10.2	9.9	Nm	10.6	7.1	7.4	9.9	9.5
Pacific Non-contiguous	14.2	13.5	12.5	12.3	10.6	10.1	12.5	12.1
US average	8.1	8.3	7.8	7.7	4.7	4.8	7.0	7.0

Source: Energy Information Administration, Form EIA-826, "Monthly Electric Utility Sales and Revenue Report with State Distributions". Downloaded on 10 June, 2003 from *www.eia.doe.gov/cneaf/electricity/epm/epmt53p1.html*.

established non-utility generators known as exempt wholesale generators (EWGs). These are exempt from PURPA's renewable fuel and cogeneration requirements. Unlike QFs, utilities are not obligated to purchase from EWGs. The EPAct also gave the Federal Energy Regulatory Commission (FERC) the authority to order that utilities provide transmission service to wholesale generators on a reasonable and non-discriminatory basis.[35] Transmission access to end-users – retail access – was not required by the EPAct; states retained discretion in this matter in their jurisdictions.

The wide variation in electricity rates across states and the emergence of a more competitive wholesale market encouraged a number of states with high prices to pursue reform at the retail level. The motivation was largely the prospect of lower prices; in fact, a component of most retail competition plans was the introduction of a baseline option for consumers involving a mandatory reduction in rates (Joskow, 2003). At the same time, however, many plans froze retail rates for a transition period at levels that were thought to be high enough to allow the utilities to recover "stranded costs" associated with earlier decisions by regulators. Experience has varied by state, but currently restructuring is largely on hold outside the Northeast and Texas, Oregon and Arizona (Figure 5.7).

Figure 5.7. **Status of state electric industry restructuring activity**
February 2003

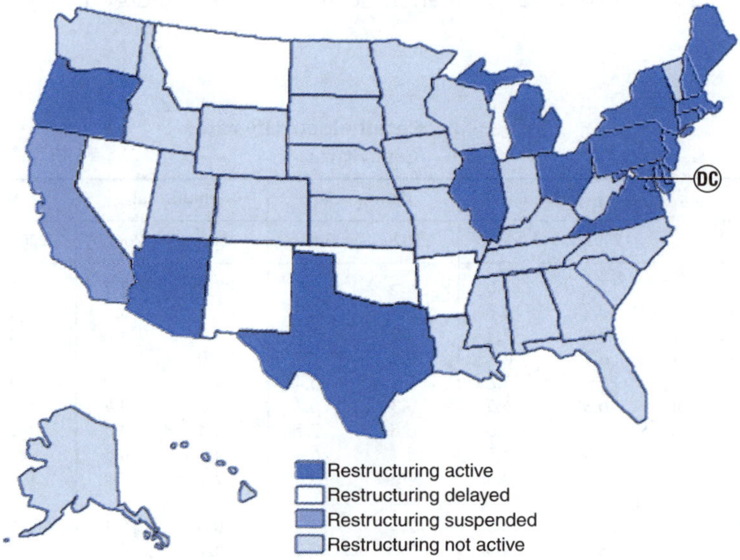

Source: Energy Information Administration (*www.eia.doe.gov/cneaf/electricity/chg_str/regmap.html*).

The experience of California demonstrates some cautionary lessons

Two words summarize the reasons behind the drop-off in reform among the states: California and Enron. The meltdown in California's electricity market over the course of 2000-01 dominated headlines and is embedded in the public's mind as the prime example of failed retail competition.[36] Enron was involved in restructuring in most states that introduced competition, and reports of its misleading actions and bankruptcy have further tainted efforts to move forward. In Enron's case, the long-term damage is probably more one of perception than substance (although its actions may have contributed to some irregularities in California).[37] California's experience provides more direct instruction on some of the features of electricity markets that make competition so difficult.[38]

The state's experiment with competition in the retail electricity market began in April 1998. Initially, default retail rates charged by the incumbent utilities were set 10 per cent below 1996 levels. The wholesale market performed as expected, at least in terms of prices, through early spring 2000. However, beginning in May, spot prices began to rise dramatically (Figure 5.8). By this point, the utility in San Diego had recovered its stranded costs and was no longer obligated to charge retail customers the legislated default rates of 10 per cent below 1996 prices; consequently, prices for end-users in its region rose dramatically and were capped by the California legislature (with a commitment to repay the losses to the

Figure 5.8. **Average wholesale price of electricity in California, 2000 and 2001**

Excludes ancillary services costs

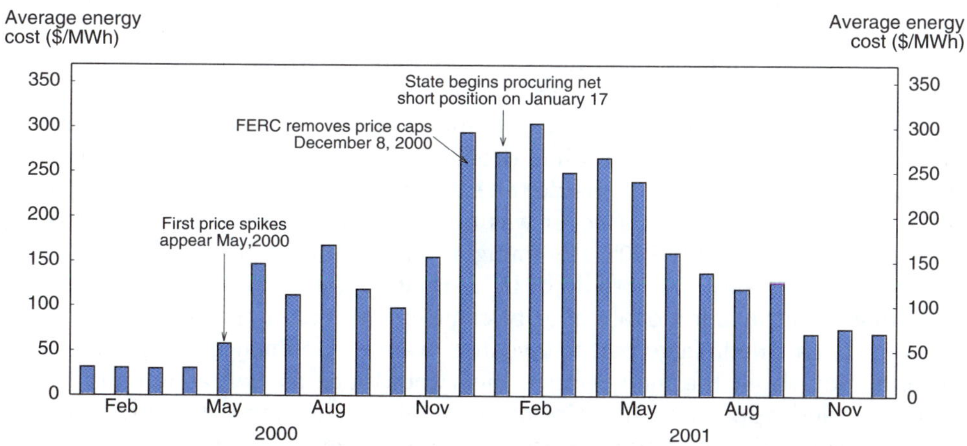

Source: Data from CA ISO (*www.caiso.com/docs/2001/03/22/2001032214552322811.pdf*) and Department of Water Resources Revenue Requirement Draft Filing (19 October, 2001). Downloaded from California Public Utility Commission on 10 June, 2003.

utility caused by the cap). The other two large utilities were still charging the low regulated retail rates and began incurring large losses. With FERC's approval, wholesale prices were capped at $250/MWh from August until December 2000. Subsequently, FERC imposed a soft cap of $150/MWh on wholesale prices; the cap could be breached if suppliers could justify the higher prices based on costs. In any event, high gas and emissions permit prices, as well as complex transactions in which power was first sold to a marketer at a higher price and then resold through the California system operator at those high rates, briefly resulted in wholesale prices in excess of $400/MWh.[39] Given that the regulated retail rates implied sales to end-users at $65/MWh, the two utilities outside San Diego were losing $50 million a day in late December; they had accumulated about $12 billion in liabilities for wholesale power charges over the previous twelve months. This burden made it progressively more difficult to finance their operations, and both were approaching insolvency at the end of the year. The lights would have gone out in California in early 2001 had the state not stepped in, first by purchasing power to meet utilities short position in power and then by entering long-term contracts to purchase electricity and acting to raise retail electricity rates by 40 per cent beginning June 2001. The crisis was over by late summer 2001. However, the state of California had entered long-term contracts (typically of about 10 years in duration) to purchase power worth approximately $45 billion. The state ended retail choice in September 2001; the experiment had been a dramatic failure.

The crisis was caused by the weaknesses in the wholesale and retail market design in California, not by the introduction of competition. That is not to say that prices would not have risen dramatically in 2000-01 even under a well-designed system; indeed, they probably would have. A number of factors contributed. Natural gas prices rose significantly, raising the costs of the marginal generators. Prices of permits for nitrogen oxide emissions also jumped in late 2000, as the number of permits fell (as had been planned for some time, consistent with the desired reduction in emissions). The impetus to higher rates from these was exacerbated by the weather; a heat wave boosted demand for electricity throughout the west, while drought conditions contributed to a drop in the available electricity from outside the state (where hydroelectricity is an important power source). And this boost was on top of a sharp uptrend in electricity demand from the mid-1990s stemming from the rapid pace of growth. The increase in demand had resulted in a relatively tight electricity market in California, as little additional capacity came on line after the mid-1990s in the western states, due in large part to investors' wariness to finance new plants, given uncertainties about the market rules they would face as well as lengthy review processes and opposition from local communities. However, it is probably not correct to conclude, as some have, that failure to approve new power plants was a binding constraint on supply and hence a key factor in the crisis. New supply in the form of QFs came on line in the early 1990s, after which there was a perception of excess supply in the market. The surge in demand led to an awareness that supply had become tighter, and the approval process was a factor that delayed new capacity coming on line until mid-2001; but the natural delays in construction and failure to forecast the surge in demand were also important (Joskow, 2001).

Elsewhere reforms have yielded more mixed results

Despite the fact that prices would have risen even under an ideal market design, it now appears that the unilateral exercise of market power by power generators was substantial during the crisis (*e.g.* Borenstein *et al.*, 2002; Joskow and Kahn, 2002; Annex 5.2). California's crisis has not been the only example where market power has boosted prices after regulatory reforms that have increased the use of markets to determine prices. Such occurrences have been common. Bushnell and Saravia (2002) documented such behaviour in New England and the PJM (portions of Pennsylvania, New Jersey and Maryland, as well as Delaware and Washington, DC), as has Wolfram (1999) in England and Wales. In fact, the Market Surveillance Committee in California repeatedly noted market-power concerns and warned that the lack of price sensitivity of demand and the absence of forward contracting could precipitate a more severe crisis (Wolak *et al.*, 1998 and 1999; Wolak 1999 and 2003b). However, experience outside of California has in general been more favourable. This may reflect, in part, greater use of forward contracts. Demand is more elastic over longer horizons, and forward contracts limit suppliers' gains in revenue from a high spot price, thereby lowering the incentives for marginal generators to withhold power supply.[40] Outside California, it was common for utilities to be required to enter forward contracts when divesting generation assets (or for divestiture not to be required, in which case a utility would have an implicit forward contract with itself to cover demand from its customers). Another factor has been the adequacy of supply: wholesale electricity markets tend to exhibit low prices during periods of excess supply, and such situations have been more common elsewhere in the United States or abroad than in California – especially in summer 2000, when the drought limited potential imports from hydroelectric sources elsewhere in the west.

More broadly, the transition to competitive markets in wholesale and/or retail electricity markets has been smoother in other countries such as Australia, England and Wales, New Zealand, Norway and Spain. An important factor has been the institutional differences between the United States and most other countries. Electricity regulation in the United States has largely been a state responsibility, making a national strategy difficult to develop. In addition, the US industry is dominated by privately owned, vertically integrated utilities; while other countries have often started with a plan to separate competitive (*e.g.* generation and marketing) and natural monopoly (*e.g.* transmission and distribution) segments and could proceed with such plans because of government ownership, such actions would involve exerting control over private property in the

United States. A concomitant constraint on competition is the relative lack of integration in transmission networks across regions (or even states). This derives from the state-by-state nature of regulatory regimes and the lack of need for strong interconnections under the vertically integrated utility model; an unfortunate effect on reform is that the number of competitors within some regions is limited and cannot be increased without investment in transmission capacity. The August 2003 blackout in the north-east showed that the US electricity system has drastic problems. A November 2003 report from a US-Canada task force investigating the blackout found that it was the result of equipment failures, co-ordination problems, violations of reliability standards and human error. The energy bill now being considered in Congress contains provisions to make mandatory compliance with existing voluntary system reliability standards and foster regional transmission integration and related investment. However, it may not address satisfactorily weaknesses in the regulatory framework, which must be fixed to enable a functioning competitive market.

Competition would be facilitated by some policy changes

The domestic and international experience points to a few changes that could improve efficiency. Reform will need to proceed flexibly because a great deal of disagreement remains regarding how best to manage the transition from a structure that is balkanised across states and dominated by vertically integrated private firms to a more regionally integrated network with separation between competitive and monopoly activities (as emphasized in, for example, Joskow, 2003). One positive step has been FERC's proposal regarding a standard market design (SMD) for wholesale markets. This plan calls for four regional transmission operators (RTOs) to manage transmission across the country. Greater regional integration and uniformity in rules across states would facilitate infrastructure investment, eliminate discriminatory practices by network owners and limit the exercise of market power (through market power mitigation measures such as price caps). Moreover, multi-state entities for planning, certification, and siting at a regional level should improve oversight of transmission investment, as such bodies are better placed to consider the regional externalities of new capacity than state commissions. Increased regional integration could result in substantial net savings to consumers after deducting SMD implementation costs (US Department of Energy, 2003).

As noted above, the spread of retail competition has stalled since the California debacle. Proponents of a continuation of reforms to encourage retail competition need to acknowledge that the short-run benefits in terms of lower prices will be limited in the low-rate states that have not begun restructuring; rather, the gains will accrue over the long run, as retail competition fosters increased use of "innovations" like demand management policies and, in conjunction with wholesale competition, provides superior signals for investments in generation and transmission capacity. Retail competition programmes could learn from the experiences of England and Wales, Texas and California. They should ensure (at least functional) separation of competitive and monopoly activities. Given the slow rate at which customers switch service providers, reform should also make full deregulation of the incumbent's retail prices wait until a competitive market has time to develop. The default service price should vary, perhaps slowly, with the wholesale rate. And customers who switch to competitive retailers should not be allowed to switch back to the regulated default service if competitive prices rise; only by creating a customer base that can be relied upon over a medium- to long-run horizon will retailers have sufficient incentives to enter forward contracts for their demand. The US experience has demonstrated that the gains from retail competition for residential and small business customers are not significant in the short run, and hence it may also be best to move forward with retail choice for larger customers first as the EU has done, as such customers can gain much more from value-added services for demand management.

Concluding remarks

In summary, as a result of reform efforts over the past two decades or so, competitive forces have been stronger in the United States than in most other OECD countries. Nonetheless, there is scope for improvements in a number of areas. Some recommendations concerning competition law, international trade, intellectual property rights and major network industries are provided in Box 5.1. These seem to be the most important issues regarding product market competition. As noted, however, others might need attention, notably the tort liability system and public procurement. Annex 5.3 provides some information on tort reform, which could enhance the proper functioning of markets and thus productivity and employment in a number of sectors, and Annex 5.4 deals with public procurement where the injection of competitive elements has been limited, especially at the state level.

Box 5.1. Recommendations regarding product market competition

Competition law and policy

The competition law combines unusually severe penalties for horizontal collusion with a complex, economically-motivated approach to monopoly and other restraints. Some remaining problems are consequences of this approach and of the roles and capacities of courts, local governments and private litigants.

- To sustain the success of the leniency programme in cartel enforcement, strong sanctions should be maintained against hard-core conduct, but provisions for private damages and other recoveries should be modified in order to preserve the incentive to be the first conspirator to come forward.
- Some anomalous exemptions and special regimes have found their way into US law, often to undo enforcement actions, sometimes in conjunction with regulatory programmes. These anomalous exemptions should be eliminated to improve coherence and to promote competition. The antitrust immunity of government enterprises should be terminated: no other member exempts government-related firms from competition enforcement. Other anomalies are the exemption of many non profit entities from the jurisdiction of the FTC and also include the remaining exemptions in the otherwise liberalised trucking industry to the treatment of insurance under the McCarran-Ferguson Act.
- The state action doctrine risks embarrassing the national commitment to competition. The OECD's regulatory reform review called for a systematic study of the doctrine's economic effects as a prelude to substantial reform. This still has not been done. State-law constraints on competition should be removed.
- The complexity and cost of litigation may result in under-enforcement of rules about non-per se conduct; on the other hand, the incentive of treble damages may encourage too much litigation over it. Clear principles for deciding about non-criminal restraints should be developed and endorsed by the courts.

Trade barriers

The US economy is relatively open to foreign competition, resulting in higher consumer welfare, and the United States is committed to pursue trade liberalisation. Nonetheless, additional efforts would be desirable.

- Heavy handed customs procedures and threatened (or levied) anti-dumping and countervailing duties cannot be justified economically, leading to higher prices for consumers and impeding necessary adjustments. Hence, policy initiatives that lower reliance on anti-dumping, countervailing and safeguard actions and similar protectionist measures should be pursued.
- Despite the relative openness of the US economy and a positive set of government proposals, US leadership to successfully conclude the Doha round is needed. Care should also be taken that multilateral liberalisation is not undermined by bilateral agreements.

Box 5.1. **Recommendations regarding product market competition** (*cont.*)

Intellectual property rights

Intellectual property rights create special challenges for competition, as their purpose is to limit competition in the short run in order to capture the long-run benefits of dynamic competition through innovation. While a broad set of specific recommendations must wait until after the ongoing study within the OECD on IPRs, innovation and economic performance, a few reforms would clearly be welfare-enhancing.

- An opposition system for patents similar to that in Europe (giving broader rights for grants to be challenged) should be considered. This would help improve the quality of the patent review process and limit the costs of subsequent litigation.
- The standards for non-obviousness and quality of patents should be raised, in particular in emerging technology fields. Limited reverse-engineering of software should be allowed to facilitate interoperability.
- Hatch-Waxman agreements that stop entry by generic drug firms through payments from branded drug firms should be illegal, although other types of settlements that facilitate resolution of patent disputes without payments from branded to generic firms would (of course) remain legal. Generic firms that abandon efforts to enter should lose their exclusive 180-day right to produce.

Telecommunications regulation

While local service competition has begun to take root, some recent policy changes have moved in the wrong direction, and new initiatives are needed to increase competition.

- Unbundling of network elements has boosted competition for local voice services and provided incentives for investment in new services; mandatory unbundling should be continued for the foreseeable future.
- The FCC should develop national performance and impairment standards to help state regulatory commissions assess whether incumbents have met their unbundling obligations.
- With a view to aiding broadband deployment, unbundling requirements for incumbent telephone carriers should be maintained, and cable firms should be required to open their lines using older technology to independent internet service providers.
- The current form of universal service fees may be distortionary. It would be better to lower or eliminate universal service subsidies and/or, when deemed necessary, to fund such subsidies from less distorting broad-based taxes.

Box 5.1. Recommendations regarding product market competition (*cont.*)

- Access charges based on jurisdictional (*i.e.* local, intrastate but not local, interstate) lines will be challenged by technological changes and create incentives to innovate around existing regulations rather than efficiently. Reviewing the inter-carrier compensation regime, including reduction of access charges, should be high on the policy agenda.

Electricity regulation

California's experiment provides an example of how reform can fail. Hence, future efforts should proceed cautiously. With that *caveat*, a number of policy changes could improve efficiency through increased competition.

- Electricity markets have developed on a state-by-state or small region basis. Efforts to increase regional integration should be considered. The Standard Market Design (SMD) initiative of the FERC is one example.
- The balkanised ownership of transmission assets, the potential for local market power and difficulties in pricing congestion over the network make it unlikely that competitive forces will spur efficient investment in transmission capacity – so called "merchant transmission investment" (Joskow and Tirole, 2003). The costs and benefits of such investment relative to a regulated monopoly transmission company (as in England and Wales) need study, as do the legal issues associated with divestiture of transmission assets and potential reforms.
- The SMD appropriately includes market power mitigation measures, such as price caps, to limit the extent to which generators can set prices above marginal cost. But such measures will also lower incentives to invest in new capacity. While there is currently excess capacity in much of the country, measures to support investment in generation through requirements that distributors contract for peak demand plus some reserve margin may be necessary.*
- Further efforts to promote retail competition should proceed first with large customers. Default service programmes should not mandate price reductions, and limits on high-frequency customer switching should be included, so that retailers have incentives to enter forward contracts.
- While many issues discussed in the OECD's *Regulatory Reform in the United States* (1999) have not been repeated to conserve space, its recommendations still need attention. In particular, distortions to competition through tax and subsidy systems should be removed (*e.g.* the differential tax treatment of public utilities). Privatisation of government-owned assets (including small public utilities and large federal entities like the Tennessee Valley Authority and the power marketing authorities) should be considered.

* California and Texas did not impose such a requirement, while the New England ISO did.
Source: OECD.

Notes

1. One further area of the US institutional framework that is both unique and costly is the tort liability system where reforms might be beneficial, especially regarding medical malpractice claims. In 2003, the Congress followed three separate tracks to enact tort reform in the areas of medical malpractice, class-action lawsuits and asbestos. All have failed thus far. For more details see Annex 5.3 and Congressional Budget Office (2003).
2. Congress has recently blocked a new FCC rule that would have let companies own TV stations serving up to 45 per cent of US viewers. The current ceiling is 35 per cent.
3. In some non-price-fixing cases, government actions have led to remedies requiring firms to disgorge unlawful gains or make restitution to victims. The sums have been very large – in one case, over $100 million. Technically, these are not considered damages, but the cases were co-ordinated with state and private claims for damages.
4. The indicators are based on detailed data collected by the OECD from national sources. Summary indicators are computed aggregating individual regulations with weights derived from factor analysis. The resulting country rankings are robust to changes in the weighting procedure.
5. Foreign competition should be understood here in broad terms. Besides the disciplinary impact of traditional imports of goods (and savings) from foreign producers, wages and prices are squeezed down to their minimum levels by intermediate or final-product imports from related parties or other parts of the value added chain that are outsourced abroad. Outsourcing, especially in the high-technology area, has become very controversial during the "jobless recovery". The US statistical agencies just announced their intention to try to track the magnitude of this growing phenomenon. And the Senate voted to prevent federal contractors from outsourcing work abroad in the FY 2004 omnibus appropriations bill that passed in January.
6. A large literature compares unit values derived from trade data to assess price gaps across countries (*e.g.* Knetter, 1994 and Swagel, 1995). Such comparisons are valuable at very detailed classification levels (for example, the 10-digit level of the harmonised trade system), but differences in goods at higher levels of aggregation make them much less informative.
7. A recent study (Danzon and Furukawa, 2003) that uses data for 1999 and concentrates on drug prices also finds that US drug prices are higher than in other countries (except Japan) but less so than Bradford.
8. A rationale for anti-dumping actions as efficiency-enhancing is particularly difficult; predatory pricing to gain a monopoly position is one such justification, but antitrust law generally (though not universally) views claims of predatory actions sceptically. Safeguard actions could be justified if, for example, an otherwise (long-run) efficient

industry faces capital market imperfections that impede it from making the adjustment to a competitive long-run position; however, this example would call for loan guarantees rather than tariffs, and it is not clear that any current safeguard action could be justified on these grounds.

9. Tarullo (2003) provides references to studies on both sides of this issue.

10. An ongoing project within the OECD on IPRs, innovation and economic performance is studying these issues in more detail.

11. A more thorough set of references to antitrust concerns and IPRs can be found in Gallini (2002).

12. Two surveys are Levin and Levin (2002) and Hall *et al.* (2003). Other studies include Janis (1997), Barton (2000 and 2001) and Wegner (2001).

13. Interoperability and interface are the abilities to work with some other patented programmes, especially operating systems but also other platforms, and to match the look of patented programmes.

14. The 2003 Medicare Prescription Drug, Improvement and Modernisation Act limits the 30-month postponement to a single delay in almost all instances (rather than having multiple consecutive postponements for multiple disputes). Moreover, the 180-day exclusivity can in certain circumstances be forfeited or be subject to co-exclusivity with other generic applicants.

15. Federal Trade Commission (2002) and Bulow (2003) provide a discussion of the issues involved.

16. One response to price regulation outside the United States has been the decision of pharmaceutical companies to refuse (or threaten to refuse) to provide products to certain countries such as Canada (Dyer, 2003) and France (Lanjouw, 2003).

17. In particular, the Senate passed a bill on 20 June 2003 that would allow pharmacists to purchase drugs in Canada and resell them in the United States; the House passed a similar provision on 25 July 2003, and such provisions have also been passed in previous years. However, it is not clear that a similar provision, even if it were to become law, would open the US market to parallel imports, as the Secretary of Health and Human Services would need to certify that the drugs imported from Canada were safe and effective; such certification has not been granted in the past.

18. While quantitative evaluations of the tradeoffs associated with lower drug prices are scarce, the presumption made by most academic experts is that such efforts would have negative long-run consequences. For an example of this view, consider Scherer (1993, p. 193): "Should a tradeoff be required between modestly excessive prices and profits *versus* retarded technical progress, it would be better to err on the side of excessive profits." There is also a distributional issue, as lower drug prices would benefit drug purchasers at the expense of owners of pharmaceutical company shares.

19. See OECD (2001), which thoroughly reviews the literature and adds more evidence on the relationship between regulation and performance in these sectors. The series of OECD *Reviews of Regulatory Reform* also constitute a rich source of information on the effects of industry-specific reforms on performance.

20. The discussion of telecommunications markets below focuses on the institutional structure in the United States and the extent to which reform measures have contributed to improved performance. While lessons from international experience are a central part of

the discussion, relatively little attention is paid to the prices of telecommunication and electricity services in the United States relative to that in other countries. This is appropriate because much of the gain from competitive provision of such services should be expected to accrue to consumers over the long run, as more efficient signals are provided for investment in new and improved services. Nonetheless, Annex 5.1 presents a comparison of relative prices. US prices are quite low for electricity and below the OECD average for voice services, albeit above those in the lowest-price Member countries. A much earlier study (Blondal and Pilat, 1997) found that the macroeconomic impact of policy changes in these sectors would be quite small as a percentage of GDP, reflecting the prevalence of competitive forces and hence low prices even prior to reform efforts. However, the effect over the long run through incentives for innovation could be larger.

21. FERC also has the ability to approve or disapprove mergers in the electric power industry, oversees the licensing of hydroelectric power projects and regulates interstate natural gas and oil transportation. Contrary to natural gas, the states have transmission siting authority for electricity.

22. More broadly, the intensity of regulatory reform in telecommunications and electricity since the mid-1990s has been accompanied by an apparent increase in the degree of political interference; some have attributed this to the role of political contributions (Hazlett, 2000; *The Economist*, 2003). The discussion below will focus primarily on economic considerations. As a result, the recent controversy over the FCC's decision to raise the maximum ownership percentage for media outlets is not discussed; this controversy stems from the priority given to diversity and other public interest goals, not from a dispute over economic efficiency.

23. The OECD review of US regulatory policies (OECD, 1999) contains a more detailed treatment of US telecommunications policy developments through 1998.

24. The consent decree required AT&T to divest its local operating subsidiaries into seven Regional Bell Operating Companies (RBOCs). It separated the country into 164 regions – Local Access and Transport Areas (LATAs), generally smaller than states – and stipulated that RBOCs could not provide services across these regions. RBOCs were forbidden from entering the competitive long-distance (inter-LATA) market to eliminate their incentive to charge discriminatory tariffs for local loop access to companies offering such services. The break-up was accompanied by price caps for AT&T on long-distance tolls (in effect until 1994) to prevent abuse of its dominant position.

25. These technological changes involved innovations that lowered the cost of facilities-based, or alternative network, competition and permitted economical "unbundling" of elements of the local network loop.

26. According to the CPI, the average price of telephone services has continued to fall and is now below the level prevailing in 1997.

27. It is interesting to recall that the cross-subsidies, relative to marginal costs, provided to residential customers by business customers reflect the preservation by regulators of AT&T's original business strategy. During the initial rollout of telephone service, AT&T figured that the value of the phone network to a business customer was greater the larger the number of residential customers, and hence it set prices low for residential customers and high for business customers.

28. Proponents of this hypothesis include Hausman (1998a), Jorde *et al.* (2000) and Crandall (2003).

29. This is consistent with the positive impact of competition on investment found for regulated industries more generally in earlier empirical work (Ahn, 2002; Alesina *et al.*, 2003).

30. A T1 line can carry 24 digitalised voice channels or data at a rate of 1 544 megabits per second.

31. Yet this penetration is still less than in Europe, probably because of the lack of a single technical standard: while most of the world uses the Global System for Mobiles (GSM) technology, US firms are split between a variant of that (GSM/GPRS), Code Division Multiple Access (CDMA) and Integrated Digital Enhanced Network (IDEN).

32. Reports in July 2003 indicated that Worldcom (now renamed MCI) was under investigation for fraud related to (alleged) efforts to re-route calls to avoid access charges. If proven, these allegations would indicate that the current structure of access charges has perverse effects beyond its presumed impact on usage, product offerings and innovation.

33. The regulatory structure, with its relatively inflexible designation of Bell companies as dominant carriers, may face other long-run challenges from technological change. Policy changes to address technological convergence in telecommunications will likely require legislative action, as the distinction between telecommunications and information services was solidified by the 1996 Act. The regulatory framework recently adopted by the European Union may provide some lessons (Marcus, 2002). It emphasizes the need for regulations to exist in situations where market power is significant; in such cases within telecommunications services, this would require dominant firms to provide non-discriminatory access to the network, as well as access to and use of unbundled network elements (UNEs). The key distinction between this framework and that in the United States lies in the presumption in US regulations that incumbent telephone carriers are dominant and hence must face restrictions on their activities. The EU framework can, in principle, adapt to technological convergence through appropriate redefinition of the relevant markets.

34. An accessible introduction can be found in Brennan *et al.* (2002). The OECD review of US regulatory policies (OECD, 1999) contains a more detailed treatment of US electricity policies through 1998.

35. FERC orders 888 and 889 (issued in 1996) implemented this authority: Order 888 required utilities to open their grids for transmission, expand capacity to accommodate new generating capacity as necessary, and unbundle wholesale power prices into rates for generation, transmission and other services; Order 889 mandated that information on capacity, prices and services for transmission be provided on a common information network (the Open Access Same-time Information System, OASIS).

36. A number of summaries are available, including Brennan *et al.* (2002), Joskow (2001) and Wolak (2003a). Much of the description of the system and crisis herein follows Joskow (2001).

37. Enron and five other companies were found by FERC to have manipulated the dysfunctional California market, and the state is slated to receive approximately $2 billion in refunds (although the exact amount has not been determined). FERC forbade Enron from selling electricity or natural gas in the United States as from 25 June 2003. This ruling is supposed to hold until Enron emerges from bankruptcy.

38. Annex 5.2 provides further details on California's reform plan.

39. On 25 June 2003, FERC demanded that more than 60 sellers, including some of the nation's largest power companies, justify why they should not be forced to give up profits obtained through improper behaviour.
40. This is not to say that forward contracting is a panacea: given underlying market conditions of high concentration and difficult entry, forward contracts will be negotiated at higher-than-competitive rates.

Bibliography

Abel, J. (2002), "Entry into Regulated Monopoly Markets: The Development of a Competitive Fringe in the Local Telephone Industry", *Journal of Law and Economics*, Vol. 45, 289-316.

Ahn, S. (2002), "Competition, Innovation and Productivity Growth: A Review of Theory and Evidence", OECD Economics Department Working Papers, No. 317.

Alesina, A. *et al.* (2003), "Regulation and Investment", NBER Working Papers, No. 9560.

Anand, B. and T. Khanna (2000), "The Structure of Licensing Contracts", *Journal of Industrial Economics*, Vol. 48, No. 1, 103-135.

Arora, A. and A. Fosfuri (2000), "The Market for Technology in the Chemical industry: Causes and Consequences", *Revue d'Economie Industrielle*, Vol. 92, 317-34.

Arundel, A. (2001), "Patents in the Knowledge-Based Economy", *Beleidstudies Technology Economie*, Vol. 37, 67-88.

Baker, D. (1996), "The High Cost of Protectionism: The Case of Intellectual Property Claims", Economic Policy Institute Technical Working Paper No. 230.

Barton, J. (2000), "Reforming the Patent System", *Science*,Vol. 287, 1933-1934.

Barton, J. (2001), "Non-Obviousness", mimeo, Stanford University Law School.

Berndt, E. (2002), "Pharmaceuticals in U.S. Health Care: Determinants of Quantity and Price", *Journal of Economic Perspectives*, Vol. 16, No. 4, 45-66.

Blanchard, O. and F. Giavazzi (2002), "Macroeconomic Effects of Regulation and Deregulation in Goods and Labor Markets", *Quarterly Journal of Economics*, Vol. 118, No. 3.

Blondal, S. and D. Pilat (1997), "The Economic Benefits of Regulatory Reform", OECD *Economic Studies*, No. 28, 7-48.

Borenstein, S. (2002), "The Trouble with Electricity Markets: Understanding California's Restructuring Disaster", *Journal of Economic Perspectives* Vol. 16, No. 1, 191-211.

Borenstein, S. *et al.* (2002), "Measuring Market Inefficiencies in California's Restructured Wholesale Electricity Market", *American Economic Review*, Vol. 92, No. 5, 1376-1405.

Bradford, S. (2003), "Paying the Price: Final Goods Protection in OECD Countries", *Review of Economics and Statistics*, Vol. 85, No. 1, 24-37.

Brennan, T. *et al.* (2002), *Alternating Currents: Electricity Markets and Public Policy*, RFF Press, Washington, D.C.

Bulow, J. (2003), "The Gaming of Pharmaceutical Patents", mimeo, Stanford Business School.

Bushnell, J. and C. Saravia (2002), "An Empirical Assessment of the Competitiveness of the New England Electricity Market", Center for the Study of Energy Markets (CSEM) Working Papers, No. 101.

Campbell, T.J. *et al.* (1995), "The Causes and Effects of Liability Reform: Some Empirical Evidence", NBER Working Papers, No. 4989.

Campbell, T.J. *et al.* (1995), "The Link Between Liability Reform and Productivity: Some Empirical Evidence", *Brookings Papers on Economic Activity: Microeconomics*, 107-148.

Coggburn, J.D. (2003), "Exploring Differences in the American States' Procurement Practices", *Journal of Public Procurement*, Vol. 3, No. 1, 3-28.

Cohen, W. *et al.* (2000), "Protecting Their Intellectual Assets: Appropriability Conditions and Why U.S. Manufacturing Firms Patent (or Not)?", NBER Working Papers, No. 7552.

Congressional Budget Office (2003), *The Economics of US Tort Liability: A Primer*, Washington, D.C., October.

Congressional Budget Office (2004), *Limiting Tort Liability for Medical Malpractice*, January.

Council of Economic Advisers (2002), "Who Pays for Tort Liability Claims? An Economic Analysis of the US Tort Liability System", April.

Crandall, R. (2003), "Debating U.S. Broadband Policy: An Economic Perspective", *Policy Brief*, No. 117, The Brookings Institution.

Crandall, R. and T. Hazlett (2000), "Telecommunications Policy Reform in the United States and Canada", AEI-Brookings Joint Center for Regulatory Studies Working Papers, No. 00-9.

Crandall, R. and L. Waverman (2000), *Who Pays for Universal Service? When Telephone Subsidies Become Transparent*, Brookings Institution Press, Washington, DC.

Crandall, R. *et al.* (2002), "The Empirical Case Against the Asymmetric Regulation of Broadband Internet Access", *Berkeley Technology Law Journal*, Vol. 17, No. 3, 953-987.

Danzon, P.M. (1997), "Price Discrimination for Pharmaceuticals: Welfare Effects in the U.S. and the E.U."*International Journal of the Economics of Business*, Vol. 4, No. 3, 301-321.

Danzon, P.M. and M.F. Furukawa (2003), "Prices and Availability of Pharmaceuticals: Evidence from Nine Countries", *Health Affairs*, October.

Dyer, G. (2003), "Astra Zeneca in limits on Canada", *The Financial Times*, 23 April.

Federal Trade Commission (2002), "Generic Entry Prior to Patent Expiration: An FTC Study".

Feldstein, M. (2003), "Why is Productivity Growing Faster?", NBER Working Paper No. 9530.

Finkelstein, A. (2003), "Health Policy and Technological Change: Evidence from the Vaccine Industry", NBER Working Papers, No. 9460.

Gallaway, M. *et al.* (1999), "Welfare Costs of US Anti-dumping and Countervailing Duties Laws", *Journal of International Economic*, Vol. 49, 211-244.

Gallini, N. (2002), "The Economics of Patents: Lessons from Recent U.S. Patent Reform", *Journal of Economic Perspectives*, Vol. 16, No. 2, 131-154.

Gallini, N. and S. Scotchmer (2002), "Intellectual Property: When Is It the Best Incentive System?", *Innovation Policy and the Economy*, Vol. 2, 51-77.

Gilbert, R. and W. Tom (2001), "Is Innovation King at the Antitrust Agencies? The Intellectual Property Guidelines Five Years Later", *Antitrust Law Journal*, Vol. 69, No. 1, 43-86.

Gonenc, R. *et al.* (2001), "The Implementation and the Effects of Regulatory Reform: Past Experience and Current Issues", OECD *Economic Studies*, No. 32, 183-227, Paris.

Grabowski, H. *et al.*(2002), "Returns on R&D for 1990s New Drug Introductions", mimeo, Duke University, Department of Economics.

Graham, J. *et al.* (2003), "Post-issue Patent 'Quality Control': A Comparative Study of U.S. Patent Re-examinations and European Patent Oppositions", forthcoming in Cohen, W. (ed.), *Intellectual Property in the Knowledge-Based Economy*, Washington, DC, National Academies Press.

Gust, C. and J. Marquez (2002), "International Comparisons of Productivity Growth: The Role of Information Technology and Regulatory Practices", International Finance Discussion Papers 727, Board of Governors of the Federal Reserve System.

Hall, B. (2003), "Business Method Patents, Innovation, and Policy", NBER Working Papers, No. 9717.

Hall, B. *et al.* (2003), "Prospects for Improving U.S. Patent Quality Via Post-Grant Opposition", NBER Working Papers, No. 9731.

Hall, B. and R. Ziedonis (2001), "The Patent Paradox Revisited: An Empirical Study of Patenting in the U.S. Semiconductor Industry, 1979-1995", *Rand Journal of Economics*, Vol. 32, 101-128.

Hausman, J. (1997), "Valuation and the Effect of Regulation on New Services in Telecommunications", *Brookings Papers on Economic Activity, Microeconomics*.

Hausman, J. (1998a), "The Effect of Sunk Costs in Telecommunications Regulation", mimeo, Massachusetts Institute of Technology, October.

Hausman, J. (1998b), "Taxation Through Telecommunications Regulation", *Tax Policy and the Economy*.

Hausman, J. (1999), "Efficiency Effects on the U.S. Economy from Wireless Taxation", mimeo, Massachusetts Institute of Technology, July.

Hausman, J. *et al.* (2001a), "Cable Modems and DSL: Broadband Internet Access for Residential Customers", *American Economic Review*, Vol. 91, No. 2, 302-307.

Hausman, J. *et al.* (2001b), "Residential Demand for Broadband Telecommunications and Consumer Access to Unaffiliated Internet Content Providers", *Yale Journal on Regulation*, Vol. 18, No. 1, 129-173.

Hausman, J. *et al.* (2002), "Does Bell Company Entry into Long-Distance Telecommunications Benefit Consumers?", *Antitrust Law Journal*, Vol. 70, 463-484.

Hazlett, T. (2000), "Economic and Political Consequences of the 1996 Telecommunications Act", *Regulation*, Vol. 23, No. 3, 36-45.

Huber, P. (1988), *Liability: The Legal Revolution and Its Consequences*, Basic Book, New York.

Irwin, D. (2003), "Causing Problems? The WTO Review of Causation and Injury Attribution in U.S. Section 201 Cases", NBER Working Papers, No. 9815.

Jaffe, A. (2000), "The US Patent System in Transition: Policy Innovation and the Innovation Process", *Research Policy* Vol. 29, No. 4-5, 531-557.

Janis, M. (1997), "Rethinking Re-examination: Toward a Viable Administrative Revocation System for U.S. Patent Law", *Harvard Journal of Law and Technology*, Vol. 11, No. 1, 1-122.

Jorde, T. *et al.* (2000), "Innovation, Investment and Unbundling", *Yale Journal on Regulation*, Vol. 17, No. 1, 1-37.

Joskow, P. (2001), "California's Electricity Crisis", *Oxford Review of Economic Policy*, Vol. 17, No. 3, 365-388.

Joskow, P. (2003), "The Difficult Transition to Competitive Electricity Markets in the United States", mimeo, Massachusetts Institute of Technology.

Joskow, P. and E. Kahn (2002), "A Quantitative Analysis of Pricing Behavior in California's Wholesale Electricity Market During Summer 2000", *The Energy Journal*, Vol. 23, No. 4, 1-35.

Joskow, P. and J. Tirole (2003), "Merchant Transmission Investment", NBER Working Paper, No. 9534.

Kessler, D.P. and M. McClellan (1996), "Do Doctors Practice Defensive Medicine?", *Quarterly Journal of Economics*, Vol. 111, 353-390.

Knetter, M. (1994), "Why are Retail Prices in Japan So High? Evidence from German Export Prices", NBER Working Papers, No. 4894.

Kortum, S. and J. Lerner (1998), "Stronger Protection or Technological Revolution: What is Behind the Recent Surge in Patenting?", *Carnegie-Rochester Conference Series on Public Policy*, Vol. 48, 247-304.

Kremer, M. (2001), "Creating Markets for New Vaccines – Part I: Rationale; Part II: Design Issues", *Innovation Policy and the Economy*. Vol. 1, 35-118.

Kruger, L. and A. Gilroy (2001), "Broadband Internet Access: Background and Issues", CRS *Issue Brief for Congress*, Congressional Research Service, The Library of Congress, 17 April.

Lanjouw, J. (2002a), "Intellectual Property and the Availability of Pharmaceuticals in Poor Countries", forthcoming in *Innovation Policy and the Economy*, Vol. 3.

Lanjouw, J. (2002b), "A Patent Proposal for Global Diseases: U.S. and International Legal Issues", forthcoming in *Harvard Journal of Law & Technology*.

Lehman, D. and D. Weisman (2001), *The Telecommunications Act of 1996: The "Costs" of Managed Competition*, Kluwer Academic Publishers, Boston.

Lerner, J. (1994), "The Importance of Patent Scope: An Empirical Analysis", RAND *Journal of Economics*, Vol. 25, No. 2, 319-333.

Lerner, J. (1995), "Patenting in the Shadow of Competitors", *Journal of Law and Economics*, Vol. 38, No. 2, 463-496.

Lerner, J. (2002), "Patent Policy Reform and Its Implications", NBER *Reporter*, Winter 2002/2003, 17-19.

Levin, R. and J. Levin (2002), "Patent Oppositions", mimeo, Yale University and Stanford University.

Lichtenberg, F. (2002), "Benefits and Costs of Newer Drugs: An Update", NBER Working Papers, No. 8996.

Lichtenberg, F. and S. Virabhak (2002), "Pharmaceutical-Embodied Technical Progress, Longevity, and Quality of Life: Drugs As 'Equipment For Your Health'", NBER Working Papers, No. 9351.

Lundsgaard, J. (2002), "Competition and Efficiency in Publicly-Funded Services", OECD Economics Department Working Papers, No. 331.

Marcus, J. (2002), "The Potential Relevance to the United States of the European Union's Newly Adopted Regulatory Framework for Telecommunications", OPP Working Paper Series, No. 36, Office of Plans and Policy, Federal Communications Commission.

National Association of States Purchasing Officials (1997),*State and Local Government Purchasing: Principles & Practices*, Lexington, NY.

Nicoletti, G. and S. Scarpetta (2003), "Regulation, Productivity and Growth: OECD Evidence", OECD Economics Department Working Paper, No. 347.

OECD (1999), *Regulatory Reform in the United States*, Paris.

OECD (2003), *The Sources of Economic Growth in OECD Countries*, Paris.

Pew Internet and American Life Project (2003), "Adoption of Broadband to the Home", May.

Scherer, F.M. (1993), "Pricing, Profits, and Technological Progress in the Pharmaceutical Industry", *Journal of Economic Perspectives*, Summer.

Shapiro, C. (2001), "Navigating the Patent Thicket: Cross Licenses, Patent Pools, and Standard Setting", *Innovation Policy and the Economy*, Vol. 1.

Swagel, P. (1995), "Import Prices and the Competing Goods Effect", International Finance Discussion Papers, No. 508, Federal Reserve Board.

Sykes, A. (2003), "The Safeguards Mess: A Critique of WTO Jurisprudence", University of Chicago Law School, mimeo.

Tarullo, D. (2003), "Paved With Good Intentions: The Dynamic Effect of WTO Review of Anti-dumping Action", Georgetown University Law Center, mimeo.

The Economist (2003), "America's Regulatory Mess", 24 July.

Tufts Center for the Study of Drug Development (2003), "Outlook 2003", Tufts University.

US Department of Energy (2003), "Report to Congress: Impact of the Federal Energy Regulatory Commission's Proposal for Standard Market Design", 30 April.

US General Accounting Office (1999), "District of Columbia Authority Needs to Improve Its Procurement Practices", GAO/GGD-99-134, August.

US Office of Management and Budget (2001), *The President's Management Agenda*.

Vernon, J. (2002), "Drug Research and Price Controls", *Regulation*, Winter 2002-2003, 22-23.

Viscusi, W.K. (1984), "Structuring an Effective Occupational Disease Policy: Victim Compensation and Risk Regulation", *Yale Journal on Regulation*, 53-81.

Wegner, H. (2001), "Invalidity Defenses to E-patent Infringement: A Comparative View of the Differing Ways to Achieve Patent Justice in the United States", Paper presented at the SOFTIC 2001 Symposium, Tokyo, Japan.

Willig, R. *et al.* (2002), "Stimulating Investment and the Telecommunications Act of 1996", mimeo, Princeton University.

Winston, C. (1998), "U.S. Industry Adjustment to Economic Deregulation", *Journal of Economic Perspectives*, Vol. 12, No. 3, 89-110.

Wolak, F. (1996), "Can Universal Service Survive in a Competitive Telecommunications Environment? Evidence from the United States Consumer Expenditure Survey", February, available at *www.stanford.edu/~wolak*.

Wolak, F. (1999), "A Report on the Redesign of California's Real-time Energy and Ancillary Services Markets", October 18, available at *www.stanford.edu/~wolak*.

Wolak, F. (2000), "An Empirical Analysis of the Impact of Hedge Contracts on Bidding Behavior in a Competitive Electricity Market", *International Economic Journal*, Vol. 14, No. 2, 1-40.

Wolak, F. (2003a), "Lessons from the California Electricity Crisis", Center for the Study of Energy Markets (CSEM) Working Papers, No. 110.

Wolak, F. (2003b), "Measuring Unilateral Market Power in Wholesale Electricity Markets: The California Market 1998 to 2000", *American Economic Review*, Vol. 93, No. 2, 425-430, May.

Wolak, F. *et al.* (1998), "Preliminary Report on the Operation of the Ancillary Services Markets of the California Independent System Operator (ISO)", August 19, available at *www.stanford.edu/~wolak*.

Wolak, F. *et al.* (1999), "Report on the Redesign of the Markets for Ancillary Services and Real-time Energy", March 25, available at *www.stanford.edu/~wolak*.

Wolfram, C. (1999), "Measuring Duopoly Power in the British Electricity Spot Market", *American Economic Review*, Vol. 89, No. 4, 805-826.

Annex 5.1

Prices for voice and electricity services

The analysis of telecommunication and electricity services in the main text focused on the challenges facing competitive provision in each market and possible policy responses. Moreover, it was emphasised that price reductions for all customers may not be the result of competition, especially in electricity; rather, reform is likely to result in a rebalancing of relative prices (for example, between low- and high-cost electricity states, or between telecommunications and information services following access charge reform). This should facilitate efficient investment and development of advanced services. A comparison with other member countries reveals that prices for residential and business voice services in the United States lie somewhat below the OECD average but well above those in the lowest-price countries; electricity rates are low in comparison to those in most member countries.

Figure A5.1.1. **OECD composite basket of residential telephone charges**[1]
November 2003

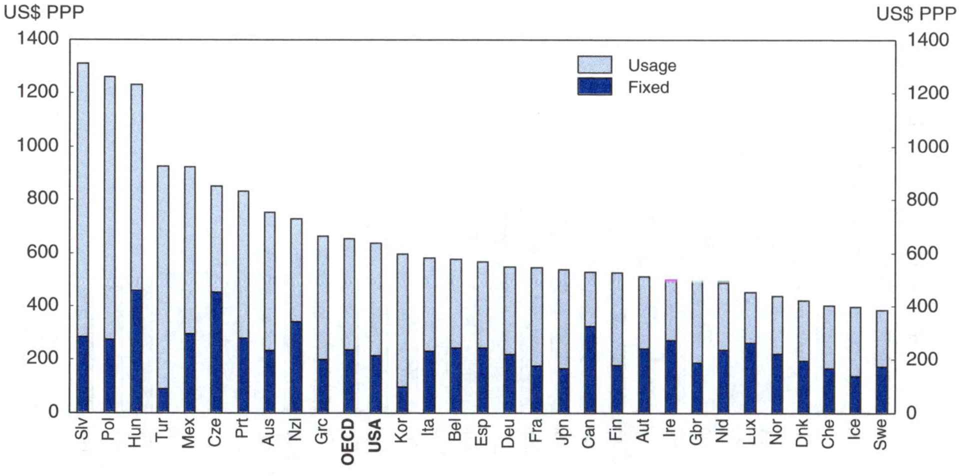

1. Composite basket includes international calls and calls to mobile networks.
Source: OECD.

Figure A5.1.2. **OECD composite basket of business telephone charges**[1]
Excluding VAT, November 2003

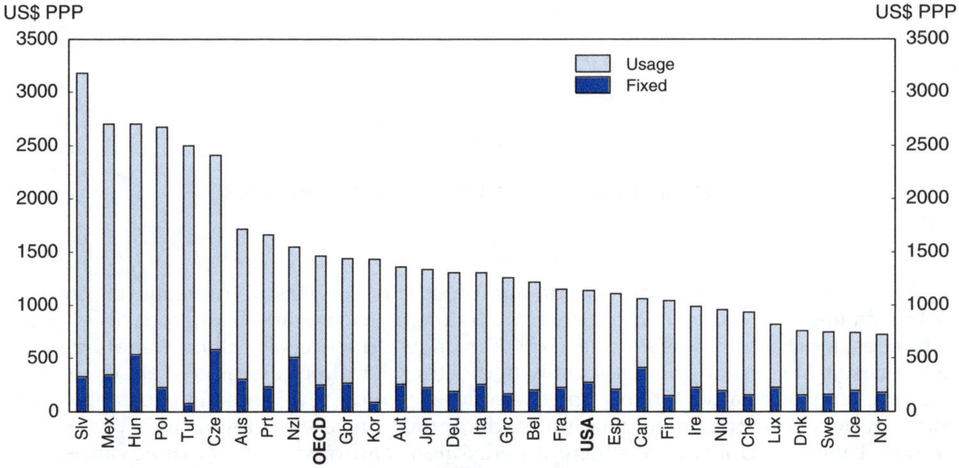

1. Composite basket includes international calls and calls to mobile networks.
Source: OECD.

Figure A5.1.3. **Electricity prices for households**
US$/KWh converted with PPP
2002 or latest available year[1]

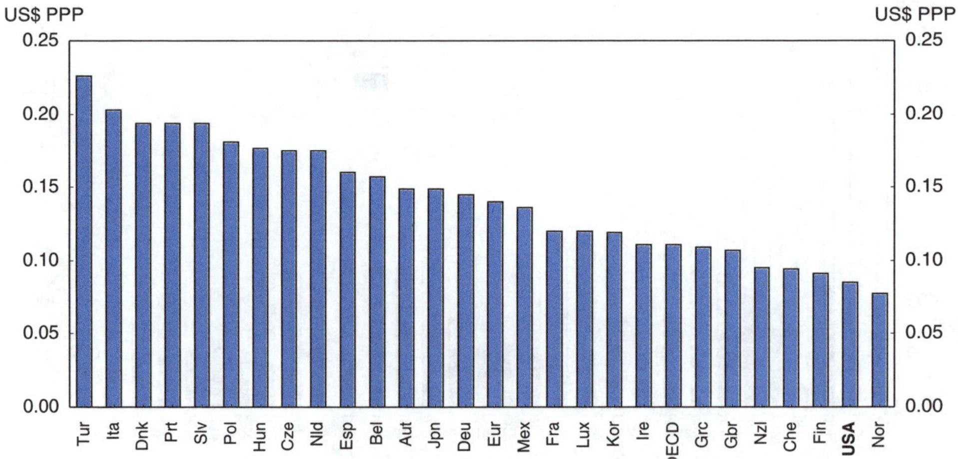

1. 2001 for Germany and Spain; 2000 for Belgium.
Source: International Energy Agency.

Annex 5.2

California's experience with reform of retail electricity markets

Prior to 1996, California's electricity industry was organized around three private vertically integrated monopolies: Pacific Gas and Electric (PG&E), Southern California Edison (SCE) and San Diego Gas and Electric (SDG&E). Their prices, costs and service obligations were heavily regulated by the state commission. In addition, these firms depended on purchasing significant amounts of power in the wholesale market in the western states, Canada and Mexico. In 1996, the state legislature passed a plan to restructure the industry. Its key components were retail customer choice through competitive entry of electricity service providers (ESPs); open access to transmission and distribution networks of the large incumbent utilities; an immediate 10 per cent reduction in retail rates from prevailing regulated prices; creation of an independent system operator (CAISO) to manage the transmission network and a power exchange (CALPX) to run a wholesale market; a requirement that the large utilities meet their default service obligations by purchasing power for those customers through the day-ahead and real-time spot market; and divestiture of at least 50 per cent of PG&E and SCE's fossil-fuel generating capacity.

Several weaknesses in California's design contributed to the subsequent crisis. The programme was too focused on the near-term drop in prices, and the mandated 10 per cent reduction in rates from 1996 levels was a mistake. The low wholesale prices in the mid-1990s reflected excess supply, and the mandatory price reduction both impeded the spread of retail competition (as entrants to retailing had to beat the lower rates) and completely insulated end-users from wholesale prices. This ensured that demand was extremely inelastic and came on top of the fact that demand is already very inelastic in the short run for most customers, because only very large consumers have real-time meters that provide price information. The inelasticity of demand, in conjunction with the physical properties of electricity, provided considerable scope for the unilateral exercise of market power: because electricity cannot be stored and demand and supply must balance in order to ensure reliability of the network, a supplier in tight market conditions can face a marginal revenue curve that is sharply decreasing in the quantity supplied, making withholding of supply very attractive (*e.g.* Borenstein, 2002). Importantly, this can occur even when a market has a large number of potential suppliers, so that simple metrics gauging competitive forces by market shares (which have been used by FERC, for example, in assessing market power) can be misleading. A number of studies have concluded that the exercise of market power was substantial during the crisis (*e.g.* Borenstein *et al.*, 2002; Joskow and Kahn, 2002). The incentives to charge prices substantially above marginal cost was further enhanced by the extensive reliance on the real-time and day-ahead spot markets for wholesale power: a supplier who realized that it could bid its power to the market at a high price would, if successful, sell all its power at the high spot price, as the largest purchasers of wholesale electricity were not allowed to enter into forward contracts hedging this risk. Although the utilities could have hedged this risk, they chose not to, perhaps because the stranded cost recovery programme guaranteed the utilities recovery through the difference between the retail rates they received and the spot wholesale price, not a price they received through a forward contract (Wolak, 2003a). The drop in prices in June 2001 – when most long-term contracts that the state entered became effective – suggests the importance of this factor. The imposition of price caps in the spot wholesale market across the west in late June by FERC may have also contributed, although by that point only a fraction of California's power needs were met through the spot market.

Annex 5.3

Tort reform

Markets require an efficient and transparent judicial system to function properly. The US institutional framework is by and large appropriate, but there are two exceptions: torts and, less clearly, bankruptcy. Both have been the object of substantial reform efforts in the Congress in recent years.[1]

Changes in the tort liability system have been particularly hotly debated in recent years, especially with regard to medical malpractice claims. The policy discussion has been driven by concerns that the current system has high costs and arbitrary distributive effects and creates a great deal of *ex ante* uncertainty regarding the risks facing both consumers and firms. Reform proposals have built on earlier efforts at the state level, including limits on punitive damages and even economic damages, caps on attorneys' fees and liability reform.[2] The latter two categories are designed to lower the costs of administering the system (in part by decreasing incentives to pursue marginal cases), while the former has been suggested as a means to lessen the arbitrary nature of certain rewards. This arbitrariness is evidenced through unusually high rewards in some cases, but also through no rewards or even failure to bring cases by some harmed individuals who are in weakened circumstances.

The system is estimated to have cost $180 billion, or 1.8 per cent of GDP, to operate in 2000; this level is double that of other industrialised nations and nearly triple that 30 years earlier (as a per cent of GDP) (Council of Economic Advisers, 2002).[3] Moreover, a substantial fraction of this expenditure is probably wasteful. Only 46 per cent of funds represent payments to claimants, with the remainder consisting of attorneys' fees and administrative costs. The cost of administering the system is clearly excessive relative to regulatory or government insurance programmes. For example, overhead in the workers' compensation system is only 20 per cent of its funds. While fault and identification of the responsible parties may be particularly easy in such cases, the 54 per cent of funds dissipated in tort actions should be reined in. In addition, tort actions may not be very efficient in those areas where they are common, such as medical malpractice and toxic waste. In both cases, determination of causation and liability can be complicated and technically demanding; these requirements may be better met through *ex ante* regulations by qualified experts (Viscusi, 1984; Huber, 1988). In this regard, most proposals for tort reform are lacking, in that they fail to address the fundamental weaknesses of the tort system that prevent agents from exercising due care and stop injured individuals from receiving just compensation. Proposals include strengthening regulation of product safety, setting up trust funds to avoid class action suits, and allowing parties to avoid the tort system through contractual arrangements. This could be justified if there were clear evidence that the system has resulted in excessive compensation (on average) and therefore less-than-optimal supply, rather than simply being inefficient at providing compensation.

Reform would have several positive effects. Cutting administrative costs by half would lower the implicit tax on economic activity by ½ per cent of GDP. Previous studies have demonstrated that the current system encourages doctors to practice defensive medicine and hence increases the cost of healthcare, without improving health; for example, Kessler and McClellan (1996) found that earlier reforms lowered medical expenditures by 5 to 9 per cent with no adverse effects. More recent studies (such as Congressional Budget Office, 2004) found somewhat smaller effects. Research has documented negative effects of the present system, and positive effects of reforms that reduce potential liabilities, on productivity and employment in a broad range of industries (Campbell *et al.*, 1995 and 1998).

Notes

1. Bankruptcy overhaul legislation that would tighten access to personal bankruptcy under Chapter 7 of the federal bankruptcy code by imposing a means test was passed by the House in March 2003. But it never progressed in the Senate because of a threat to amend it so as to prevent abortion protesters from filing for bankruptcy to escape civil fines and judgements. Some observers have also complained about the unfairness of Chapter 11 under which firms can gain cost advantages and then cut prices; a prime example is commercial aviation. As regards tort reform there have been three separate efforts, and all have stalled. First, a bill to establish a $108 billion fund to pay asbestos claims according to medical criteria has not yet been brought to the floor after Committee passage in July 2003; no legislation has yet been introduced in the House. Second, once again the House passed legislation to cap non-economic damages for pain and suffering and punitive damages in medical malpractice lawsuits in March 2003, but a similar bill has gone nowhere in the Senate. Finally, a bill to reform class-action lawsuits by making it easier to transfer them from state to federal courts passed the House in June 2003, but a Senate motion for cloture failed in October.
2. A current proposal, passed by the House, would place a cap not only on punitive damages but also on non-economic damages.
3. A more recent figure practiced by the private consultancy Tillinghast-Towers Perrin in December 2003 put the cost at $233 billion (2¼ per cent of GDP) in 2002, up 13 per cent on the year.

Annex 5.4

Public procurement

Competitive sourcing of publicly provided services has been a high priority since the mid-1990s, and the current Administration's management agenda has pushed even harder to bring the discipline of competition to services provided by the federal government. Nearly half of federal employees perform tasks available in the commercial marketplace, and competition between public and private parties has often resulted in cost savings of 20 to 50 per cent for such functions (US Office of Management and Budget, 2001). But the extent of competition has been limited; as a result, the Administration announced changes to the federal government's competitive sourcing programmes last spring.[1] These changes simplify the definition of activities that are "inherently" governmental and streamline the administrative process associated with conducting competitive bidding. While previous procedures could take as long as four years, the revised guidelines limit the process to one year. These are positive steps. However, the cost savings realised from earlier instances may not be representative of future efficiency gains, as experience remains limited; moreover, international experience suggests that savings have clustered between 10 and 30 per cent (Lundsgaard, 2002).

Introducing competition to primary and secondary education remains a challenge. As discussed extensively in the previous *Survey*, the No Child Left Behind Act introduced a number of accountability measures designed to increase parental awareness of school quality and to allow choice among public schools to those whose children attend institutions of low quality. Unfortunately, one response at the state level – where standards are set – has been to lower the threshold for low-quality schools, thereby limiting choice. (This reaction may stem, in part, from funding problems; the federal mandate to facilitate choice for those in failing schools was not accompanied by additional funding, and states have been struggling to balance their budgets). Vouchers or other financial assistance to spur greater competition and choice between public and private schools have not spread widely. One positive development in this area was the recent Supreme Court decision which determined that voucher programmes such as that in Cleveland, which are used to attend church-affiliated schools (as well as others, although in some areas most private schools have a religious affiliation), are constitutional.

Procurement policies at the state level have not shifted toward competitive provision to the same extent as those at the federal level. A majority of states have introduced reforms to allow agencies to enter cooperative purchasing agreements, to make purchases based on criteria involving quality and price and to gain greater independent authority based on past cost-savings or quality improvements (Coggburn, 2003). But a systematic account of reforms or efforts to delineate inherently governmental functions as at the federal level is lacking (National Association of State Purchasing Officials, 1997).[2]

Notes

1. The Office of Management and Budget issued a revised Circular No. A-76, which governs federal policy for competition of commercial activities, on 29 May 2003.
2. Although it is clear that certain state or local government practices have fallen short of standards for transparency and accountability in their procurement policies (*e.g.* US General Accounting Office, 1999).

BASIC STATISTICS

BASIC STATISTICS:

INTERNATIONAL COMPARISONS

	Units	Reference period[1]	Australia	Austria	Belgi
Population					
Total	Thousands	2000	19 157	8 110	1022
Inhabitants per sq. km	Number	2000	2	97	33
Net average annual increase over previous 10 years	%	2000	1.2	0.5	0.
Employment					
Total civilian employment (TCE)[2]	Thousands	2000	9 048	3730 (99)	385
of which:					
Agriculture	% of TCE	2000	4.9	6.2 (99)	2.
Industry	% of TCE	2000	22.0	30.6 (99)	24.
Services	% of TCE	2000	73.1	63.2 (99)	68.
Gross domestic product (GDP)					
At current prices and current exchange rates	Bill. USD	2000	388.5	188.7	228.
Per capita	USD	2000	20 158	23 270	22 33
At current prices using current PPPs[3]	Bill. USD	2000	507.6	219.0	268.
Per capita	USD	2000	26 338	27 001	26 19
Average annual volume growth over previous 5 years	%	2000	3.9	2.6	2.
Gross fixed capital formation (GFCF)	% of GDP	2000	22.7	23.6	20.
of which:					
Machinery and equipment	% of GDP	2000	...	8.0	9.
Residential construction	% of GDP	2000	4.5	5.4	4.
Average annual volume growth over previous 5 years	%	2000	0.5	0.2	0.
Gross saving ratio[4]	% of GDP	2000	18.3	21.8	26.
General government					
Current expenditure on goods and services	% of GDP	2000	18.2	19.0	20.
Current disbursements[5]	% of GDP	2000	32.1 (98)	46.9	46.
Current receipts[6]	% of GDP	2000	33.7 (98)	47.1	47.
Net official development assistance	% of GNI	2000	0.27	0.23	0.3
Indicators of living standards					
Private consumption per capita using current PPPs[3]	USD	2000	15 829	14 910	13 83
Passenger cars, per 1000 inhabitants	Number	1999	510 (98)	496	44
Internet subscribers, per 100 inhabitants	Number	2000	12.7	6.00	10.
Television sets, per 1000 inhabitants	Number	1998	548 (97)	331	34
Doctors, per 1000 inhabitants	Number	1999	2.5 (98)	3.0	3.
Infant mortality per 1000 live births	Number	1999	5.7	4.4	5.
Wages and prices (average annual increase rate over previous 5 years)					
Wages (earnings or rates according to availability)	%	2001	2.8	2.5	2.
Consumer prices	%	2001	2.3	1.6	1.
International trade[7]					
Exports of goods, fob	Mill. USD	2000	63 920	64 226	187 95
As % of GDP	%	2000	16.5	34.0	82.
Average annual increase rate over previous 5 years	%	2000	3.8	2.2	1.
Imports of goods, cif	Mill. USD	2000	67 742	69 058	177 12
As % of GDP	%	2000	17.4	36.6	77.
Average annual increase rate over previous 5 years	%	2000	3.4	0.8	2.
Total official reserves[8]	Mill. SDR's	2000	15 455	11 017	7 96
As ratio of average monthly imports of goods	Ratio	2000	2.7	2.1	0.

1. Unless otherwise stated.
2. According to the definitions used in OECD *Labour Force Statistics*.
3. PPPs = Purchasing Power Parities.
4. Gross Saving = Gross national disposable income minus private and government consumption.
5. Current disbursements = General government final consumption expenditure plus subsidies plus property income plus current taxes on income, wealth, etc. plus social benefits other than transfers in kind plus other current transfers.
6. Current receipts = Operating surplus plus taxes on production and imports plus property income plus current taxes on income, wealth, etc. plus social contributions plus other current transfers.

Questionnaire on the quality of OECD publications

We would like to ensure that our publications meet your requirements in terms of presentation and editorial content. We would welcome your feedback and any comments you may have for improvement. Please take a few minutes to complete the following questionnaire. Answers should be given on a scale of 1 to 5 (1 = poor, 5 = excellent).

Fax or post your answer before 31 December 2004, and you will automatically be entered into the prize draw to **win a year's subscription to *OECD's Observer magazine*.***

A. Presentation and layout

1. What do you think about the presentation and layout in terms of the following:

	Poor	Adequate		Excellent	
Readability (font, typeface)	1	2	3	4	5
Organisation of the book	1	2	3	4	5
Statistical tables	1	2	3	4	5
Graphs	1	2	3	4	5

B. Printing and binding

2. What do you think about the quality of the printed edition in terms of the following:

Quality of the printing	1	2	3	4	5
Quality of the paper	1	2	3	4	5
Type of binding	1	2	3	4	5
Not relevant, I am using the e-book	❑				

3. Which delivery format do you prefer for publications in general?

Print ❑ CD ❑ E-book (PDF) via Internet ❑ Combination of formats ❑

C. Content

4. How accurate and up to date do you consider the content of this publication to be?

1 2 3 4 5

5. Are the chapter titles, headings and subheadings…

Clear	Yes ❑	No ❑
Meaningful	Yes ❑	No ❑

6. How do you rate the written style of the publication (*e.g.* language, syntax, grammar)?

1 2 3 4 5

D. General

7. Do you have any additional comments you would like to add about the publication?

....

....

....

Tell us who you are:

Name: .... **E-mail:** ....

Fax: ....

Which of the following describes you?

IGO ❑ NGO ❑ Self-employed ❑ Student ❑
Academic ❑ Government official ❑ Politician ❑ Private sector ❑

Thank you for completing the questionnaire. Please fax your answers to: (33-1) 49 10 42 81 or mail it to the following address:
Questionnaire qualité PAC/PROD, Division des publications de l'OCDE
23, rue du Dôme – 92100 Boulogne Billancourt – France.

Title: OECD Economic Surveys 2002-2003 – United States

ISBN: 92 64 01578 7 **OECD Code (printed version):** 10 2004 07 1 P

* Please note: This offer is not open to OECD staff.

Questionnaire on the quality of OECD publications

Printing and binding

Content

General

OECD PUBLICATIONS, 2, rue André-Pascal, 75775 PARIS CEDEX 16
PRINTED IN FRANCE
(10 2004 07 1 P) ISBN 92-64-01578-7 – No. 53503 2004
ISSN 0376-6438